The Art of Critical Pedagogy

Studies in the
Postmodern Theory of Education

Joe L. Kincheloe and Shirley R. Steinberg
General Editors

Vol. 285

PETER LANG
New York • Washington, D.C./Baltimore • Bern
Frankfurt am Main • Berlin • Brussels • Vienna • Oxford

JEFFREY M. R. DUNCAN-ANDRADE
AND ERNEST MORRELL

The Art of Critical Pedagogy

Possibilities for Moving from Theory to Practice in Urban Schools

PETER LANG
New York • Washington, D.C./Baltimore • Bern
Frankfurt am Main • Berlin • Brussels • Vienna • Oxford

Library of Congress Cataloging-in-Publication Data

Duncan-Andrade, Jeffrey M. R.
The art of critical pedagogy: possibilities for moving from theory to practice
in urban schools / Jeffrey M. R. Duncan-Andrade, Ernest Morrell.
p. cm. — (Counterpoints: studies in the postmodern theory of education; v. 285)
Includes bibliographical references and index.
1. Education, Urban—United States. 2. Critical pedagogy—United States.
I. Morrell, Ernest. II. Title.
LC5141.M67   370.11'5—dc22   2007051208
ISBN 978-1-4331-0031-4 (hardcover)
ISBN 978-0-8204-7415-1 (paperback)
ISSN 1058-1634

Bibliographic information published by **Die Deutsche Bibliothek**.
Die Deutsche Bibliothek lists this publication in the "Deutsche
Nationalbibliografie"; detailed bibliographic data is available
on the Internet at http://dnb.ddb.de/.

Cover art by Refa One

The paper in this book meets the guidelines for permanence and durability
of the Committee on Production Guidelines for Book Longevity
of the Council of Library Resources.

© 2008 Peter Lang Publishing, Inc., New York
29 Broadway, 18th floor, New York, NY 10006
www.peterlang.com

Printed in the United States of America

To Vien (BBB) & to Mom and Dad,
and to all my students here and gone.
—JEFF DUNCAN-ANDRADE

To Paulo Freire and to Grandma,
and to all of my students past, present, and future.
—ERNEST MORRELL

Contents

Preface

There has been much discussion concerning critical pedagogy and its practical applications to urban contexts in the generation following the publication of such seminal works as Paulo Freire's *Pedagogy of the Oppressed* (1970), Henry Giroux's *Theory and Resistance in Education: Toward a Pedagogy for the Opposition* (1983/2001), and Peter McLaren's *Life in Schools: An Introduction to Critical Pedagogy and the Foundations of Education* (1994/2003b). While honoring the tremendous contributions that each of these works has made to educational theory and practice, this book addresses two looming, yet underexplored, questions that have emerged with the ascendancy of critical pedagogy in the educational discourse:

What does critical pedagogy look like in work with urban youth, specifically in the context of urban schooling in the United States?

How can a systematic investigation of critical work enacted in urban contexts simultaneously draw upon and extend the core tenets of critical pedagogy?

The book reports from a theoretically informed, inquiry-based practice that is a direct response to Freire's (1997) call for critical and reflective journaling of the pedagogical process. It is a systematic analysis of our theoretically inspired practice in urban education; that is, we have developed a text that challenges and reconsiders critical theories of teaching in urban contexts through the examination of actual practices with urban youth. This book addresses several tensions inherent in enacting a critical practice in traditional institutionalized settings, such as between the efforts to disrupt oppressive structures and to navigate oppressive structures successfully. It also addresses tensions surrounding the role of the urban teacher in critical pedagogy and the tensions of enacting critical pedagogies within the current, standards-driven climate. As authors, we do not claim to resolve these tensions, yet by naming and exploring them we seek to generate authentic internal and external dialogues among educators who mine the educational discourse in search of texts that offer guidance for teaching for a more socially just world.

1

The Challenges and Opportunities of Urban Education

We begin this chapter by articulating some key ideological and structural dilemmas in urban education that result in a lack of funding, high dropout rates, excessive teacher attrition, and low standardized test scores. Rather than taking a defeatist tone, we address these dilemmas in order to situate critical pedagogy as a viable force for confronting them. We conclude the chapter with an outline of the remaining chapters in the book.

Let us begin by rethinking the position that urban schools are failing. Given the overwhelming body of evidence that reveals decades of funding and structural inequalities between schools in high- and low-income communities (Akom, 2003; Anyon, 1997; Darling-Hammond, 1998; Kozol, 1991, 2005; Noguera, 2003; Oakes, 1985), it is illogical to compare schools across these communities and then decry urban schools as failures. When one set of schools is given the resources necessary to succeed and another group of schools is not, we have predetermined winners and losers. In this scenario, failure is not actually the result of failing. This is the paradox facing urban school reformers. On the one hand, urban schools are producing academic failure at alarming rates; at the same time, they are doing this inside a systematic structural design that essentially predetermines their failure. This is where the urban school reform rhetoric has missed the mark. It has presumed that urban schools are broken. Urban schools are not broken; they are doing exactly what they are designed to do.

This argument is not meant to excuse the academic failure in many urban schools. Instead, it is meant to shake up and radicalize the business-as-usual approach to improving urban schools by shifting the blame from the victims of an unjust system onto the fiscal, political, and ideological policies that deliberately undercut and demean urban schools. It challenges the rhetoric of "fixing failure" that has driven countless reform measures aimed at improving the achievement of the country's most disenfranchised youth, particularly poor non-white youth. These efforts have produced some individual success stories, sometimes improvement across an entire school, but none of these reforms has produced systemic change in urban schools. Instead, while one school improves, another school that serves a remarkably similar group becomes worse. This virtual zero-sum game—the ebb and flow of failure in schools serving poor communities around the country—is tolerated for two reasons. It is important that we analyze these reasons if we are to move toward a set of structures and critical educational practices in urban schools that give young people a reason to invest in the education their schools offer, an education that challenges and transforms social, economic, political, and educational injustices through critical pedagogies that are ideologically, culturally, and locally relevant.

The Politics of Failure

Perpetual urban school failure is tolerated because deep down our nation subscribes to the belief that someone has to fail in school. In fact, this quasi-Darwinian belief system is built into most schools through the existence of a largely unchallenged pedagogical system of grading and testing that by its very design guarantees failure for some. For some time, this system for perpetuating unequal educational outcomes has been justified by racist and classist pseudo-scientific theories, sometimes referred to as deficit models (Hull, Rose, Fraser, & Castellano, 1991; Valencia & Solórzano, 1997). These models reached the height of their popularity in the early 1960s, but they have a historical trail that stretches back for as long as educational and intellectual potential have been discussed and measured. The contemporary version of these theories suggests that educational failure is the result of cultural deficiency on the part of the student, the family, and the community—de facto, educational attainment is attributed to cultural superiority or assimilation into culturally superior ways (D'Souza, 1995; Herrnstein & Murray, 1994; Ogbu, 1990). The most notable recent resurgence of the theory of cultural deficiency came with the publication of *The Bell Curve* (Herrnstein & Murray, 1994), whose authors suggest that blacks and Latinas/os are intellectually inferior to whites. Although the theories posited in the book have been thoroughly refuted, the book was a national bestseller.

The Economics of Failure

The second reason educational failure of poor and non-white children is tolerated is rooted in economics. The general public acknowledges, sometimes explicitly and sometimes tacitly, that schools are this country's de facto socio-economic sorting mechanism. Under this logic, schools are the primary place where economic futures are cast and people are sorted into their roles in society (Anyon, 1981; Carnoy & Levin, 1985; Finn, 1999). In short, some people must fill the least desirable places in society, and it is important that they feel they deserve to be in those positions or, at the very least, that there is a formal mechanism to justify their place there (Bowles & Gintis, 1976; MacLeod, 1987).

In effect, the high-stakes nature of this sorting process plays itself out like a rigged game of Monopoly. Let us draw this simile out to explain the role of school in socioeconomic reproduction. Monopoly is a board game where each player begins at the same place ("Go") on the board with the same amount of Monopoly money to work toward economic domination over the other players. The goal of the game is to combine strategy and luck to move around the game board building your individual wealth through the acquisition of property and rent from other players. Like Monopoly, the rhetoric of school-based meritocracy suggests that everyone starts at "Go" with equal chances to move around the board and capitalize on the opportunities that abound. However, a relatively simple comparison of the rhetoric of educational meritocracy with the reality of schools across communities suggests that this game is rigged to create an unfair competition. Whereas the outcomes in Monopoly are largely random, heavily influenced by the roll of the dice, educational outcomes are much more predictable. In the game of education, groups with high levels of social, political, and economic capital move around the same game board as the rest of the population, supposedly competing under the same set of rules, but they afford themselves a supplemental bankroll that guarantees an unfair competition, one that for centuries has produced the same unequal outcomes in schools and in the larger society.

To a large degree, the public discourse recognizes but leaves unchallenged the fact that wealthier communities have better educational opportunities. However, this public discourse remains largely dismissive of the nefarious impact of this rigged game on poor communities by standing behind the rhetoric of opportunity and the myth of meritocracy. The few exceptional students who combine fortitude and fortune to succeed in under-resourced urban schools play an important role in this myth making. The time-honored tradition of publicizing rags-to-riches stories (Horatio Alger narratives) confirms for the public that opportunity exists for anyone who wants it bad enough. This is, of course, untrue. The stratified nature of our current society creates a social pyramid that has no room at the top for the masses. This structure requires people to be sorted, and schools are the mechanism used to resolve this messy social conundrum, which was previously accomplished through overtly racist and classist social policies (for historical analyses of such policies, see Acuña, 2003; Loewen, 1995; Zinn, 1995). The fact that opportunity exists (currently defined as all children having access to public schools) helps maintain the rhetoric of a democratic and meritocratic society where competition churns the cream to the top, ultimately benefiting society as a whole by rewarding the most deserving. And it just so happens that the overwhelming majority of those who benefit most from this sorting process are those who look, talk, think, and act most like those who already have power. And it just so happens that the overwhelming majority of those who benefit least from this sorting process are those who come from different backgrounds and communities than those who already have power. This is not by chance, and it is not democratic. It is inequality by design, it is well documented, and schools play a central role in the perpetuation of this rigged social lottery (Fischer et al., 1996).

If school achievement were an accurate measure of intellect, achievement patterns would more closely mirror the random distribution of intellect that genetic scientists report in human populations (Gould, 1996; Zuberi, 2003). Instead, the results of schools are quite predictable. This is true largely because the nation's poorest young people are the most likely to be denied access to a quality education and then to be blamed (implicitly and explicitly) for their academic "failure." The predictability of these trends results in an almost permanent underclass. With remarkable consistency, schools serving low-income, non-white children disproportionately produce the citizens who will spend most of their adult lives in the least desirable and least mobile socioeconomic positions (prison, low-ranking military positions, and service labor). There is little to no social outrage over these conditions, which have been likened to a system of "academic apartheid" (Akom, 2003) and referred to as a "crisis of civil rights" (Harvard Civil Rights Project, 2005). In the end, schools produce very little mobility for the communities most in need and are the stamp of justification on one's position in the labor force and society.

Embracing the Truth: Urban Schools Are Not Failing

On the one hand, this analysis of the role of public schools can lead to the conclusion that urban public schools are bankrupt institutions. To the degree that we continue to operate within the paradigm that urban schools are failing, this is an accurate conclusion. It makes sense that a school system designed to justify social and economic stratification would least serve the

population with the greatest needs and the smallest amount of social, political, and economic capital to meet those needs. If urban schools have been
decried for decades as "factories for failure" (Rist, 1973), then their production of failures means they are in fact successful at producing the results they
are designed to produce. To the degree that we continue to misname this
problem by calling schools designed to fail "failing schools" we will continue
to chase our tails.

We could cite a litany of research data and evidentiary claims to support
the arguments that school is a rigged game, but what would be the point?
How long must we continue to argue over common sense? Poverty and the
gap between the haves and the have-nots is the enemy of every nation. We
must not be distracted from this point. Our nation's least desirable stations
(prison, military, low-semi-skilled labor) are overwhelmingly and disproportionately occupied by residents emerging from our poorest communities. The
only difference between this nation and those that openly support a social
caste system is the de facto nature through which we achieve these outcomes.
At some point we must come to grips with the fact that we are not a nation
of opportunity for all but a nation built upon grand narratives of opportunity
for all. It is no accident that for centuries our non-white and poor communities have been disproportionately represented among our perpetually poor
and poorly educated. It is no accident that those born into poverty overwhelmingly remain in poverty and those born into wealth overwhelmingly
remain wealthy and that the gap between these two groups is at an all-time
high. The predictability of this inequality is not borne from a system of meritocracy but from a system of oligarchy. We must address this structural reality if we are ever to develop a system of education that is meaningful for
economically disenfranchised communities.

Beyond the Dollars and Cents of Urban School Reform

Academic failure in urban schools persists despite increasing attention to the
problem from a variety of sources. This failure is most pronounced in urban
high schools, where dropout rates are consistently above 50% and college-
going rates are below 10% (Harvard Civil Rights Project, 2005). Strategies
aimed at addressing these issues are debated in and across research, policy,
and practice circles but have made little to no impact on the educational attainment of poor, non-white children in the past twenty years. Major reform
plans such as those funded by the Carnegie Corporation (2001) and the

Gates Millennium Foundation (American Institutes for Research, 2003) have allocated millions of dollars to innovative programs that have not substantially improved achievement in urban schools.

In seeking a more fruitful direction for urban school reform, it is important to consider briefly where such previous plans may have missed the mark. To be sure, efforts that increase the resources being allocated to urban schools should be applauded and supported. However, it has become increasingly clear that this formula for urban school reform is not a panacea. As suggested by Rothstein (2004), the failure of these efforts can largely be traced to the fact that the resources they produced have not been used to address the context of urban life and poverty directly. Rather, much of the logic behind increasing material resources has been rooted in notions that urban schools fail because they lack the resources and support that suburban schools receive—that is, they fail because they are not like suburban schools. This thinking has led to a growing number of reform plans that reduce larger and more pressing social and systemic issues of poverty (nutrition, health, environment, violence) to the more quantifiable issue of material resources. Following this logic, urban school reform has committed itself to supplementing a wide range of institutional material resources as the cure-all for low achievement: rolling out high-stakes testing and test preparation programs, decreasing school and class sizes, increasing the number of computers per student, increasing the number of textbooks per student, implementing scripted literacy and math programs, and improving facilities. Sadly, none of these efforts has produced notable gains in urban high school student engagement or achievement on the state or national level.

The failure of increased material resources to produce commensurate academic growth should not be misinterpreted to mean that material resources are unimportant. In point of fact, a number of studies (Ferguson & Ladd, 1996; Greenwald, Hedges, & Laine, 1996) have disproved economist Eric Hanushek's (2001) position that the accumulated research suggests there is no clear systematic relationship between resources and student outcomes. One need look no further than the unwavering commitment of wealthy communities to the maintenance of highly resourced schools to understand the importance of material conditions in schools. Where resource models for urban school improvement have missed the mark has been in the way they have outlined the purpose of these resources and the measurement of their impact. To date, most resource-based efforts in high schools have focused on improving instruction and learning conditions, with the goal of increasing the number of students who are able to "escape" poverty and attend college—to "better themselves" or to "move up." Valenzuela (1999) has called this a subtractive model of schooling, one where urban students are asked (sometimes tacitly, sometimes explicitly) to exchange the culture of their home and community for the higher culture of the school in exchange for access to college. This approach to schooling often reduces the life choices for urban non-white youth into a false binary—that of choosing between staying behind as a failure and "getting out" as a success. Faced with the prospect of leaving their communities behind to be successful, many non-white youth opt out of school. They choose to retain an urban and cultural identity that they perceive to be in conflict with the expectations of schools, even if the cost of that choice is educational marginalization (MacLeod, 1987; Valenzuela, 1999; Willis, 1977).

To be effective, urban education reform movements must begin to develop partnerships with communities that provide young people the opportunity to be successful while maintaining their identities as urban youth. This additive model of education focuses on the design of urban school culture, curriculum, and pedagogy that identifies the cultures and communities of urban students as assets rather than as things to be replaced (Moll, Amanti, Neff, & Gonzalez, 1992; Valenzuela, 1999). The unique lives and conditions of urban youth deserve an education system that accomplishes two goals in concert with one another: preparation to confront the conditions of social and economic inequity in their daily lives and access to the academic literacies (computational and linguistic) that make college attendance a realistic option.

This approach to urban education reform is a double investment in urban communities. It provides pedagogy and curricula that lend immediate relevance to school in the lives of urban youth. It also works to break the cycle of disinvestment of human capital in urban communities by creating graduates who recognize their potential agency to improve urban centers, rather than seeing them as places to escape. These prospects offer urban youth a renewed sense of purpose with regard to school, and the community the necessary human and institutional capital to contribute to its social, economic, and political revitalization.

Confronting the Urban in Urban Schools

The Gates Foundation, the Carnegie Corporation, and others carrying out similar initiatives are finding that one of the biggest challenges facing urban school reformers is the development of secondary instructional practices that encourage students to invest in schools as a viable social institution. In their independent studies and reform efforts, these organizations have identified a glaring need for institutional support of teaching and leadership practices that promote a new vision for urban high schools.

In an executive summary of its small school reform efforts, the Gates Foundation reports:

> Many of the small schools were still struggling with putting consistent, innovative instructional practices in place as their first year drew to a close. ... Many teachers told us that they lacked models and ready-to-use curricula for project-based learning and that their students came to the school lacking the basic knowledge and skills that this instructional approach requires. As a result, most of the start-up schools we visited found themselves introducing more structure and direction for incoming students than they had originally planned. (American Institutes for Research, 2003; italics in original; p. 2)

The findings from Carnegie's "Schools for a New Society" also indicate that the most challenging reform efforts have been in the area of pedagogical vision. Carnegie's research suggests that urban school reform must draw from "new leadership strategies and a new and dynamic vision of the high school" (Carnegie Corporation, 2001, p. 1). It goes on to conclude that this requires collaboration with community stakeholders to focus the high school's mission more directly on the needs of the community (pp. 1–2).

A new vision for urban school reform must continue the work of Gates and Carnegie, insisting on equitable material resources in all schools. However, their findings suggest that these resources must be used to address directly the context of urban life and poverty that shapes the lives of students and the surrounding community. In the few places where there have been consistent successes with urban students, this is the clear epistemological pattern. In efforts such as Columbia University's Cross-City Campaign, the University of California, Los Angeles, Institute for Democracy, Education, and Access (IDEA) Summer Seminar (Morrell, 2004a), and New York's Educational Video Center (Goodman, 2003), the focus remains on pedagogies that challenge the social and economic inequities that confront urban youth. For these successes to become more widespread, more attention must be paid to helping schools, and teachers most directly, in the development and implementation of pedagogy and curricula that address the conditions of urban life and develops a sense of agency among students for altering those conditions.

To institute this more critical pedagogy, we suggest moving beyond the pedagogical reform efforts of the multicultural education movement, which has also failed to deal with the conditions of modern urban life. Reform-minded individuals and collectives must be better equipped to identify the most acute issues in the social context of urban schools. Teachers, and schools more generally, need support to develop and implement pedagogy that investigates and draws from the social contexts of the lives of urban youth. Luis Moll (2000) has referred to these contexts as a student's "funds of knowledge"; that is, rather than presenting the community as a place to rise above, schools must equip themselves to draw from the knowledge that students bring with them to school—knowledge that is often not in their textbooks but is acquired from the streets, family cultural traditions, youth culture, and the media. Ladson-Billings (1994) has referred to this as "culturally relevant pedagogy," and, like Ladson-Billings, Carol Lee (2004) suggests that teachers must be better equipped to investigate what is going on in the lives of their students generally so that their curriculum and pedagogy can be reflective of those lives. With this deeper understanding of their students' lives, schools are in a much better position to appreciate and positively influence how these social contexts affect the educational outcome for urban youth.

This project of addressing the urban in urban schools must take place on various levels, foremost of which is work with teachers and school leaders. There is virtually no disagreement from any political persuasion that access to quality teachers can level the educational playing field (Schrag, 2003). For this reason, more attention must be paid to the type of training, development, and support that are given to urban teachers and school leaders. This is particularly important if educators are to develop a pedagogy, curriculum, and school culture that heed Carnegie's call for schools that are more attentive to the most pressing needs of the community. In addition to this in-service support, significant focus must also be given to the recruiting and preparation efforts in schools of education committed to preparing people to work in urban schools. In effect, meaningful urban school reform means ramping up efforts in all phases of the educational profession: recruiting, pre-service training, and in-service support and development.

Beyond Structural Determinism: Creating Pedagogies of Possibility

The paradox of educational inequality is that schools remain among the few institutions that produce opportunities to contest structural inequalities. Some have argued that the increasing standardization of pedagogy through undue attention to scripted curriculum and standardized testing threatens to reduce dramatically these opportunities to contest (Oakes & Lipton, 2001). We agree with these concerns and believe it is imperative that teachers and teacher educators develop a concrete counter-strategy to these increasingly popular state and national reform policies. Toward the development of this counter-strategy, this book argues for pedagogical practices situated in critical analyses of the role of urban schools in social inequality. Furthermore, a transformational critical pedagogy in urban education develops academic skills among populations that have traditionally been failed by these urban schools. In this way the pedagogy develops necessary skills among individuals within a context of social critique and struggle for social change.

We argue, as mentioned, that urban schools are not failing; they are doing precisely what they are designed to do. How does this premise change our approach to working in urban schools? First, it shifts the rhetoric of failure from young people and caring teachers onto an inequitable system designed to concretize failure in poor communities. Creating the conditions for suffering communities to hold structural and material inequities up to the light of inquiry is the first step in a critical pedagogy. Brazilian critical pedagogue Paulo Freire (1970) suggests that the first step toward liberation from oppression is being able to identify and name your oppression.

This urban critical pedagogy sees the recognition of the conditions of inequality and the desire to overturn those conditions for oneself and for all suffering communities as the starting point and motivator for the urban educator and for the urban student. For both educator and student, this means discarding the framework of meritocracy and critically embracing the role of the underdog. It means framing a classroom and school culture that utilizes critical pedagogy to critique notions of equal opportunity and access, making education a weapon to name, analyze, deconstruct, and act upon the unequal conditions in urban schools, urban communities, and other disenfranchised communities across the nation and the world. The liberal model of urban education reform makes the mistake of attempting to replicate the schooling ideology of the middle class, foregrounding a "college-going culture." In so doing, it all but ignores the material conditions of urban communities, which are more pertinent to the lives of students and are far removed from the rhetoric of college.

Let us be clear. We believe that urban students should go to college at rates equal to their more affluent counterparts. We also believe that a schooling environment that foregrounds the relationship between education and the most pressing conditions in the community, an education with relevance, is most likely to produce notable increases in college eligibility. We advocate for an urban education model that utilizes critical counter-cultural communities of practice (4Cs), developing a critical and engaged citizenry with a democratic sensibility that critiques and acts against all forms of inequality.

In short, communities of practice can be defined as follows:

- Who: "groups of people who share a common concern or a passion for something they do and who interact regularly to learn how to do it better"
- What is it about: it's a *joint enterprise* as understood and continually renegotiated by its members
- How does it function: *mutual engagement* that binds members together into a social entity
- What capability does it produce: the *shared repertoire* of communal resources (routines, sensibilities, artifacts, vocabulary, styles, etc.) that members have developed over time (Wenger, 1998).

A counter-cultural community of practice recognizes the existence of a dominant set of institutional norms and practices and intentionally sets itself up to counter those norms and practices. In urban classrooms, a counter-cultural community of practice responds directly to structural and material inequalities in the school and the larger community. The developing counter-cultural community of practice intentionally targets alienation, intellectual disenfranchisement, despair, and academic failure to be replaced with large quantities of community, critical consciousness, hope, and academic achievement.

To develop these critical counter-cultural communities of practice in our own work with urban youth, we attempted to employ the five steps of the cycle of critical praxis (see Figure 1.1).

As educators, drawing upon the cycle of critical praxis helps us to create a dynamic curriculum that is directly responsive to the needs of any given community. For instance, when the curriculum begins with a problem or issue that is identified in collaboration with youth, there is no doubt as to its

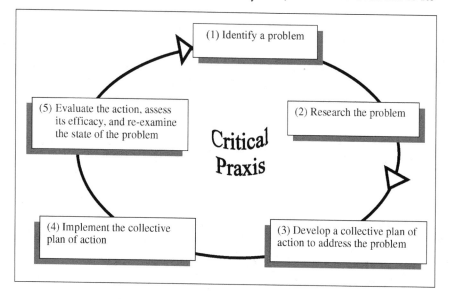

Figure 1.1. Cycle of Critical Praxis

relevance or its authenticity. In Chapter 6, for instance, we describe the work of a summer research seminar where young people learned the tools of critical research, which they immediately used to investigate problems in their city schools.

The second step, researching the problem, implies an action that can guide the curriculum and lead to praxis. In that same seminar, for example, once the problems were identified, the next step entailed conducting research into these problems. During one seminar, students investigated the access that urban students had to quality learning resources, quality teachers, and rigorous college-bound curricula in their schools. They visited school sites, talked to teachers and administrators, and conducted a comprehensive survey among their peers. Their findings were ultimately shared with a wide audience of practitioners, researchers, and policymakers.

Research in and of itself, while valuable, is not enough. Once a problem has been identified and researched, the next step involves developing collective action that addresses the problem. For the students in the seminar who researched educational inequality this meant advocating for changes in educational policy. Their research fueled the creation of a bill that championed the rights of California students. For the girls' basketball team that we discuss in Chapter 4, this plan of action entailed putting on basketball clinics for other young girls in the city who did not have access to quality coaching at a young age.

Once a plan has been developed, it needs to be implemented. In the case of the seminar students, this meant lobbying legislators or organizing with parents and teachers to march on the state capitol. For the girl basketball players, this meant actually putting on basketball clinics. For the students at Northeast Community High School, this translated into an organized protest. Students at East Bay High School created a magazine that they planned to distribute to their peers. (See "Sites and Participants" below for an introduction to these schools.)

The final step in the process is a reassessment of the problem and a renewed commitment to remedy the problem. Critical praxis involves continued action for social justice, but it also involves continued reflection on the actions necessary to deal effectively with the problems that have been identified.

Each of the steps in the cycle of critical praxis reveals powerful opportunities for critical pedagogy with urban youth. The cycle breaks down the inherent power relations in traditional pedagogy and identifies students as collaborators with adults. This does not negate the important and crucial role that educators play in this process (we discuss this important role throughout the book), but it fundamentally repositions students as actors and as contributors to the struggle for social change. Furthermore, the cycle identifies youth popular culture as a legitimate site for engagement and curriculum development. While youth will need to learn about world history, and while they will need to be exposed to the literary canon, they can learn most of the core academic skills that they need by engaging their own social worlds. We will show throughout our descriptions and analyses of the pedagogical interventions how youth developed sophisticated academic skills while being involved in this sort of work.

As we transition into a description of our methodology and provide an overview of the remaining chapters, we want to be explicit in acknowledging that this is not the first book to propose, in theory, a critical pedagogy for urban youth. What makes this book different is that the middle chapters report on educational contexts where we implemented these theoretical principles with urban youth. We began this work over a decade ago, drawing upon many of the theoretical tenets that have inspired other critical educators as well. What we provide here is a comprehensive analysis of the projects that were developed in response to that theory. In many ways, this book represents the final stages in our own cycle of critical praxis.

The critical pedagogy we discuss here is one that sees education as a tool for eliminating oppressive relationships and conditions. To that end, this book is profoundly hopeful and humanistic because it articulates pedagogical practices situated in the civic responsibility of an educational system intolerant of the suffering of anyone. Educating young people this way should not be a particularly complex endeavor. It is, however, profoundly difficult if one does not recognize the ways in which the current system of education is rigged to produce unequal outcomes. It is our hope that reading about the shape that our work has taken over a decade of critical praxis with urban youth inspires others to go through the same process and articulate their own grounded theories of critical praxis, for we know that it is only through our continued engagement and reflection on that engagement that we have a chance fundamentally and radically to alter the nature of contemporary academic instruction. The following brief overview of the methodology includes a description of our sites, our participants, and our methods of data collection and analysis.

Methodology

Critical Research Tradition

This study is centered firmly within what we call the critical research tradition. Since the Age of Reason, many thinkers (and scientists in particular) have set out in search of universal truths that are derived from rigorous and objective research. Indeed, the term "scientific research" has come to be synonymous with this notion of enlightenment. Quality scientific scholarship is defined by its objectivity, by the disinterestedness and distance of the researchers from the research itself, and by its external validity—the ability of any outside researcher to come to the same general conclusions were she or he to follow the same steps.

In its defense, social science has often pushed upon these narrow definitions of scientific research. Anthropology, for instance, is largely informed by participant-observation research methodology, which acknowledges that ethnographers are not only observers but also participate in the cultural contexts that they investigate. However, for the most part, the same rules apply.

The researcher, even in social science research, is supposed to remove herself or himself from the data as much as possible and should not have a vested interest in the outcome of the research.

Critical research, in contrast, is defined by the interestedness of the researcher, more specifically by the explicit desire to use research as a tool for social change (Carspecken, 1996; Cushman, 1998; Kincheloe & McLaren, 1998; Morrell, 2004a; Oakes, Rogers, & Lipton, 2006). Critical research is usually conducted with or on behalf of marginalized populations, the work itself is collaborative in nature, and the work is geared toward producing knowledge in the pursuit of action for change.

The work reported here is critical research in each of these respects. In each of the interventions one or both of us served as primary educators in some respect, meaning that we were participants with an interest in creating conditions for powerful learning to occur. We were heavily involved with the students, teachers, and parents whom we talk about in subsequent chapters. We are unabashed to admit that we loved (and continue to love) our research subjects, who often participated as collaborators and friends. This very context, this very engagement, and these very relationships form the bedrock of our critical research enterprise. Without them we would have been unable to develop the five projects that we talk about, and we would not have had access to the powerful and evocative data that we collected across each of these projects. With this in mind, we transition to a brief discussion of our research sites, along with an explanation of our data collection and strategies for analysis and an overview of the remaining chapters in the book.

Sites and Participants

The projects that we discuss were carried out across three major sites: a high school English classroom and basketball team at East Bay High School, a college access program at South City High School, and a summer research seminar operated through a major university in Southern California. East Bay High School is a large comprehensive high school located in Oakland, California. Oakland, one of the more diverse cities in California, is home to a large population of African Americans, many of whom migrated west (from the small towns of the South) during the years immediately before World War II. The city has also witnessed huge waves of immigrants from East Asia and Latin America that started in the 1970s and continue through the present. The demographics over the ten years that one or both of us worked with the school reveal a population of about 50% Asian American students, 30–40% African, and 10–20% Latino. The population of white students at the school was negligible during this entire period (even though the population of the city has remained more than 25% white). More than three-quarters of the students attending East Bay High School came from families that qualified to receive AFDC (Aid to Families with Dependent Children), and students scored far below state and national norms on standardized tests and college admissions exams. Finally, the graduation rates and college-bound rates for this school were far below state and national norms. From every statistical indicator, and from our personal experience, we designate East Bay High School an under-resourced and under-achieving urban high school. The participants at East Bay High include a 12th-grade English class (Chapter 3) and a girl's varsity basketball team (Chapter 4). The demographics of the class and the team mirror exactly the larger composite demographics of the school.

South City High School is located in a neighborhood in Southern California that brings together a diverse population of extremely wealthy (and largely white) residents with a population of working poor (largely Latino and African American). The school reflects these demographics (indeed, the school is far more ethnically and socioeconomically diverse than the city) and was almost evenly split between a wealthy population of white and Asian students and a working-class population of African Americans and Latinos. Many of the African American and Latino students at the school either come from a small section of the city known to have higher poverty rates or on transfer from poorer areas of the city because their parents feel that South City represents a safer and more rigorous academic environment than their own district schools.

Unfortunately, South City remains an extremely academically segregated learning environment. African American and Latino students rarely enroll in the most challenging classes at the school, and their achievement and college-bound rates are far lower than those of their white and Asian counterparts at the school. The principal of the school at the time of this research referred to this as the "two school phenomenon": one school for the students from wealthy families and one for students from lower-income families. As is normally the case, race and class were closely correlated, giving the classrooms in South City the appearance of academic apartheid. While it would be a stretch to classify South City as "urban," there is no question that the racial and socio-economic demographics and academic achievement of students in the "second school" closely mirrored those in urban schools throughout the region. The college access program we conducted at South City consisted only of students who would be categorized within this "second school." Our participants consisted of twenty-seven working-class African American and Latina/o students who participated in a four-year college access program that we labeled as the Futures program. These students were randomly selected from a larger population of students identified as being at risk of not graduating from high school. This is significant because four years after this designation, all but one of the Futures students had graduated from high school and most were attending postsecondary schools throughout the region. We talk more in Chapter 5 about the pedagogical conditions that facilitated these impressive outcomes.

The summer research seminar, which ran for six consecutive summers between 1999 and 2004, drew 150 students from the most under-performing schools in Greater Los Angeles to participate in a six-week intensive program at a local university. Throughout their six weeks in the program the students learned the tools of critical research, designed research studies, and carried these studies out in teams within the neighborhoods and schools of urban Los Angeles. Textual/media products included research reports, PowerPoint presentations, and short films. Students also produced individual essays describing the experience of becoming a critical researcher. Since then the students' research has been featured at local and national conferences, in an Internet journal, in peer-reviewed professional publications, and in local and national media. The students have also presented their work to university professors and elected officials. Students were selected on the basis of their willingness to participate in the seminar's activities. Many were recommended by teachers, counselors, administrators, and peers as young people in need of our program. The socio-economic demographics of the students matched those of the urban schools they were attending. These students also represented a wide range of academic achievement, with grade point averages spanning from 1.0 to well over 4.0.

Data Collection and Analysis

Throughout our substantive involvement across these various projects, we collected a massive data set that included observational field notes, videotapes of classroom interactions, samples of student work, interviews, and academic achievement data (grades, course taking, graduation, and college admission). We analyzed this data in terms of academic development, critical consciousness, and action toward social change. This three-part approach is rooted in our belief that the desired outcome of critical pedagogies in urban education is multiple and that it must impact academic achievement, identity development, and civic engagement. We further believe that any powerful pedagogy in urban education (or all education for that matter) should address each of these crucial areas. We do not do our students any favors if we let them matriculate through our schools without the development of core academic skills that will allow them to access postsecondary education and professional work in our postindustrial age. Too often, we believe, critical pedagogies focus on the rhetoric of social critique to the exclusion of the development of sophisticated literacy and numeracy skills.

That being said, education cannot be articulated only as the mastery of discrete facts and skills. We know only too well that students can master these skills and succeed academically at great personal and social costs that include alienation from family, language, community, and progressive social values. A critical pedagogy in urban education strives to create spaces for students to learn as they also embrace and develop affirmed and empowered identities as intellectuals, as urban youth, and as members of historically marginalized ethnic groups. Finally, the true value of a public education can be measured only to the extent that it makes public life better for all citizens. This means more than simply preparing select individuals to enter the elite professions. Our goals as educators, and as an educational system, should include the development of competent and humane citizens who are proactive participants in social life.

When analyzing student work and student discourse, we employed a new literacy studies framework that allowed us to examine the myriad literacy events that occurred across these pedagogical interventions for evidence of academic skill development (Barton and Hamilton, 2000). We used this framework to address the following questions: To what extent do these samples reveal that students are emerging as competent readers and writers working at sophisticated levels? To what extent does the outcome in the academic settings meet or even exceed content area standards in the disciplines? And to what extent do the students who experience these pedagogical interventions make more quantifiable academic transformations, including raised grade point averages and test scores and admission into colleges and universities?

We employed a community of practice framework (Lave & Wenger, 1991; Wenger, 1998) to investigate the development of empowered and affirmed identities among the students who participated in these interventions. In particular, we wanted to understand the various roles that students embraced as they became involved in the activities that we explore in subsequent chapters. To what degree, we wondered, did the change in roles over time serve as evidence of the development of affirmed and empowered identities? Drawing from the work of Jean Lave (1996), we were interested in what the students were "becoming" as they changed in participation over time in these counter-cultural communities of practices. We also analyzed student work and student interview data to get a sense of whether they saw themselves differently as a result of these critical interventions.

We also drew on the community of practice literature to examine the nature of the practice itself; that is, we were interested not only in the changing identities of the students who participated but also in the actual work in which the students took part. Toward these ends, we examined the relationships between the critical teaching events, the students' skill and identity development, and real work for social change. In particular, how did the students as individuals and collectives participate differently in social life? In what activities did they engage? What, if any, evidence exists of a social impact as a result of these new ways of participating? Each of these analyses provided important insight for unpacking the relationship between these four pedagogical interventions and powerful learning outcomes for the students. Before embarking on our ten-year journey with urban youth, Chapter 2 unpacks the traditional and contemporary theories that inform our conception of critical pedagogy. Each of the middle five chapters reports on a pedagogical intervention. Chapters 8 and 9 return to a grounded theory of critical pedagogy with urban youth.

Overview of Book Chapters

Chapter 2 is an investigation of the post-philosophical foundations of critical pedagogy, paying particular attention to those Marxist-inspired critical pedagogues who have emerged in the Freirean tradition (Aronowitz & Giroux, 1991; Darder, 1991; Freire, 1970, 1997, 1998; Freire & Macedo, 1987; Giroux, 1988, 1996; hooks, 1994a, 1994b; McLaren, 1994, 2003b; Shor, 1992) and highlighting both their similarities and differences. The chapter also looks to theorists and practitioners who may not be traditionally associated with critical pedagogy (Frantz Fanon, Ché Guevara, W. E. B. Du Bois, Subcommandante Marcos, Edward Said, Carter G. Woodson, and T. Trinh Minh-ha) yet who have much to offer to the current discourse.

Chapter 3 highlights our six years of teaching English at East Bay High. As colleagues and, ultimately, as co-teachers and research partners, we designed units that incorporated elements of youth popular culture and film to encourage the students to participate as critical social theorists and social advocates. Relying heavily on critical pedagogy strategies, we attempted to equip our students with critical media literacy skills to allow them to navigate omnipresent twenty-first-century media texts more effectively. In this chapter we analyze video transcripts, student interview data, and student work to answer questions about the appropriateness of critical pedagogy as a strategy for increasing academic literacy, critical thinking, and commitment to social justice in English classrooms.

Chapter 4 investigates the potential of youth culture to increase the connectedness of urban high school students to their academic and personal lives. Through critical qualitative investigation, this chapter examines a year-round sports program (a varsity women's basketball team at East Bay High School) for its effectiveness in overtly using participation in sports to increase the academic performance and social growth of a group of urban high school students. Relying on scholarship that views youth culture as a powerful, but oftentimes under-utilized, point of intervention for schools (Apple, 1990; Darling-Hammond, 1998; Delpit & Dowdy, 2002; Gans, 1999; Giroux, 1996; Ladson-Billings, 1994), this study seeks to understand whether the group of young women who participated were affected academically and socially by the program's intervention and whether there is an impact that warrants the increased use of critical pedagogy and youth culture as intervention strategies in urban schools.

Chapter 5 examines the practice of critical pedagogy in a college access intervention program that targeted the low-income students of color attending South City High School. Morrell worked with a team of university researchers who combined the normal work of college access programs with a curriculum that apprenticed these students as critical researchers of equity and access in urban schools. Centered at the nexus of critical pedagogy (Freire, 1970; McLaren, 1994, 2003b) and socio-cultural theory (Lave & Wenger, 1991), this research apprenticed students of color as critical sociologists to develop academic and critical literacy while also promoting meaningful college access. Through our examination of a two-year data set that includes student work, student reflections, interviews, ethnographic field notes, and videotapes of classroom instruction and student participation in a research seminar, we attempt to articulate a theory of practice that challenges a myopic or idealistic implementation of critical pedagogy in oppressive institutions such as urban schools while not losing sight of the proponents' ideals of enacting a liberating and humanizing practice with marginalized student populations. Our goal in analyzing the work of this project is to demonstrate that it is possible to fashion a college-bound culture and to develop college-readiness skills among urban youth within a context of research and action for social change. Indeed, it may only be such a practice that will effectively engage and motivate urban secondary students to overcome a history of academic marginalization and to be willing simultaneously to navigate and to confront the institutions that have facilitated this academic marginalization.

Chapter 6 examines the practice of critical pedagogy in a summer research seminar that brought together urban teens from a large metropolitan area in Southern California to learn the tools of critical research and to conduct critical research studies on issues of importance to urban schools and communities. In this chapter we examine field notes, interview and survey data, videotaped classroom sessions, videotapes of students involved in the research process, students' essays, and student-generated research reports. Our goal was to understand the relationship between engagement in critical research, critical pedagogy, the development of academic and critical literacies, and the struggle for social and educational justice. We also wanted to contribute to a model of educational reform that involves young people as intellectuals and collaborators in the process. In addition, we wanted to understand the role of critical pedagogy in this development.

Chapter 7 examines the possible intersection between critical pedagogy and ethnic studies at the high school level. We begin with the premise that the connections between critical pedagogy, racial identity, and academic achievement are under-explored. We then articulate a framework for critical pan-ethnic studies that we play out across two contexts: (1) a Sociology course at an urban high school that was part of the small schools movement and (2) a research seminar where young people are apprenticed as critical public historians investigating the history of race and education in their city. We sought to understand the role of critical pedagogy in providing space for the development of empowered ethnic and intellectual identities in the course of work that sheds light on the history of race and racism in our society. We further wanted this praxis to be situated in collective cross-racial conversations and cross-racial action for change. Given that our schools are rarely mono-racial environments, and given that many racially marginalized groups experience injustice in similar ways, we felt strongly about putting forth a pan-ethnic studies approach that allowed students to see themselves and each other as implicated in the same sets of historical problems.

Chapter 8 addresses the current tenor of educational discourse that is focused on standards and standardized tests. We address the tensions associated with being critical of such standards and tests while acknowledging that the future of marginalized students depends on being able to navigate these oppressive standards and exams. We attempt in this chapter to offer examples of how the critical pedagogical interventions we describe connect to disciplinary standards in English/Language Arts, Social Studies, and Mathematics. At the same time, we provide a critique of an over-reliance on standards and standardized tests and offer other possibilities for measuring student competence and disciplinary knowledge.

We conclude this work with a grounded theory of practice that juxtaposes the theoretical and historical traditions of critical pedagogy with the context of ten years of practice in urban schools. The intention of this final chapter is not to be dismissive of foundational texts or to provide a one-size-fits-all model of critical pedagogy in urban contexts. Rather, we seek to convince readers that critical pedagogy is a viable practice in urban contexts by providing enough substantive examples of critical pedagogy in action to generate discussion, debate, and, most important, future critical practices. In this final chapter we review the principles of our grounded theory of critical pedagogy in urban education; we also consider the implications of this grounded theory for educational policy, for educational practice in K–12 contexts, and for the preparation of the next generation of urban educators. We conclude by appropriately situating our model of critical pedagogy within a larger context of revolutionary action for social change. Transforming one classroom or the lives of a handful of students is not the goal of a radical theory of critical pedagogy. Only when all students, all people, have equitable access to their humanity and to the full material resources available will our work be done. That sort of change comes only with revolution.

2
Contemporary Developers of Critical Pedagogy

This chapter discusses the foundation of our understanding of critical pedagogy. It pays particular attention to critical pedagogues emerging from the Freirean tradition (Freire, 1970, 1998; Freire and Macedo, 1987; Shor, 1992; Darder, 1991; McLaren, 1994, 2003b; Giroux, 2001, 2003; hooks, 1994a, 1994b). It also discusses educators, scholars, theorists, and revolutionaries not traditionally associated with critical pedagogy (Carter G. Woodson, Lolita Lebrón, Frantz Fanon, Reies Tijerina, Audre Lorde, Gloria Anzaldúa, and Subcommandante Marcos). Finally, it addresses critiques of critical pedagogy from both the right and left in attempting to contextualize the current educational discourse.

Critical pedagogues, drawing on social and critical educational theory and cultural studies, examine schools in their historical context and as part of the existing social and political fabric that characterizes the dominant society. They challenge the assumption that schools function as major sites of social and economic mobility. Instead, they suggest that schooling must be analyzed as a cultural and historical process in which students are positioned within asymmetrical relations of power on the basis of specific race, class, and gender groupings. A major task of critical pedagogy has been to disclose and challenge the reproductive role schools play in political and cultural life. Although differences exist in their analysis, these critical thinkers are united in their belief that any genuine pedagogical practice demands a commitment to social transformation in solidarity within subordinated and marginalized groups.

Critical pedagogies can provide teachers and researchers with a better means of understanding the role that schools play within a race-, class-, and gender-divided society. This promotes the questioning of student experiences, texts, teacher ideologies, and aspects of school policy that conservative and liberal analyses too often leave unexplored. Further, critical pedagogues aim to pry theories away from the academics and incorporate them into educational practice. They set out to "relativize" schools as normalizing agencies that essentially bring legitimacy to existing social relations and practices, rendering them normal and natural by dismantling and rearranging the artificial rules and codes that make up classroom reality (McLaren, 1994, 2003b).

Paulo Freire

There is no agreement about who originated critical pedagogy, but Paulo Freire is considered the most likely candidate. Freire, a Brazilian educator, was an important mentor to many of the critical pedagogues in the United States. He is best known for his book *Pedagogy of the Oppressed* (1970), which has sold upward of 750,000 copies and is a seminal text for the study of critical pedagogy. In it, Freire juxtaposes the banking metaphor for education with his recommended problem-posing education. He explains that the banking model of education leads to

> [e]ducation becom[ing] an act of depositing, in which the students are the depositories and the teacher is the depositor. Instead of communicating, the teacher issues communiqués and makes deposits that the students patiently receive, memorize, and repeat. (p. 72)

For Freire, this model of education is the greatest tool in the hands of the oppressor. It is a weapon used to prepare the oppressed to adapt to their situation as the oppressed rather than to challenge the situation that oppresses them.

The antithesis to the banking model of education is critical pedagogy, which Freire calls problem-posing education:

> In problem-posing education, people develop their power to perceive critically *the way they exist* in the world *with which* and *in which* they find themselves; they come to see the world not as a static reality, but as a reality in process, in transformation. (p. 83)

Problem-posing education is education for freedom and emphasizes that teachers must see themselves in a partnership with their students. As part of this relationship, the teachers must see themselves as teacher-student, ready to accept that their students possess knowledge and solutions they can share with the teacher. Such an approach to education emphasizes learning for freedom rather than learning to earn (to enter the economy). This, Freire says, is the "pedagogy of the oppressed, which is the pedagogy of people engaged in the fight for their own liberation" (p. 53).

At the core of Freire's critical pedagogy is the concept of praxis, the process by which teachers and students commit to education that leads to action and reflection on that action. This process has five stages:

1. Identify a problem.
2. Analyze the problem.
3. Create a plan of action to address the problem.
4. Implement the plan of action.
5. Analyze and evaluate the action.

The process is intended to be cyclical (see Figure 1.1). Students are encouraged to become social agents, developing their capacity to confront real-world problems that face them and their community. The reflective part of the process develops the understanding that complex problems require complex solutions that must be revisited, revised, and re-implemented to reach a full solution.

Freire describes three major challenges to the effective implementation of a critical pedagogy. The first challenge to be overcome is the tendency of the educator to revert to the banking model of education:

> in their desire to obtain the support of the people for revolutionary action, revolutionary leaders (teachers) often fall for the banking line of planning program content from the top down. They approach the peasant or urban masses with projects that may correspond to their own view of the world, but not to that of the people. They forget that their fundamental objective is to fight alongside the people for the recovery of the people's stolen humanity, not to "win the people over" to their side. (p. 94–95)

Most teachers, even those with justice and liberation at the heart of their educational program, were educated in a banking model system. Nowhere is this barrier more pronounced than for the K–12 educator. Faced with the challenge of preparing for a classroom of youngsters, there is little to fall back on except their training as students, which has most certainly prepared them to reproduce the banking model.

The second obstacle to the implementation of critical pedagogy is something Freire calls false generosity.

> Any attempt to "soften" the power of the oppressor in deference to the weakness of the oppressed almost always manifests itself in the form of false generosity … in order to have the continued opportunity to express their "generosity," the oppressors must perpetuate injustice as well. An unjust social order is the permanent fount of this "generosity," which is nourished by death, despair, and poverty. That is why the dispensers of false generosity become desperate at the slightest threat to its source. (p. 44)

converts [to problem-solving education] truly desire to transform the unjust order; but because of their background they believe that they must be the executors of the transformation. They talk about the people, but they do not trust them; and trusting people is the indispensable precondition for revolutionary change (pp. 94–95).

Freire suggests that educators must constantly reflect on their pedagogy and its impact on relationships with students. They should strive not for affirmation of their own generosity but to destroy the causes of false generosity. This, *true generosity*, is a commitment to pedagogy that develops hands— of individuals or groups—that "need be extended less and less in supplication, so that more and more they become human hands which work [to] transform the world" (p. 45).

A third major challenge that Freire describes to the full implementation of a critical pedagogy is a phenomenon he calls the sub-oppressors, oppressed groups who become oppressors themselves. Freire suggests that this almost always is the case in the initial stages of critical awareness because the structure of the situation that has shaped their identity has normalized the oppressor–oppressed paradigm, and to be free is to be on the oppressor side of that dichotomy: "Their ideal is to be men; but for them, to be men is to be oppressors. This is their model of humanity" (p. 45).

This creation of the sub-oppressor can result in a "horizontal violence" whereby people striving for freedom see themselves as getting ahead when they take advantage of other oppressed peoples. This association of freedom with the power to oppress can also lead oppressed groups to simply invert the oppressor–oppressed paradigm, seizing power and then oppressing the people who formerly oppressed them. Freire describes both of these outcomes as part of a "colonized mentality" and says that critical pedagogues must encourage oppressed people to challenge the tendency to associate one's freedom with the ability to oppress others (p. 62). For this reason, a Freirean critical pedagogy involves the process of freeing oneself, other oppressed people, and, ultimately, one's former oppressors (p. 62).

For Freire, the pursuit of a fuller humanity is the purpose of education. He believed that educators who rise to the challenge of critical pedagogy create a humanizing pedagogy. His life's work bordered on an obsession with the exploration of the concept of pedagogy, something for which he was totally unapologetic. Five of his book titles begin with *Pedagogy of ...*, and each further reflects upon and refines his earlier analyses of pedagogy. His last book, published posthumously, was titled *Pedagogy of Freedom*. It provides no silver bullet for the persistence of inequality and injustice. Instead, it simply suggests that we understand three core principles about pedagogy: (1) There is no teaching without learning; (2) teaching is not just transferring knowledge; (3) teaching is a human act (Freire, 1998, vii–viii).

These principles are explored in separate chapters in *Pedagogy of Freedom*. In sum, they are the anchors of a humanizing education that develops a critical literacy for students and teachers. This literacy revolves around the five stages of critical praxis. It creates a cycle of awareness, action, and reflection whereby people are empowered constantly to analyze and act upon the material conditions of their own lives—what Freire called "reading the word and the world" (Freire & Macedo, 1987). People involved in this style of education establish a symbiotic relationship between the word and the world. Their relationship with literacy is no longer mechanical—learning to earn. Instead, literacy is an interchange where their understanding of the world allows them better to understand the word, and the word allows them better to understand their world. This is learning for freedom.

Freire's critical literacy is at the heart of his vision for effective pedagogy. It results in an educative process that leads to actions, ideally collective in nature, guided by love and aimed at producing a more just society. These acts of love are followed by reflection in order that the next actions are better informed. This is Freire's concept of praxis, it is his concept of constantly reading the word and the world, and it is his concept of pedagogy for freedom. This, Freire believed, can make teachers and students into "permanent re-creators" of their own knowledge and reality, resulting in a "committed involvement" by the oppressed to the liberation of all peoples (Freire, 1970, 69).

The significance of Freire's work to our modern understanding of critical pedagogy cannot be overstated. Our attention to his work in this small section could never adequately capture the breadth of his thought on the matter. Yet it seems appropriate to conclude our discussion by pointing out that after a lifetime during which the world became a less humane place by most standards of measure, Freire remained unshakably committed to the establishment of a humanizing pedagogy. In *Pedagogy of the Oppressed* he wrote:

> As individuals or as peoples, by fighting for the restoration of their humanity they will be attempting the restoration of true generosity. Who are better prepared to understand the terrible significance of an oppressive society? Who suffer the effects of oppression more than the oppressed? Who can better understand the necessity of

liberation? They will not gain this liberation by chance but through the praxis of their quest for it, through their recognition of the necessity to fight for it. (p. 45)

Problem-posing education does not and cannot serve the interests of the oppressor. No oppressive order could permit the oppressed to begin to question: Why? While only a revolutionary society can carry out this education in systematic terms, the revolutionary leaders need not take full power before they can employ the method. ... They must be revolutionary—that is to say, dialogical—from the outset. (p. 86)

Almost thirty years later, he wrote:

I cannot be a teacher if I do not perceive with ever-greater clarity that my practice demands of me a definition about where I stand. A break with what is not right ethically. I must choose between one thing and another thing. I cannot be a teacher and be in favor of everyone and everything. I cannot be in favor merely of people, humanity, and vague phrases far from the concrete nature of educative practice. Mass hunger and unemployment, side by side with opulence, are not the result of destiny, as certain reactionary circles would have us believe, claiming that people suffer because they can do nothing about the situation. The question here is not "destiny." It is immorality. Here I want to repeat—forcefully—that nothing can justify the degradation of human beings. Nothing ... I refuse to add my voice to that of the "peacemakers" who call upon the wretched of the earth to be resigned to their fate. My voice is in tune with a different language, another kind of music. It speaks of resistance, indignation, the just anger of those who are deceived and betrayed. It speaks, too, of their right to rebel against the ethical transgressions of which they are the long-suffering victims. (p. 93)

In these two passages we see that Freire's commitment to those who have the least remains unwavering. So does his belief that teachers practicing critical pedagogy with their students are central agents of radical social change. What is new in the second passage is adamancy that his message not be misinterpreted or watered down. This is a response to educators around the globe who have appropriated the concept of critical pedagogy while maintaining lifestyles far removed from those of people who suffer under oppressive social conditions. Freire's final thoughts on critical pedagogy demand harsh self-reflection for educators who find comfort in the rhetoric of a progressive pedagogy. He has taken away the middle ground and demanded that to earn the title "teacher" is to permanently occupy a place alongside the "wretched of the earth."

Ira Shor

Shor (1992) combines critical educational theories such as those of Freire, Giroux, and Dewey with Piaget's theories of learning and development that advocate a reciprocal relationship between teacher and student (as opposed to teachers merely transferring knowledge to students via lecture) to analyze the impact of critical pedagogy and empowering education on classroom practices. Empowering education, as Shor defines it, is

> a critical-democratic pedagogy for self and social change. It is a student-centered program for multicultural democracy in school and society. It approaches individual growth as an active, cooperative, and social process, because the self and society create each other. … The goals of this pedagogy are to relate personal growth to public life, by developing strong skills, academic knowledge, habits of inquiry, and critical curiosity about society, power, inequality, and change. (p. 15)

Teaching inside of this paradigm is not a neutral act. A curriculum that avoids questioning school and society is not, as is commonly supposed, politically neutral. It cuts off the students' development as critical thinkers about their world. According to Shor, there are eleven values of empowering education: "participatory, affective, problem-posing, situated, multicultural, dialogic, de-socializing, democratic, researching, interdisciplinary, and activist" (p. 17).

Empowering Education (1992) provides an explicit critique of traditional education. Shor argues that traditional education suppresses, instead of develops, skills and intellectual interests; it relegates students to positions of powerlessness, setting them up to accept powerlessness as adults; it fails to acknowledge the strengths and cultures and prior knowledge of the students; and it gives teachers the ultimate authority. It leads students and teachers to feel disconnected and alienated from the curriculum and schooling. It promotes failure for a large segment of the population, facilitates cultural and social reproduction, and doesn't accurately measure cognitive skills.

Shor's work also points to the difficulties that emergent critical educators may face, provides strategies for dealing with these challenges, and advocates for empowering educators to become classroom researchers. By becoming researchers of their classrooms, educators can reflect on their practice and influence the research-driven discussions about effective pedagogy. They can challenge the "zero pardigm" which supports inequality by delivering a "Eurocentric syllabus that silences critical thinking about society and ignores the culturally diverse languages and experiences of students" (p. 202). The first responsibility for critical teachers creating an empowering curriculum is to "research what students know, speak, experience, and feel" (p. 202). This allows teachers to create what Shor calls a "critical paradigm" that respects the experiences, languages, and experiences of students.

Antonia Darder

Darder, a student of Paulo Freire, has theorized extensively on critical pedagogy. Some of her more recent work has looked closely at Freire's lifelong commitment to articulating critical pedagogy as an act of love (Darder, 2002a, 2002b). In her book examining the work of Freire, *Reinventing Paulo Freire: A Pedagogy of Love*, Darder draws on interviews from eight of Freire's former students. The book uses first-person narrative to emphasize the impact of Freire's own practice on the lives of his students. As the title suggests, a major conclusion of the narratives is the centrality of love to the practice of critical pedagogy. If there is a central tenet of critical pedagogy, Darder's work suggests that it is love.

Darder has also articulated the importance of complicating the concepts of democracy and race in discussions of critical pedagogy. She draws from Gramsci's statement that true democracy does not use education to move the worker-citizen from unskilled to skilled. Instead, democracy relies on education to position every citizen to govern. Darder argues that critical pedagogues must be more attentive to facilitating this preparation in their classrooms. She argues that the challenge for educators is to "delve rigorously into those specific theoretical issues that are fundamental to the establishment of a culturally democratic foundation for a critical bicultural pedagogy in the classroom" (Darder, 1997, 331). She is emphatic that this process is not meant to help teachers prepare a one-size-fits-all recipe for classroom practice. On the contrary, practicing critical pedagogy requires educators to work collectively with their students, colleagues, and the larger school community. This collaboration is essential for educators to "move beyond the boundaries of prescribed educational practice" to develop classroom pedagogy that serves their students' context-specific needs (cultural, linguistic, social, political, economic) (p. 350). For Darder, this project of democratic education can be carried out only by educators with a "critical commitment to act on behalf of freedom and social justice that serve as a model for their students to discover their own personal power, social transformative potential, and spirit of hope" (p. 350).

Darder's work also encourages critical pedagogues to complicate their thinking about race as an absolute marker for liberating struggles. She argues that while race is a critical factor in the marginalization of people everywhere, it has been over-simplified in educational discourses on multiculturalism:

> [T]he process of racialization, with its reified commonsense notions of "race," fails to challenge fundamental structural inequalities inherent in the mode of production of capitalist relations. ... As a consequence, contemporary society has become entrenched in the language of "race" as destiny, with an implicit dictum that membership in particular "races" enacts social processes rather than ideology and material conditions of survival. (p. 7)

Too often, the focus of multicultural educators has not been on the structural inequalities and massive wealth disparities that result from modern capitalistic practices. Thus, much of the educational discourse on race has "failed to generate any real or lasting structural change" for widespread equity (p. 8). It has, instead, instantiated an expansion of a non-white elite class as evidence of the social progress of the country. The challenge for critical pedagogues, then, is not to eliminate educational discourse on race but to shift the attention to "the malignant ideology of racism that sustains the economic conditions of segregation" (p. 8). Darder's work challenges critical pedagogues to focus on exploitation and inequality to "revive an emancipatory politics of collective self-determination" (p. 13). This requires critical pedagogues to understand racism as an "inherent political strategy of exclusion, domination, marginalization, violence, and exploitation [not to] be separated from its economic imperative" (p. 6). In this way, critical pedagogues shift the educational discourse away from multiculturalism and illuminate the connections between race and social, political, and economic inequities.

Peter McLaren

McLaren (2003b) asserts that critical pedagogy is simultaneously concerned with the details of what students and others might do to create change together and the cultural politics that support such practices. Critical educational theorists, he claims, have responded to the new right by arguing that the increasing adoption of management-style pedagogies and accountability schemes to meet the logic of market demands has resulted in policy proposals that actively promote the deskilling of teachers.

McLaren was also a student of Paulo Freire. His most widely recognized work in the area of critical pedagogy is *Life in Schools*, where attempts to address how "critical educators can create a language that enables teachers to examine the role that schooling plays in joining knowledge and power to capitalist social relations of production" (2003b, xxxiv). These teachers employ critical pedagogy with the dual purpose of empowering themselves and teaching for empowerment.

McLaren's work has given considerable attention to articulating a framework for critical pedagogy. His framework suggests that educators intending to facilitate critical pedagogy must first become critical theorists. That is, critical educators endorse theories that "recognize the problems of society as more than simply isolated events of individuals or deficiencies in the social structure" (2003a, 69). This training in critical theory prepares educators to examine and act upon the relationships between knowledge, power, curriculum (formal and hidden), and social reproduction.

For McLaren, critical pedagogues understand that schools have the capacity to construct knowledge in three different ways: technical, practical, and emancipatory. Technical knowledge values empirical, analytical methods to construct forms of knowledge that can be measured and quantified (e.g., reading scores, SAT results) (2003a, 73). The growing culture of testing has placed technical knowledge at the center of the professional discourse in most schools. Practical knowledge "enlightens individuals so they can shape their daily actions in the world" (p. 73). This form of knowledge describes and analyzes societal conditions with the intention of helping students develop practical situational skills that will be transferable to their role in society (e.g., functional literacy, conflict resolution, time management). Emancipatory knowledge "creates the foundation for social justice, equality, and empowerment" (p. 73) and is the primary goal of critical pedagogy. It is rooted in the study of past and existing social conditions in order to change circumstances of irrationality, domination, and oppression through collective action. By emphasizing critical thought, action, and liberation, it transcends the false binary that suggests that school knowledge is either technical or practical.

For McLaren, the development of these liberating classroom conditions requires educators to engage in an ongoing analysis of the relationship between power, knowledge, and curriculum. Such an analysis presumes awareness that the knowledge schools tend to value (mostly technical) is linked to the maintenance of existing social and power relations. For this reason, critical pedagogues do not develop classrooms that construct knowledge as something to be consumed and regurgitated. Instead, they see knowledge as something that should "help students participate in vital issues that affect their experience on a daily level rather than simply [to] enshrine the values of business pragmatism" (pp. 85–86).

To accomplish these liberating educational goals, McLaren notes, critical pedagogues must respond to two forms of curriculum, formal and hidden, which are carefully selected to reinforce and normalize the dominant culture (p. 86). The formal curriculum is what is taught—the program of study. The hidden curriculum consists of standardized learning conditions, teaching styles, rules of conduct, and grading procedures. To disrupt these two forms of curriculum, educators must practice a critical pedagogy that prepares students to act for racial and social justice in their lives, their communities, and the larger society.

Ultimately, McLaren's framework for critical pedagogy requires educators to engage in an analysis of and action against social reproduction. This compels educators to "explore how schools perpetuate or reproduce the social relationships and attitudes needed to sustain the existing dominant economic and class relations of the larger society" (p. 89). As educators uncover the conditions for social reproduction they must be critically self-reflective, raising their own awareness of how they are sometimes complicit in over-valuing certain ways of talking, acting, and dressing and certain language practices and values. This heightened awareness is crucial for educators to understand student resistance when it does occur. According to McLaren:

> Critical pedagogy does not guarantee that resistance will not take place. But it does provide teachers with the foundations for understanding resistance, so that whatever pedagogy is developed can be sensitive to socio-cultural conditions that construct resistance, lessening the chance that students will be blamed as the sole, originating source of resistance. No emancipatory pedagogy will ever be built out of theories of behavior which view students as lazy, defiant, lacking in ambition, or genetically inferior. A much more penetrating solution is to try to understand the structures of mediation in the socio-cultural world that form student resistance. (p. 93)

McLaren's point here is an important one, and one often left out of the discussion on critical pedagogy in K–12 contexts. Students will sometimes find even the most engaging critical pedagogy uninteresting. To stay true to critical pedagogy does not mean that students are permitted to misbehave; instead, educators should engage in a deeper analysis of the source of the students' resistance. Critical pedagogues must resist the temptation to fall back on institutional norms that permit teachers to punish or tolerate student resistance. Instead, critical pedagogy demands that educators help students redirect their resistance to make it transforming and liberating for themselves, the class, the community, and broader society.

Henry Giroux

Giroux has been prolific in articulating the importance of critical theory in education. He argues that critical theory has the potential to lead educators toward a radical pedagogy that would reveal repressive ideologies (capitalist, racist, classist, sexist) and reconstruct more emancipating relationships (Giroux, 2001, 237). He also insists that we should not expect critical pedagogy to be a magic bullet for a society rife with inequality. Instead, critical education "represents both an ideal and a strategy in the service of struggling for social and economic democracy" (p. 239).

Educators who draw from critical theory to guide their pedagogy develop a radical view of knowledge. Their critical pedagogy values radical knowledge by offering instruction on the specific relations of domination and subordination that lead to conditions of oppression. This can be thought of as a pedagogy of appropriation, positioning oppressed groups to claim the "most progressive dimensions of their own cultural histories" as well as restructuring and appropriating "the most radical aspects of bourgeois culture" (Giroux, 2003, 50). Ultimately, critical pedagogy must be motivational enough to move students and teachers beyond critique and into actions that "explode the reifications of the existing society," replacing them with socially just relations (p. 50).

The major flaw that Giroux sees in radical pedagogy is its over-emphasis on cognition, to the exclusion of the sensual and imaginative in education (Giroux, 2003, 53). He argues that educators must "become more knowledgeable about how teachers, students and other educational workers become part of the system of social and cultural production, particularly as it works through the messages and values that are constituted via the social practices of the hidden curriculum" (p. 54). This approach requires teachers and communities to fight for control over the organization of school knowledge to develop pedagogy focused on the needs of the least advantaged. This calls for teachers to investigate, value, participate in, and incorporate the cultural norms and resources of the community in their classroom pedagogy. Giroux emphasizes that this process requires critical pedagogues to become partici-pating researchers of ethnic, linguistic, and popular cultural practices in their students' communities. Finally, this process compels teachers to resist stan-dardized curriculum and testing. They should, instead, practice a radical pedagogy that undermines "repressive modes of education that produce social hierarchies and legitimate inequality" and provides students with the "knowl-edge and skills needed to become well-rounded critical actors and social agents" (Giroux, 2001, xxvi).

bell hooks

In her work on critical pedagogy, hooks (1994a) advocates for an "engaged pedagogy." She warns that this is more demanding than critical or feminist pedagogies because it requires teachers to be "actively committed to a process of self-actualization that promotes their own well-being if they are to teach in a manner that empowers students" (p. 15). That is, teachers must be committed to their own spiritual, emotional, and physical well-being to posi-tion themselves properly to educate students in liberating ways. In short, educators who are "teaching to transgress" forms of oppression (racism, clas-sism, patriarchy, hetero-normativity) must be living examples of their politics (p. 48).

hooks's discussions of critical pedagogy focus heavily on the importance of confronting class in the classroom. She became acutely aware of class dif-ferences in education as an undergraduate at Stanford University, having grown up with a "nonmaterially privileged background" (1994a, 177–178). She entered Stanford thinking class was about material possessions but be-came increasingly conscious of the fact that "class was more than just a ques-tion of money, that it shaped values, attitudes, social relations, and the biases that informed the way knowledge would be given and received" (p. 178). hooks points out that Stanford was like most any mainstream schooling in-stitution in its unwillingness to mount a critical analysis of the significance of class in education or the larger society. She argues that schools effectively marginalize poor and working-class students by ignoring the ways that bour-geois class biases shape educational norms, particularly pedagogical practices. This normalizing of bourgeois class values in schools "create[s] a barrier, blocking the possibility of confrontation and conflict, warding off dissent" (p. 178). To combat this, hooks believes educators should employ a critical pedagogy that confronts class and other forms of inequality. This pedagogy

would encourage profound, emotional responses to the material being studied, allowing for unrestrained laughter, deep-seated rage, and all the emotions that rest in between (hooks, 1994a). Critical educators

> encourage students to reject the notion that they must choose between experiences.
> [Students] must believe they can inhabit comfortably two different worlds, but they
> must make each space one of comfort. They must creatively invent ways to cross
> borders. They must believe in their capacity to alter the bourgeois settings they en-
> ter. (pp. 182–183)

hooks (2000) contends that this pedagogy requires educators to maintain
a "solidarity with the poor," which she distinguishes from empathy for the
poor. Empathy for the poor comes when "people feel sorry for the poor or
identify with their suffering yet do nothing to alleviate it" (p. 130). Solidarity
with the poor is "rooted in the recognition that interdependency sustains the
life of the planet" and is practiced by the repudiation of all forms of exploitation in one's words and deeds (p. 130).

Most of hooks's discussions of critical pedagogy are in the context of the
university classroom, but they provide important insights for all educators.
As with each of the critical pedagogues discussed here, hooks was deeply influenced by Freire's work. She has taken the lessons of Freire's work with
economically poor adult farmers and mapped it onto places of privilege in the
United States. Like that of any pedagogue who challenges the status quo,
hooks's work has undergone intense scrutiny and received its share of negative feedback and pressures (hooks, 1989, 103). These challenges are partly
connected to the fact that she has carried out her pedagogical efforts in places
of extreme privilege, including Duke University and Yale University (p. 103).
In her discussions of teaching in universities, she notes that privileged students can have very different reactions to critical pedagogy than oppressed or
colonized peoples:

> Oppressed peoples] may begin to feel as they engage in education for critical con-
> sciousness a new found sense of power and identity that frees them from the coloni-
> zation of the mind, [whereas] privileged students are often downright unwilling to
> acknowledge that their minds have been colonized, that they have been learning
> how to be oppressors, how to dominate, or at least how to passively accept the
> domination of others. (p. 102)

hooks's insistence that students with class privilege must also be educated
with critical pedagogical strategies sets her work apart from most discussions
of critical pedagogy. It does, however, fit with her thoughts on the larger

body politic of our society. Drawing from Martin Luther King's essay "Facing the Challenge of a New Age," hooks concludes her book *Outlaw Culture* by stating that true liberation leads us "beyond resistance to transformation" (p. 250) and that this is only possible with love. Her work, then, like that of most critical pedagogues, is deeply embedded with a critical hope that the world can be a place opposed to domination and oppression and that critical education can trigger all people, privileged and oppressed, to "act in ways that liberate ourselves and others" (1994b, 250).

Critical Pedagogues Who Are Not on the Radar

The educators, activists, theorists, and scholars discussed in this section are rarely mentioned in discussions of critical pedagogy. This oversight can be attributed in part to the fact that only a few of them speak directly about schools, and even fewer about classroom practice. However, a major aim of critical pedagogy is to produce educators and students who commit their lives to the fight for racial and social justice. To this end, it is important that critical pedagogues investigate people who have engaged in such revolutionary acts beyond the classroom. There are many freedom fighters whose efforts would make any critical pedagogue proud. Here, we highlight the efforts of a few of these lived examples of critical pedagogy to emphasize that critical pedagogy is more than just a teaching strategy—it is a personal, financial, political, emotional, and spiritual commitment to prioritizing the needs and liberation of people who are suffering under various forms of oppression.

Carter G. Woodson

The second African American to receive his Ph.D. from Harvard University, Woodson authored 16 books, more than 100 articles, and more than 125 book reviews. His most relevant work, a discussion of critical pedagogy, is *The Miseducation of the Negro* (2000). The title is telling, as the book is highly critical of the treatment of African Americans in the U.S. educational system. For Woodson, education has played a central role in the ongoing marginalization of African Americans in the United States, consistently failing to deliver on the promises of freedom and equality it proposes to bring to the community. On the back cover of a recent edition (2000) of the book, Woodson is quoted as having stated:

> When you can control a man's thinking, you do not have to worry about his actions. You do not have to tell him not to stand here or go yonder. He will find his "proper

place" and will stay in it. You do not need to send him to the back door. He will go without being told. In fact, if there is no back door, he will cut one for his special benefit. His education makes it necessary.

Woodson's commentary is a double-layered critique of the educational system. First, like many critical pedagogues, he is arguing that the schooling system is designed to operate in collusion with larger social inequalities. Thus, schools serving black students offer opportunities for social mobility to very few. The majority of students are trained to occupy the social margins—their "proper place." For the most part, students emerge from the system with an education that has offered them little more than a belief system to justify the social inequalities they will experience for the rest of their lives.

The second layer of Woodson's critique is his alarm over the lack of concern with this cycle of social reproduction. He is particularly critical of those who emerge from the education system with some relative social mobility but fail to use that power to uplift less fortunate members of the community. He suggests that this absence of social responsibility to one's community is trained into those who are granted upward mobility. They are conditioned to believe that they are leaders of the people rather than servants, and they aim to reproduce socially unequal relationships where they act out the part of the elite. Education, according to Woodson, should prepare people to disavow such inequalities in social status, instead grooming them to serve their communities:

> The servant of the people, unlike the leader, is not on a high horse elevated above the people and trying to carry them to some designated point to which he would like to go for his own advantage. The servant of the people is down among them, living as they live, doing what they do and enjoying what they enjoy. He may be a little better informed than some other members of the group; it may be that he has had some experience that they have not had, but in spite of this advantage he should have more humility than those whom he serves, for we are told that "Whosoever is greatest among you, let him be your servant." (p. 131)

Woodson's hope for this type of education is based on his belief that the revolutionizing of the social order must come from the educational system. Anything short of accomplishing this task marks the system as "worthless" (p. 145). The potential to achieve this goal rests primarily in the hands of teachers. They must confront the fact that schools charged with educating black youth are largely committed to teaching imitation rather than critical thought. This prepares black children to do what they are told, leaving them "well prepared to function in the American social order as others would have [them do]" (p. 134). Teachers must discard the dominant pedagogy, which has permitted people to exploit, oppress, and exterminate others and still be regarded as righteous (p. 150). In its place, teachers should use a critical pedagogy that develops enlightened youth, with a nobleness of soul and the power to "perform in society a part of which others are not capable" (p. 151).

Lolita Lebrón

Lebrón is included in this section because her life exemplifies an uncompromising commitment to justice, a central tenet of critical pedagogy. Many of the theorists on critical pedagogy discussed here talk about the importance of living radical lives and acting upon our convictions. Lebrón has done just that for the better part of her life. As a member of the Puerto Rican Nationalist Party, Lebrón has fought relentlessly to free Puerto Rico from U.S. commonwealth status. On March 1, 1954, she led a group of party members in an attack on the U.S. House of Representatives. The goal of the attack was to bring worldwide attention to the struggle for Puerto Rican independence. The attack cost Lebrón and her comrades twenty-five years in prison. She was pardoned in 1979 by President Jimmy Carter and immediately returned to her work as a freedom fighter for Puerto Rico.

As a witness in the 2000 International Tribunal on Violations of Human Rights in Puerto Rico and Vieques, Lebrón ended her deposition by saying:

> I had the honor of leading the act against the U.S. Congress on March 1, 1954, when we demanded freedom for Puerto Rico and we told the world that we are an invaded nation, occupied and abused by the United States of America. I feel very proud of having performed that day, of having answered the call of the motherland. (Joubert-Ceci, 2000)

Less than a year later, in June 2001, Lebrón went back to jail for another sixty days for protesting the U.S. navy occupation of Vieques. In May 2003, the navy left Vieques and turned over their facilities to the Puerto Rican government. This small victory against U.S. occupation can be, at least partially, attributed to Lebrón's tireless commitment to resistance for freedom on behalf of Puerto Rico. Now in her late eighties, Lebrón continues to participate in pro-independence activities.

Lebrón's persistent outspoken resistance to U.S. imperialism is an excellent example of the critical awareness and action critical pedagogues aim to develop in their students. Critical pedagogues should learn from and share her lifelong commitment to fight for justice. Lebrón's courage frees us up to conceptualize more radical forms of resistance so that her drastic and largely isolated actions can become contagious, more collective, and less marginalized.

Franz Fanon

Fanon, like Ché Guevara, became a doctor, rejected the bourgeois lifestyle of his middle-class family, and fought and died for the liberation of a country where he was an immigrant (Algeria). Much has been written on Fanon as a radical thinker and revolutionary actor for the freedom of colonized peoples around the world. He is an excellent example of a critical pedagogue for his lifelong commitment to the cycle of critical praxis. Fanon's praxis led him to reflect constantly on the challenges facing the most oppressed groups in his society. These reflections resulted in a grounded theoretical analysis of such challenges that guided his acts of resistance. His actions led to deeper reflections and analyses of the problems, which ultimately resulted in more informed acts of critical resistance.

Fanon's efforts focused primarily on the plight of colonized peoples in Africa, predominantly in Algeria, although his work is widely recognized for its relevance to colonized peoples everywhere. His work took shape in three principal stages:

1. The search for black identity, as presented in *Black Skin, White Masks* (1967), the stunning diagnosis of racism that Fanon wrote while he was studying medicine and psychoanalysis

2. The struggle against colonialism, as explained in *A Dying Colonialism* (1970) and *Toward the African Revolution* (1968), collections of essays Fanon produced when he was actively engaged in Algeria's war of independence

3. The process of decolonization, as analyzed in *The Wretched of the Earth* (2004), the book that extended insights gained in Algeria to Africa and the Third World (Wyrick, 1998, 3).

Fanon's influence on revolutionary actors has been significant, particularly in the United States. Chicano activists and Black Panther leaders regularly invoked Fanon's work, particularly *The Wretched of the Earth*, as central to the development of their theory of action. Mainstream sources such as

Time magazine branded Fanon "an apostle of violence" and "a prisoner of hate" (Wyrick, 1998, 155) and used this reading of his work to position these revolutionary groups as threats to the social order. However, a more thorough reading of Fanon's work suggests that he was guided by a deep commitment to humanity aimed at ending violence and oppression. It is likely that Fanon was seen as threatening to the mainstream because he contended that the European economic model was the primary cause of suffering around the world. He argued that the economic strategies of many European nations and the United States were dependent on valuing profits over people. He concluded that the masses of people suffering under these economic models could be liberated only if they rejected them and pursued instead economic principles that emphasized humanity above all else:

> But what matters now is not a question of profitability, not a question of increased productivity, not a question of production rates. ... The notion of catching up must not be used as a pretext to brutalize [people], to tear [them] from [themselves] and [their] inner consciousness, to break [them], to kill [them].
>
> No, we do not want to catch up with anyone. But what we want is to walk in the company of [humanity], every [person], night and day, for all times. ... For Europe, for ourselves and for humanity, comrades, we must make a new start, develop a new way of thinking, and endeavor to create a new [person]. (Fanon, 2004, 238–239)

This kind of thinking significantly influenced the work of Guyanese theorist Walter Rodney, who coined the term "guerrilla intellectual," which accurately captures Fanon's lifelong commitment to socially engaged scholarship. At only eighteen years old, Fanon responded as follows to a philosophy professor at the lycée who said that World War II was not their war: "Each time liberty is in question, we are concerned, be we white, black, or yellow; and each time freedom is under siege, no matter where, I will engage myself completely" (Wyrick, 1998, 10).

Thus, from his earliest work as an intellectual, Fanon rejected the traditional separation of theory and practice. He believed true intellectualism means embracing the responsibility of engaging and affecting material conditions. He saw the notion of objective distance as an unthinkable strategy for doing work that mattered to the world. He believed, instead, that an individual's responsibility was to engage daily in the struggle for justice.

Reies López Tijerina

Often excluded from Chicano history and discussions of the Xicano power movement, Tijerina has been called "the most charismatic of the Chicano leaders" (Acuña, 2003, 340). Tijerina became known as El Tigre for his passionate resistance to what he termed the United States' defrauding of the Mexican people of *ejido* land (communal or village land) (p. 340). He rigorously studied the Treaty of Guadalupe Hidalgo and believed that it illegally took land away from Mexicans. His convictions led him to form La Alianza (Alliance of Towns and Settlers), a group that fostered heritage pride and fought for land rights for native New Mexicans. By 1966, four years after its inception, La Alianza had 22,000 members and Tijerina had started radio and television shows, *The Voice of Justice*, because they provided the best medium to reach the community about the issue of land. With the backing of these supporters, Tijerina engaged in a series of land rights marches and actions, the most well known being the occupation of the Echo Amphitheatre (New Mexico) in 1966. Tijerina, along with 350 other protestors, declared that 1,400 acres of the Kit Carson National Forest was stolen territory and asserted the revival of *ejido* land rights to reclaim that land for the Pueblo de San Joaquín de Chama (Acuña, 2003). As mainstream politicians denounced and distanced themselves from Tijerina's actions, he continued to fight business-as-usual politics in New Mexico and nationally. Tijerina also served as the elected leader of the Chicano contingent during the 1968 Poor People's Campaign march on Washington where he helped build alliances between black, American Indian, and Chicano leaders. Tijerina's uncompromising fight to redress the material inequalities of New Mexico natives resulted in a range of detractors, some of whom pursued criminal charges against him which resulted in him being incarcerated on multiple occasions. In response to his critics and the conditions of suffering that plagued the community, Tijerina wrote a letter to the *Albuquerque Journal* which was published May 1, 1968. The contents of the letter exemplify his commitment to the struggle to end the suffering of all poor people:

> ...to know the poor people, one must know the reasons for the poverty in which they live...
>
>   It is true that I am in trouble with the establishment, and with the enemies of the poor who are in power. But I am also proud to be in this position [Chairman of the Poor Peoples' March] because of the poor...

Besides, for the poor I am more than ready to get in trouble. No poor man can accuse me of fooling him, lying, taking his land, violating international treaties, such as the Treaty of Guadalupe Hidalgo, or burning and destroying the documents and records of Spanish and Indian *pueblos*...

I cannot be accused of raping and attacking the culture and national characteristics of any people...not can I be accused of converting justice into state welfare powdered milk.

So...I am taking part in the poor peoples' march because from the beginning it was I who began the coalition philosophy between the brown and the black people and the Indian people and the good whites. So the fact that the Indians and Spanish Americans are taking part in the poor peoples' march in Washington is proof that I've been interested in unity of all people and justice for all people. (Blawis, 1971, 113-114)

Audre Lorde

Lorde's work is informed by multiple standpoints—black woman, lesbian, feminist, mother, daughter of Grenadian immigrants, educator, cancer survivor, and activist. She considers herself not a writer of theory but a poet (Lorde, 1984, 7). However, she has significantly impacted feminist theory by insisting that feminists examine their differences and include significant input from poor, non-white, and developing world women and from lesbians. She made this position most clear in her comments at the Second Sex Conference:

It is learning how to stand alone, unpopular and sometimes reviled, and how to make common cause with those others identified as outside the structures in order to define and seek a world in which we can all flourish. It is learning how to take our differences and make them strengths. *For the master's tools will never dismantle the master's house.* They may allow us temporarily to beat him at his own game, but they will never enable us to bring about genuine change. (p. 112)

Lorde believes that women are often taught to ignore their differences, or to treat them as causes for separation and suspicion. These politics of difference replicate the divide-and-conquer politics of the mainstream (the master's house). They create opportunities for temporary victories for *some* women, but they do not build community, and "[w]ithout community there is no liberation, only the most vulnerable and temporary armistice between an individual and her oppression" (p. 112).

Lorde has consistently argued that critical thinkers must recognize and value difference as the "raw and powerful connection from which our personal power is forged" (p. 112). She chastises academic critical theorists for developing rhetoric of social critique that fails to recognize that racial and economic groups experience oppression differently. For academics to resolve this tension, Lorde argues, they must "live and love in the trenches … to remember that the war against dehumanization is ceaseless" (p. 119). This is a challenge she issues to people of color, as well as whites, because "our [people of color's] struggle does not make us immune to the errors of ignoring and misnaming difference" (p. 119).

For Lorde, the goal of critical work should be the construction of an empowered community that resists all forms of oppression. However, for those endeavoring to undertake this challenge she draws upon Freire (1970) for some words of caution. To build this community we must find the courage to overcome "the piece of the oppressor which is planted deep within each of us, and which knows only the oppressor's tactics, the oppressors' relationships" (p. 123). This requires us to avoid confusing unity with homogeneity so that we work and struggle together with "those whom we define as different from ourselves, although sharing the same goals" (p. 123). Lorde concludes that this growth will be painful, but it is the path to our survival.

Gloria Anzaldúa

Anzaldúa was a Chicana feminist whose work fits into the traditions of critical pedagogy for its commitment to challenging patriarchy, white supremacy, and homophobia. Much of her work developed an analysis of the various borderlands into which people find themselves socialized in U.S. society. For Anzaldúa, these borderlands are predominantly occupied by people of color, who often find themselves cut out of the mainstream cultural norms through social divisors such as skin color, language, class, education, and immigrant status. What's more, inside of groups of color, Anzaldúa exposed the presence of borderlands by expanding the list of social divisors to include gender and sexual orientation. She wrote:

> The world is not a safe place to live in. … Alienated from her mother culture, "alien" in the dominant culture, the woman of color does not feel safe within the inner life of her Self. Petrified, she can't respond, her face caught between *los intersticios*, the spaces between the different worlds she inhabits. (1987, 20)

Similar to Freire and other critical pedagogues, Anzaldúa argued that critical literacy was a weapon with which to combat the injustice of being pushed to the borderlands. In one of her most famous works, *This Bridge Called My Back: Writings by Radical Women of Color* (Moraga & Anzaldúa,

1984), Anzaldúa wrote that her words compensated her for what the real world did not give her, because writing "put order in the world" and gave it a "handle so [she could] grasp it" (Anzaldúa, 1984, 169).

Anzaldúa used critical literacy to challenge Western notions of being that presented people with binary ("either-or") options for their identities. She introduced the term *mestizaje* to represent a way of being in the world that transcends binaries and allows for all of a person's identity to mesh together all of his or her complexities (racial, sexual, social, economic):

> So don't give me your tenets and your laws. ... What I want is an accounting with all three cultures—white, Mexican, Indian. I want the freedom to carve and chisel my own face, to staunch the bleeding with ashes, to fashion my own gods out of my entrails. And if going home is denied me then I will have to stand and claim my space, making a new culture—una cultura *mestiza*—with my own lumber, my own bricks and mortar and my own feminist architecture. (1987, 22)

Such stances that balance critique, hope, and action are representative of the best traditions of critical pedagogy. Anzaldúa did not simply stand at a distance to lob critiques at the society in which she lived. She employed her critical sensibilities to challenge the injustices that confronted her and members of other oppressed groups. While she is probably best known for having done this through her political and academic writing and speaking, it is worth noting that Anzaldúa was also a teacher and the author of bilingual children's books (*Friends from the Other Side/Amigos del Otro Lado*, 1997; *Prietita and the Ghost Woman/Prietita y La Llorona*, 1996/2001) in which she brought these ideas of cultural freedom and the *mestizaje* to young people.

Subcommandante Marcos

No one is certain of Marcos's true identity, although he admits to being a university graduate, and it is widely accepted that he studied liberation theology and philosophy in Mexican universities. Marcos identifies himself as the spokesperson for the Ejército Zapatista de Liberación Nacional (EZLN), a Mayan indigenous revolutionary group from Chiapas, Mexico. When Marcos came to Chiapas from the city in 1992, his life was changed forever by the suffering that he saw among the Mayans living there. He stayed on in Chiapas and began organizing with the indigenous people to fight for land rights and economic justice for indigenous people of the Chiapas region and oppressed groups around the globe.

In the documentary film *A Place Called Chiapas* (Wild, 1998), Marcos explains that the suffering in Chiapas shaped his outlook on life as a revolutionary for social justice:

> People here coexist with death ... especially the little ones. Paradoxically, death begins to shed its tragic cloak, death becomes a daily fact. It loses its sacredness. ... You don't lose your fear of death, but you become familiar with it. It becomes your equal. Death, which is so close, so near, so possible, is less terrifying for us than for others. So, going out and fighting and perhaps meeting death is not as terrible as it seems. For us, at least. In fact, what surprises and amazes us is life itself. The hope of a better life. Going out to fight and to die finding out you're not dead, but alive.

This kind of connection to the struggle for social and economic justice has led him to be incredibly prolific as a writer and speaker. Since 1992, he has responded to local and global conditions of social inequality by writing more than 200 essays and at least 21 books.

As an outsider to Chiapas, Marcos has had to earn his place in the community. He has accomplished this by immersing himself in the material conditions of the people and fighting alongside them. As testament to this, a Mayan woman from Chiapas says of him:

> We don't see his face like we see ours. Ours we see clearly, but his stays covered. We can't see him. Whatever the poor eats, he eats. When he's here, is he going to eat better food? What we eat, he eats. We eat vegetables, he does too. We don't believe he's from the city. We can't believe it. (Wild, 1998)

The reference made here to Marcos's face being covered is due to the fact that he wears a black mask in public, a symbolic gesture he believes makes him no one and everyone. This is meant to indicate the alignment of the Zapatistas' struggles with those of all suffering people. In keeping with this effort to support worldwide struggles for liberation, many of Marcos's communications (co-edited by the Zapatista leadership) are addressed "to the people and governments of the world."

Like many critical pedagogues, Marcos is deeply committed to the principles of liberatory education with the aim of aiding young people to become the vehicles for justice. In a letter to a thirteen-year-old boy, Marcos wrote that the EZLN fights so that one day the young man will realize "men and women like us exist, without faces and without names, who have left everything behind, even life itself, so that others (children like you and those not like you) are able to get up in the morning without being told to shut up, and with no need for masks to confront the world" (Marcos, 1995, 167). According to Marcos, this dream cannot happen unless we "teach [children] that there are so many words like colors and that there are so many thoughts because within them is the world where words are born. ... And [if] we teach them to speak the truth, that is to say, to speak with their hearts" (Vodovnik, 2004, 584).

Ultimately, Marcos contends, the struggle for justice requires one to march with love and pain (*amor y dolor*) simultaneously. To make this march, alongside "those with nothing, for the eternal losers, those without names, without faces," is to stand for the dignity of everyone (Marcos, 1995, 168–169). At the end of his letter to thirteen-year-old Miguel, Marcos explains the paradox of his current position: he is a soldier whose sole aim is to end the need for soldiers. This kind of soldier, Marcos concludes, should

> not be afraid of anything but surrender, of remaining in our seats and resting while others struggle, sleeping while others are on watch. ... Dignity, Miguel, is the only thing that must never be lost ... ever. (p. 169)

Marcos says that his profession is hope (p. 167). It is this hope, which lies in the struggle for dignity and justice for oppressed people everywhere, that links the work of all the men and women discussed in this section to the action of critical pedagogy.

Critics of Critical Pedagogy

While this book clearly supports the use of critical pedagogy, we would also like to acknowledge that critical pedagogy has critics in the educational community. By critics from the conservative right to self-proclaimed radicals, critical pedagogues have been derided for being overly idealistic and theoretical (Ravitch, 2000) or for promoting pedagogy that de-emphasizes the role of the educator in imparting important skills that the poor and students of color must learn if they are to be successful in K–12 and postsecondary education. Delpit (1987, 1988, 1995) claims that it is racist to not teach students of color the skills that they need to get into and succeed in college. She critiques "open and progressive" education that does not teach students how to write a sentence. Delpit recalls her early years as a teacher in Philadelphia during the early 1970s. Her attempts to employ a student-empowering pedagogy resulted only in her students continually lagging behind their white and wealthy counterparts attending school in the suburbs. Her students did not improve until she decided explicitly to teach them the skills that they needed to access and navigate the culture of power. From her research, Delpit has surmised that many white progressive educators think they are freeing students of color from a racist educational system by allowing them to express themselves without learning to read, write, or speak Standard English. Delpit argues that these students will not be able to enter the mainstream of society without these skills.

Delpit's comments must be taken seriously by educators who plan to use critical theory to engage urban youth. We must resist the urge to focus only on the emergence of critical consciousness without finding ways to link this consciousness to the development of academic skills. For this reason, this book focuses on the development of academic *and* critical literacy in an attempt to link critical consciousness with academic skill development.

It is also important to be critical of stances that are themselves somewhat uncritical of the existence of schools as mechanisms of social reproduction. Teaching poor urban students of color to think, act, and speak like wealthy, suburban, and white students is not going to ensure success for those students. Moreover, an uncritical approach could be dangerous to students' sense of self to the extent that it is uncritical of the status quo in education and fails to make explicit the dominant hegemony of schooling. We are, however, in agreement with some of the critics of critical pedagogy that critical discourse should seek to transform identities and empower previously oppressed students while promoting critical reading and writing skills. Further, critical educators should work to create curricula that illuminate the culture of power while also honoring the tradition of ethnic and cultural studies.

3
Critical Pedagogy in an Urban High School English Classroom

Critical pedagogy is hotly discussed and highly debated in the academy. Its proponents draw upon important scholars (Freire, 1970; McLaren, 1994, 2003b; Giroux, 2001; hooks, 1994; Darder, 1991; Kincheloe, 2004; Shor, 1992) to argue for an approach to education that is rooted in the existential experiences of marginalized peoples; that is centered in a critique of structural, economic, and racial oppression; that is focused on dialogue instead of a one-way transmission of knowledge; and that is structured to empower individuals and collectives as agents of social change. Increasingly, critical pedagogy is being discussed as a potential component of urban school reform. Again, educators and researchers look to critical pedagogy as they consider ways to motivate students, to develop literacies and numeracies of power, and to engage students and their communities in the struggle for educational justice. We certainly applaud these goals, but we also feel as though the field at present insufficiently explores the applications of critical pedagogy to urban education.

For the past dozen years we have been dedicated to the enterprise of designing and investigating classroom interventions that are built upon the core principles of critical pedagogy. In our joint efforts we have worked across multiple settings, from English classrooms to basketball teams to summer research programs. Our goal in this research is to develop a grounded theory of practice (Strauss & Corbin, 1997), that is, a theory that begins with the core principles of critical pedagogy but uses empirical data from theoretically informed practice to develop a more nuanced and particular theory of critical pedagogy as it applies to urban education in new-century schools. In this chapter we describe applications of critical pedagogy to a secondary English class in Oakland, a Northern California urban center, that we co-taught for three years. We begin with the underlying principles that simultaneously honored the spirit of the discipline of secondary English, our commitment to academic excellence, and our belief in the practice of education for individual and collective freedom.

Underlying Principles

Though we didn't always agree with traditional definitions and measures of academic literacy, we remained committed to facilitating academic skills and academic achievement in our classrooms. We understood the promotion of literacy development and academic achievement to be part of our mandate—from the profession, from the students, and from their families. Without agreeing on much else, we could agree with our colleagues in the English department at East Bay High, our on-site administrators, and state administrators that students needed to achieve academically in our schools. Regardless of our philosophical foundation, we understood that our students existed in a world where they would be expected to take and perform well on standardized tests that served as gatekeepers to postsecondary education and, as a consequence, professional membership.

We also knew that our students would need to understand, interpret, and produce in the Language of Wider Communication (LWC) (Smitherman, 2001), or what others might refer to as Standard English; they needed to develop linguistic competencies and literacy skills for academic advancement, professional employment, but also for civic participation. If students were going to acquire capacities required of critical citizens, they needed strong literacy skills, including the ability to read and write in the LWC. Though critical literacy remained a goal of our pedagogy, we understood that critical literacy also demands a knowledge of and facility with the language of power. It is impossible to critique or refute texts that one does not understand; comprehension is an important prerequisite for critique. Through our reading of critical theory and our work with urban adolescents we came to understand the importance of studying dominant texts to the development and maintenance of a revolutionary consciousness for both teachers and the students in their classrooms (Freire, 1997).

As English teachers and former English students at the undergraduate and postgraduate levels, we also knew that our students would be expected to demonstrate knowledge of canonical literature to pass Advanced Placement exams or to succeed in college-level coursework in the discipline. Again, these literacies of power, though sometimes problematic, were important for our students and not unimportant for the development of critical consciousness. With respect to canonical literature, Nobel Laureate author and activist Toni Morrison reminds us that national literatures reflect what is on the national mind. Studying canonical texts is an important strategy for understanding the values and ideologies of dominant groups at various points in history. For example, we would often tell our students that literary texts such as *The Scarlet Letter* and *The Adventures of Huckleberry Finn* offered more insights into the American psyche than most texts on U.S. history. When engaging these texts, however, it became important to include critical literary theories and multicultural readings of canonical texts that empowered students as readers and did not defer to the authority of the texts.

Toward these ends, we made a concerted effort to incorporate canonical pieces from British and classical literature (the 12th-grade mandate in our district) alongside post-colonial literature and popular cultural texts. Our senior syllabus has included *Beowulf, The Canterbury Tales, Othello, Pygmalion,* and *Heart of Darkness* in addition to popular films and hip-hop music, which we discuss later in this chapter. We also developed vocabulary units and units that prepared students for the SAT and ACT exams as well as the Advanced Placement examinations offered each spring. Furthermore, we placed a premium on academic writing, focusing on expository essays and research reports, and on academic speaking (or persuasive rhetoric) in the form of presentations and debates. Though we did not use the language of rhetoric, we wanted students to be able to present themselves powerfully and persuasively across multiple written genres as well as through formal and informal oral presentations.

In no way, shape, or form did our focus on academic literacy compromise our commitment to critical pedagogy and to literacy education for individual freedom and social change. In fact, we felt that it was only within a pedagogy firmly committed to freedom and social change that we were able to motivate students to develop sophisticated academic literacies. On this point we were in accord with the Cuban ministers of education who centered all academic content within a framework of praxis-oriented pedagogy to increase students' sense of commitment to upholding the values of the Cuban revolution while simultaneously making connections with real local and global demands for knowledge accumulation and production (Kozol, 1978). In addition, we were able to honor the existential experiences of our students and to work toward the development of academic literacies by complementing the canonical literature with popular cultural texts from music, film, mass media, and sports. More important, though, we were able to situate all texts and curricula within a critical pedagogy that was explicitly aware of issues of power, oppression, and transformation, that honored the non-school cultural practices of the students, and that included the students in authentic dialogue about inequity and advocacy for justice.

One of the core foundational philosophical principles of classroom pedagogy and practice was a belief that multiculturalism was more closely related to pedagogy than to curriculum. Although we were firm believers in foregrounding popular cultural texts in our curricula, we did not shy away from the "classics." The curriculum that we taught to a diverse population at East Bay High included canonical texts such as *Beowulf, The Canterbury Tales, Othello, Macbeth, Hamlet, The Odyssey*, Romantic poetry, and Joseph Conrad's *Heart of Darkness*. We were able to apply multicultural readings to these texts, having the students pay close attention to the treatment of those who were distinguished as cultural "Others," such as the Canon Yeoman in *The Canterbury Tales* and the natives in *Heart of Darkness*. We firmly believed that literacy educators could encourage a multicultural reading of any text (Nieto, 1992), even one several thousand years old, such as *The Odyssey*.

By the same token, we were wary of those educators and literary theorists who equated multiculturalism with simply offering texts written by people of color or featuring people of color as protagonists. As students and educators, we witnessed practices around these so-called multicultural texts that were equally, if not more, disempowering of students of color than more traditional and less diverse texts. An oppressive rendering of a culturally diverse text is still oppressive.

This is not to suggest that the sole purpose of interacting with literary texts was to pick them apart or to tear them down. We believed that, to the extent that students were exposed to literature of other times and places, they would begin to make connections to their own everyday experiences while gaining an understanding of similarities across time and cultures. This certainly happened in our Poet in Society unit, where students were able to make connections between classic poets such as Shakespeare and John Donne and contemporary hip-hop artists such as the Fugees. These connections also occurred during conversations on heroism and sexism in *The Odyssey* or on violence in *Beowulf*. Nothing promotes border crossing or tolerance more than helping students to arrive at an implicit understanding of what they have in common with those they have been taught to perceive as different. Anthropologist Clifford Geertz claims that the more we study the cultural practices of others, the more these practices seem logical to us (2000, 16) and the more they help us to understand our own practices as equally unique and equally meaningful—one practice among many meaningful practices. Indeed, such cross-cultural literary study may allow us to see ourselves in others even as we see these others as different in important and extraordinary ways.

We would label these practices in our secondary English classrooms critical pedagogy because they promoted a sense of empowerment in readings of traditional texts. Creating classroom learning spaces where a sixteen-year-old student can see herself as having something to say to an author like Shakespeare is itself an empowering act that has implications not only for future readings of Shakespeare but for future engagements with any texts that have the aura of immutability or ultimate authority. Hegemonic texts such as local, state, and national legislation, corporate by-laws, labor-management agreements, professional contracts, mortgage offers, and school report cards, to name a few, are those "sacred" texts that emerge in the everyday lives of citizens and that serve to limit, constrain, or control actions or thought. These are the very texts that need to be critiqued, contextualized, and ultimately re-written by critically empowered and critically literate citizens, which is what we want our students to become and how we want them to act. These practices are also instantiations of critical pedagogy: they encourage readings that are themselves critical of traditional approaches to multicultural readings, in that students are asked to find commonalities across multiple cultural contexts instead of solely highlighting differences that can be primarily ascribed to ethnic affiliation. Critically literate students should feel empowered to enjoy texts that more politically correct environments would pressure them to disdain. Our purpose as educators is not to replace one dominant ideology with another. Rather, we agree with the assertion of Italian Marxist social theorist Antonio Gramsci (1971) that the ultimate goal of a proletariat education is to help make students more critical consumers of all information that they encounter in their daily lives and to give them the skills to become more capable producers of counter-information. The goal is not to make them slaves to a different (and more politically correct) ideology, even if it happens to be one that we agree with.

We also endeavored as educators to question and expand the literary canon; critical pedagogy in urban secondary English necessarily entails questioning what actually constitutes a text worthy of study. While we respected and honored much of the current literary canon and encouraged our students to gain a mastery and appreciation of it, we also recognized that the canon could be limiting in ways that were problematic and ultimately disempowering to our students. In particular, the existing literary canon was most problematic in its exclusions. Our students, we felt, were being given implicit and explicit messages about which texts were aesthetic or intellectual (coded definitions of the popular use of the term "literary") in ways that excluded, even condemned, the traditional and new media texts that they interacted with daily. Nowhere was this more evident than in the treatment of "popular culture" in secondary academic settings. Cultural theorists (Adorno & Horkheimer, 1999; Docker, 1994; Storey, 1998; Strinati, 2000) have pointed toward the hierarchy that has been articulated between elite culture and popular culture, where the former holds society's most idealized values and the latter is held to be base, common, and unsophisticated. Clearly, one of the core purposes of industrial schooling (and literacy education in particular) has been to expose children to the "best" the culture has to offer to elevate them from their often vulgar and "un-American" backgrounds (Tyack, 1974). It's easy to understand why little popular culture has been sanctioned in traditional primary and secondary educational spheres. The irony here is that popular culture has always found a central place in the most elite of postsecondary educational institutions, and popular culture has consistently been a site of study by the most elite of society's philosophers and cultural theorists in the twentieth (and now twenty-first) centuries.

We sought to counter these traditions in our curriculum development and our pedagogies, and we sought to situate our work conceptually and empirically. To do so we chose a different tack, one more in line with the work of Russian psychologist Lev Vygotsky (1978), who drew from his cultural historical research and his experiments on language development, cultural transmission, and the relations between mothers and children to advocate for instruction that draws upon the everyday experiences or the known worlds of children. We do not agree with all aspects of Vygotskian cultural psychology; for instance, we do not envision the hierarchical relationship between everyday activities and higher-order thinking skills as Vygotsky did. However, we recognized the pedagogical potential of tapping into young people's everyday experiences as participants in popular culture to scaffold academic literacies. At the same time, we draw from Freire and Macedo's (1987) dialectical relationship between reading the world and reading the word, where readings of the word informed readings of the world in a dialectic cycle.

As teacher-researchers, we devoted significant time and resources to understanding the nature of youth involvement in popular culture and the extent to which systematic involvement with popular culture in academic settings could facilitate the development of academic skills and critical faculties. It is important to note that our definition of popular culture differed greatly from "popular" conceptions of the term. We drew upon the work of sociologists and cultural theorists who envisioned popular culture as a set of cultural practices that were both influenced by and influencing everyday culture and the culture industries that market and co-opt this culture. For instance, Frankfurt School theorists Max Horkheimer and Theodor Adorno believed that elite interests used the culture industries (film, radio, etc.) to promote dominant values. In a similar vein, Gramsci (1971) viewed emergent media as instruments of hegemony, and Louis Althusser (2001) viewed the media as an ideological state apparatus through which the state could inculcate in its citizens ideologies that promoted the reproduction of state interests. There have also been cultural theorists, notably from the Birmingham Centre for Contemporary Cultural Studies, who have identified mass culture as a site of working-class struggle and resistance. Most contemporary theorists acknowledge popular culture as a site of both resistance and dominant hegemony or even as a site of conflict between these forces (Storey, 1998).

As a result of this work, we developed classroom units that coupled the study of film, newspapers, magazines, and music with the study of traditional novels, poems, and plays. We also created opportunities for students to study their own everyday culture, whether as students attending urban schools or as citizens of a metropolitan community.

Finally, we were very much influenced by Paulo Freire's (1970) critiques of the banking metaphor for education, where teachers treat students as passive, empty receptacles and schooling becomes a process whereby knowledgeable experts "deposit" bits of information into the impoverished minds of students. Instead, Freire advocated a pedagogical practice centered upon dialogue, inquiry, and the real exchange of ideas between teachers and students, who, he felt, had a great deal to offer one another. We took this idea of a dialogic or problem-posing pedagogy to heart when designing activities within our various units.

The final assignments for these units usually consisted of some sort of performance or presentation that allowed students to take ownership of the knowledge production process. There was also some form of interrogation built into these presentations, usually from the students who were not presenting. One common format was to divide a major work into sections or themes and divide the class into groups of five or six. Usually we would give the groups a week to work together on their particular section or theme. The groups would need to perform research, assign roles and responsibilities, prepare a presentation, rehearse that presentation, anticipate possible questions from the audience, and prepare answers to them. Individual non-presenting class members' responsibilities entailed preparing at least three questions that they could ask of the presenting group during the Q&A sessions. This would build upon work early in the year in which we helped students understand the difference between critical questions and questions of fact.

Each group would then receive one class period in which to present. The hour-long periods were divided equally between group presentation and question-and-answer sessions. During the presentation, other class members were required to take copious notes, which would be handed in for grading at the end of the unit. Needless to say, there was a huge incentive for the groups to prepare themselves well. At the culmination of these activities, students would hand in outlines of their group's presentation along with a brief description of their role in the preparation and presentation. They would also hand in their notes and questions for the other groups. Final grades would be divided into thirds between preparation, presentation, and participation in other groups' presentations. We felt that this structure allowed us to evaluate the students' content knowledge while also encouraging the dialogue and inquiry that are essential to any critical pedagogy.

We began with the fundamental knowledge of the disconnect between the skills and sensibilities we encouraged and our grading rubrics. Initially, we would call for active participation in discussions, but we would turn around and grade only final written products. This was a disservice to the students who worked diligently to contribute to the intellectual development of their peers and the class as a whole. Writing was not forgotten; it is just that we sought to develop a grading system that honored skills no longer emphasized in many classrooms, such as working well with classmates, presenting one's ideas orally, and engaging in respectful, yet critical, conversations with teachers and classmates.

Pedagogical Practices

Savage Inequalities in Urban Schools

Our first unit of the year strayed a little from the traditional content of a high school English class. We began with a unit that brought together Jonathan Kozol's (1991) *Savage Inequalities* and the 1988 film *Stand and Deliver* to study the material conditions and pathways to academic achievement in urban schools. In brief, *Savage Inequalities* is a book that offers an excellent example of new journalism and sociology of education research. Kozol visits several metropolitan areas throughout the country to document the drastic differences in spending, in curricular offerings, and in attitudes toward students in America's wealthiest and poorest schools. Kozol's thoroughly researched and rhetorically powerful tract shows a clear correlation between parental income, race, and quality of educational resources. He also shows very clearly that not only are the schools of the urban poor unequal, but they are in many cases inadequate and physically and psychologically unhealthy places for anyone's children to be.

Stand and Deliver, by contrast, is a story of triumph in the face of adversity. It relates how Jaime Escalante, a computer engineer, becomes a substitute math teacher at an impoverished school in East Los Angeles. Within a few years, Escalante is able to help students who were failing Algebra to pass the Advanced Placement examination in Calculus.

By pairing the book with the film, we wanted the students to have a sense both of the harsh realities of urban schools and of the possibilities to transform and transcend those realities. After all, we were reading Kozol's *Savage Inequalities* in a school that was similar in every respect to the failing schools depicted in the book. Our classroom had no windows, and often no heat in the winter; the carpet was held together in places by duct tape; the moveable chalk board possessed only two of its original four wheels, and a crack ran the full length of the board. Moving the chalkboard involved lifting the side without wheels and pushing it sideways. Also, the classroom has no computers, and the library had only one computer, which students could sign up to use for ten-minute sessions. The challenge for these students was that the Internet connection was so slow that it required more than ten minutes to dial into America On Line. We saw many a student kicked off that machine with their first page only partially loaded.

At the same time, we saw our goals as consistent with Jaime Escalante's up to a point. We wanted our students to envision themselves as having academic potential, and we wanted to create a curriculum that enabled our students to compete on equal academic footing with their counterparts who were attending the nation's elite schools. Indeed, many of these students did go on to take the Advanced Placement examination in English, and a large percentage of them were able to matriculate to four-year universities, where they were able to compete with peers who had attended better-funded, more highly regarded secondary institutions.

Our goals differed, though, to the extent that we foregrounded social critique and social praxis in our curriculum and pedagogy. We would not have been content, for instance, had our students achieved academically without a language to make sense of the material conditions that separated their school from one of the wealthiest high schools in the nation, which was less than four miles away. While we wanted students to have a sense of their own agency to resist, to subvert, and to transcend, we also understood that agency is enacted within and against structural contexts. In this case, it would be dishonest to promote a pull-yourself-up-by-your-bootstraps approach within a structural context that facilitated academic under-achievement. At the same time, it would be unconscionable to give students an excuse to fail. Rather, we sought to encourage a critical dialogue whereby our students would understand that they possessed the individual and collective ability to achieve even within a structure that can only be labeled as oppressive. At the same time, we hoped that the dialogue would be generative in producing a transformational praxis. We hope that the life of our classroom, the lives of our students, our lives, and the words in this book serve as evidence of that praxis.

Toward these ends, we created a space for discussion and action related to the conditions of urban schools. Naturally, a great deal of conversation pertained to comparisons between the conditions of schools in *Savage Inequalities* and *Stand and Deliver*. Students were critical of teachers and administrators who either contributed to inequitable conditions or stood idly by without trying to change them. We knew that we needed to be careful with the nature of our classroom conversations, though. It requires a delicate balance to encourage a critical discussion of schooling conditions with students without having them indict their teachers and administrators. We did our best to focus conversations on structural issues instead of individuals, but, honestly, several colleagues so closely resembled the antagonists from the book and film that not making comparisons required conscious effort.

At the conclusion of the unit we wanted an assignment that moved from talk to action, so we placed student groups in the position of policymakers and had them consider the policy implications of the unit from local contexts to federal initiatives. Students researched school spending policies and interviewed administrators and local politicians. It just so happened that a wealthy nearby school was in the process of constructing a $5-million stadium while our students did not have books that they could take home with them in their math and science courses. Interestingly, students chose to interview peers and administrators in both the wealthy school and their own. Students also drew upon photographs, video footage, and other artifacts to exemplify the conditions of the various schools.

Students began using these critical media literacies for political advantage in fighting for social and educational justice. For example, when it looked as though the school was planning to serve lunch even though over an inch of sewage from a nearby backup covered the kitchen and cafeteria floor, the students called local media outlets to convene a press conference in the sewage-filled halls of the school. Both lunch and school were subsequently cancelled.

Throughout the year a number of students became involved in citywide politics, urging council members to support an initiative to put "children first." Once the initiative was passed, two students continued to serve on the advisory board of the city council. Students, however, continued to experience the savage inequalities of East Bay High for the rest of their tenure at the school. The wealthy school up the hill finished its $5-million stadium and, to this day, continues to score in the 99th percentile on state standardized tests. What did change noticeably, however, was the relationship between the students and their school. Everyone on campus from the principal to the teachers was on notice that, if something was not right, the students would get to the bottom of it. This did not always make like enjoyable for us, their teachers, or for the students themselves. The stinging backlash became a frequent sensation. However, there is ample evidence and testimony to support the charge that the students felt empowered to challenge conditions that were seemingly innate and immutable.

Teaching Hip-Hop Music and Culture

Other teachers and members of the larger society perceived many of the students in our classes as functionally illiterate and lacking in intellect. These detractors relied on traditional school-based measures (past school performance, test scores) to support their claims and their resultant behavior toward (more like against) these youth. These assessments, however, ran counter to our observations of our students' sophisticated literacy practices that accompanied their participation in hip-hop culture. The same students portrayed as uninterested in literacy would come into our classrooms capable of reciting from memory the lyrics of entire rap albums. They voraciously read popular hip-hop magazines and transcribed song lyrics, and several carried their own rap composition books. Even those students who were not so deeply involved with hip-hop culture regularly listened to popular radio stations that programmed predominantly hip-hop and accessed magazines and CDs.

To tap into this literacy-rich youth cultural activity, we developed a seven-week poetry unit that paired hip-hop texts with canonical works of poetry. The goal of the unit was to play on students' heavy investments in hip-hop to create deeper understandings of school-based forms of poetry. We aimed to help students see the timelessness of the literary themes present in both canonical texts that they were mostly unfamiliar with and some of the music they listened to daily. We made explicit the fact that the literacy skills and knowledge that they exhibited in their interactions with hip-hop texts were not far removed from the skills required to succeed in analysis of poetry.

After pairing eight traditional poetry texts with eight rap songs, we divided our classes into groups of four or five students. Each group was responsible for preparing a class lesson on its pair of works. They were given relative autonomy for the form of their presentation, but each presentation was to have the following three elements:

1. analysis of the literary themes of each work (we gave students a list of common themes but encouraged them to develop others as they saw them emerge in the work)

2. comparative analysis of the two works (how are the works similar, how are they different, how do the authors use similar or different devices to deliver their message?)

3. guiding questions for class discussion (we had modeled complex, open-ended questions throughout the year and encouraged students to design similar questions)

In addition to preparing the group presentation, each student was expected to prepare an analysis of the other seven poem/song pairings to participate in class discussions. We had worked hard all year on developing a classroom culture where student participation in dialogues about literary themes was normalized. This, along with the use of hip-hop texts that drew students' attention, made the prospect of out-of-class preparation more likely, as the class came to enjoy challenging and broadening the literary analysis of their peers.

For the first two weeks of the unit, we spent class time going over poetic forms (sonnet, haiku, free form, prose) and poetic devices (rhythm, rhyme, meter, imagery, word choice, theme). We used examples from the eight pairings to teach these concepts, discussing with students their presence in music and traditional poetry. Students were also encouraged to bring passages from favorite songs or poems that displayed the ideas we were learning. During this time, students also began developing their poetry portfolios, writing poems that employed the concepts and forms that were discussed.

During the second two weeks of the unit, students continued developing their own poems while they worked in class with their groups and the teacher, preparing the analysis and presentation of their assigned pair. Class time was split between sharing and receiving feedback on their poems among peers and on preparing for their upcoming class presentations.

During the fifth and sixth weeks of the unit, each group was assigned one day to present its analysis and to lead the class in discussion about its pair. Presentations ranged from traditional stand-and-deliver approaches to more creative approaches where students brought in music videos and film clips or utilized interactive activities.

The remaining week-and-a-half was used for poetry readings. Each student was required to choose at least one poem to read in front of the class. These were often some of the most personally revealing and moving moments in the class. Putting the unit toward the end of the school year afforded many students the comfort level to risk sharing poems that revealed some of their most personal life experiences.

Race and Justice in Society Unit

We started each spring semester with a unit on race and justice. We waited until the second semester for several reasons. Though the topic of race certainly cropped up in earlier discussions, we wanted to ensure the development of a critical classroom culture and make certain that the students had prior experience with our brand of film study, which we describe in more detail below. The spring semester was also the time our department considered ideal to teach Richard Wright's *Native Son* (1940/1989). The unit opened with a collective viewing of *A Time to Kill* (Schumacher, 1996) and ended with a classroom court trial to decide the fate of Bigger Thomas. It is important to state up front that we watched film not merely as entertainment but as an intellectual activity. In the classroom, we watched with the lights on and notebooks out for about half of the period and spent the next half reviewing the segment, discussing interpretations and reactions to the text in terms of both the technical and thematic aspects of the film.

One incident we would like to recount occurred during a viewing of the segment of *A Time to Kill* where there are racial riots surrounding the trial of Carl Lee Hailey, a black man who is on trial for killing the two white men who raped his daughter and left her for dead. As the trial approaches in the film, racial tensions escalate. The National Association for the Advancement of Colored People (NAACP) comes from up North to lobby on the side of Carl Lee, and the Ku Klux Klan (KKK) comes from the Deep South to lobby on the side of the two white men who were killed.

As the racial tensions escalate in the movie, the class becomes more emotionally charged and begins to identify with the African Americans in the film and to root for them. Students begin to chant with the protesters and yell disapproval at the screen. Obviously, this is more than a dispassionate viewing of a class assignment or an opportunity to sit back and be entertained. The class, in this example, is beginning to relate the film to their everyday lives as citizens in a racially charged society. They are also using this understanding to facilitate textual analysis as well as a critical engagement with the text. This is a film, and the story is fictional, and the characters are fictional, but the emotion surrounding the issues of racism and justice where the students are upset with characters and clapping and cheering and pumping fists shows that the students are politicizing this film and relating it to similar issues in their own lives. This relevance, we argue, leads to a deeper understanding that, in turn, facilitates a more personal and deeper analysis of the themes of race and justice found in the text.

Freeing Carl Lee, for these students, is victory for the African Americans, who are the oppressed group in the film. As members of oppressed groups within society, this perspective informs the students' identification with and analysis of the text. Several of the students have claimed that the torching of the Klan wizard is justice and any exoneration of Carl Lee's actions is a victory for the oppressed. Their willingness to identify with this text enables them to bridge their worlds and the film text and to embrace the text at a critical level. Rather than looking at Carl Lee and the others as fictional characters, they are looking at what they represent to their own lives in creating that universal plane of knowledge. As they begin to relate the characters to their own lives, they bring their daily life experiences into their critical interpretation of this text.

During the post-film discussion, Morrell asks whether the African American male who killed the Klan wizard was guilty of murder. The point gets made that the guilt of blacks and whites in the scene is not equivalent, since the whites have power, privilege, and a stake in the status quo while the blacks are largely reactionary. Morrell grants that Stump Sisson, the wizard, was wrong, but says he didn't deserve to die. On the other hand, the boy who killed him wasn't necessarily guilty of first-degree murder. This problematizes simplistic notions of right and wrong and sets the stage for future discussions and debates.

As we discuss our impending reenactment of the Bigger Thomas court trial, the connection is made between Clanton, Mississippi, and the city where the school is located. One student recalls a recent incident between African Americans and Latinos at the school where the police were called to intervene. Another tells a story about how two Asian American friends of hers were victims of attacks by African Americans. A third asks for more details about the incident as the class listens attentively. Although we cannot agree on whether there can be a single conception of justice for all, the entire class agrees that what happened to the Asian American students was wrong.

Throughout the many times that we taught this unit, there were incidents similar to the one just described. Students had personal and meaningful transactions with the film that facilitated a healthy dialogic space and the completion of superior academic work. One class went so far as to create a newsletter that challenged the school's approach to issues of culture and power. These students interviewed their peers, teachers, and administrators, and candidates for the office of mayor. They also collected video footage of the campus climate that they offered to local news agencies. Most important, the students were able to learn about themselves and each other and cross fairly entrenched racial and cultural lines to come together as a class committed to cultural acceptance and affirmation.

Critical English teachers can use films such as *A Time to Kill* to promote reader response or the use of critical literary theories (feminist, Marxist, postcolonial, psychoanalytic) in secondary English classrooms. Students can use film as a springboard to reflect upon their experiences as involuntary participants in a racialized society. Through the sharing of these personal transactions, students can acquire a sensitivity to and understanding of cultures different from their own. They can also use cultural studies to make sense of how society creates categories of self and other around a host of identifiers such as race, class, gender, sexuality, home language, and religion. Students can discuss how those classified as "Other" are portrayed and treated in popular media and in everyday life.

It is important to highlight that watching film together in a classroom is a social activity that is different from reading a text privately and then discussing it publicly. If film watching is done appropriately, it becomes a public viewing in a unique social space. The class members, as a community of practice, participate together in the activity of making sense of this text. These young people are also able to come together as members of a common culture, a youth popular culture that frequently transcends race and class. The film text is a great equalizer in that more students have a schema for the critical analysis of film and more experience with this literacy practice in their everyday lives.

It is also important to recognize the power of the visual imagery associated with the film medium to engender critical dialogue about race. Sometimes it is more difficult for students to engage older texts such as *Huckleberry Finn* because they are from eras that students can easily dismiss. More contemporary films that deal with the experiences of women, of people with disabilities, or of people of color have a greater chance of being perceived as relevant. These popular texts, however, can be used to create bridges to older, canonical texts, much as we did with *A Time to Kill* and *Native Son*.

By no means are we advocating that educators subordinate the canonical to the popular. Rather, we are encouraging the creation of meaningful links between the worlds of the students and the worlds of canonical texts. Many socio-cultural theorists influenced by the work of Vygotsky have promoted authentic learning environments that draw upon the strengths that students bring from home and community and allow students to learn through legitimate peripheral participation in communities of practice. Moll (2000), for example, argues that educators become ethnographers who seek to understand and affirm the community's funds of knowledge when designing curricula. We agree with Moll and contend that any ethnographic investigations of the lives of young people would reveal that film plays a central role in their emergent understandings of themselves and their world.

Though we are absolutely convinced of the transformational possibilities associated with this innovative approach to English education, we want to address issues of appropriateness and communication. Because of the connotations of the medium and also because of its evocative nature, controversies and challenges are certain to arise. It is one thing to read about oppression or violence in a book; it is another experience entirely to watch these acts manifested through a film or video text. Teachers need to be prepared for the emotions that will be evoked by the visual text. They also need to be ready to communicate with other teachers, with administrators, with parents, and with students about the importance of utilizing this medium to teach about issues related to diversity. Educators, however, should not shy away from these encounters, nor should they be apologetic about the use of film in their classrooms. The imperative of our moment demands that we push the envelope to discover novel approaches that allow us to accomplish our multiple goals of developing students who have the skills to function academically and professionally in a complex world and also the sensitivities needed to function as critical citizens in a multicultural democracy.

Serious Voices for Urban Youth

It was during the final presentations of the Race and Justice film unit that one of the students stopped the discussion of the film to ask her classmates, "Do we have justice here at East Bay High?" The response was swift and certain. The students knew that they did not, in fact, receive justice at their high school. Students shared narratives of receiving an inferior education, of being treated as prisoners and second-class citizens. They talked about being harassed by campus security, about being corralled into holding rooms when they were a few minutes late to class. One student commented on the greasing of the fences to prevent students from climbing them during school hours, the locked gates that went against the fire codes. "If there's a fire in here we're all gonna die; there's no way we can get out," a student correctly remarked.

Other comments addressed the lack of textbooks in Chemistry courses—so few, in fact, that students could not take the texts home. They would have to devote class time to writing down the problems they needed for homework. If, at home, they required some sort of explanation, they were just out of luck. These comments continued in fervor and intensity until Jasmine asked her classmates what they planned to do about this injustice. It was April of their senior year, six short weeks until their graduation. For these students, it was now or never, their final chance to leave a legacy to the students who followed them.

What emerged from this discourse was a magazine project to which the students devoted their final six weeks as students of East Bay High. The project ultimately became known as *Serious Voices for Urban Youth* and included articles, poems, and drawings. The students selected themes and issues that they wanted to cover and chose peers to take on assignments. Some of these assignments included interviews with prospective mayoral candidates about the state of the high school, personal narratives about experiences in schools, portraits of inspiring teachers, letters of guidance and inspiration to successive classes at the school, and artwork depicting the conditions of the school.

Implications

We could have taught any of these units using more traditional methods and curriculum. This would, however, run counter to our philosophy that the most important ingredient of an effective classroom is engaging pedagogy and curriculum. Our sense about the development of this approach to teaching is that it must value the cultural sensibilities and interests of students. While this is not a particularly new idea, we would argue that the relative failure of this multicultural (Banks, 1994) or culturally relevant (Ladson-Billings, 1994) approach to education has stemmed from the misapplication of these principles.

In short, the practice of multicultural education has employed an all-too-narrow definition of culture. The term "culture" in school curricula has largely been a proxy for "race/ethnicity," and while this has resulted in some attention to a more ethnically and gender-diverse set of readings and perspectives, it has not considered other central aspects of culture. To understand this interpretation and application of modern multicultural and culturally relevant pedagogy theory, we can use John Dewey's notions about the importance of a democratic education.

In the early 1900s, Dewey suggested that educational theory had trapped teachers in a false binary when it came to pedagogy (Dewey, 1938). That is, Dewey believed that teachers were asked to choose between a classical curriculum and a curriculum focused on the lived experiences of their students. More often than not, teachers selected the former as it was traditional and, ergo, professionally more acceptable. Dewey's work argued that, rather than think of curriculum as an either/or proposition, we should always see it as a both/and endeavor. Dewey believed that the child should be at the center of the curriculum, such that the school curriculum draws from the lived experiences of the child to expand into broader horizons. This approach does not attempt to replace the knowledge that children bring with them to school; it builds on it. Dewey believed that this would make the relevance of school immediately apparent to the student, given that they would be engaging school knowledge through the lens of their lived social reality. We agree, and we developed our pedagogy and curriculum accordingly.

4
What a Coach Can Teach a Teacher

In 1996, we were both teaching English at East Bay High School. Candace,[1] the star girls' basketball player, was a student in my (Duncan-Andrade's) 11th-grade English class. In late September, she asked me to become the varsity head coach because their coach had just resigned. As a former high school basketball player, I knew taking over a program a month before the season began was equivalent to coaching suicide, especially in a highly competitive basketball league like the Oakland Athletic League. Having coached boys' basketball during my first four years of teaching, I also knew that coaching was a powerful way to educate young people. I told Candace that if she could convince Morrell, also a high school basketball player, to coach the team with me, I would commit to an interim position with the program while the athletic director conducted a search for a full-time replacement. No replacement was found, and we both ended up heavily investing in the development of the basketball program: Morrell coached in the program from 1996 to 2000 and I stayed with the program from 1996 to 2002. Over those years, the program had tremendous social, academic, and athletic success, due in large part to the principles of critical pedagogy infused into the program's ideology and structure. This chapter reports from portions of a four-year study of that program that I conducted between 1997 and 2001.

Sports and Social Resistance

The basketball gym is probably not the first place most people would go to see critical pedagogy in an urban high school. Sports, particularly revenue sports such as basketball and football, are often criticized by liberal thinkers as tools for the maintenance of conservative and patriarchal value systems. There is plenty of validity in those critiques. However, the potential of using sports as a vehicle for resistance, empowerment, and collective change should receive more scholarly attention.

The recent publication *What's My Name Fool* (Zirin, 2005) documents numerous examples of athletes using the notoriety of sports as a vehicle for raising voices of resistance and social critique. Zirin's commitment to capturing moments of social resistance by athletes continues beyond his book. He also writes weekly articles that provide a critical analysis of society through the lens of sports (http://www.edgeofsports.com). Such efforts are important because they draw attention to the fact that sports have been, and continue to be, a site for raising social consciousness.

Unfortunately, Zirin's work is limited by the fact that most of the examples he provides are instances of individual resistance. Most of his cases where sports were used as a vehicle of social critique came about because individual athletes use their notoriety to bring their political views into public purview. It is true that some of the most memorable moments of resistance in sports are the result of athletes connecting their personal views with the views put forth by larger social movements (Tommie Smith and John Carlos in solidarity with the Black Power movement and Muhammad Ali with the anti–Vietnam War movement). However, it is not typical for the commentaries of these athletes to be deliberately linked to long-term organizing and resistance strategies of movements for social change.

In relationship to their sport and their team, most acts of social resistance by athletes end up being individualized because they are not an intentional outcome of their athletic training. Such actions are not part of a collective team effort, and they are not the result of a critical political agenda on the part of the team or the coach. But what if they were? Could sports be used to develop a collective culture that aims to transform oppressive social norms? Can critical pedagogy help coaches to foster such a critical collective consciousness and agency with their teams? This chapter discusses our use of three pillars of critical pedagogy (organic intellectualism, praxis, and counter-hegemony) in the Lady Wildcat Basketball Program (LWBP) to develop a powerful counter-narrative to urban school failure. The success of the program suggests that there are fundamental principles in this work that can inform the development of similar cultures in other urban school programs and classrooms.

Vehicles for Engagement: Practicing What We Preach

Reading the world always precedes reading the word, and reading the word implies continually reading the world.

—*Freire & Macedo, 1987, 35*

Aspiring critical pedagogues are quick to teach students to "read the world and the word," but they are less likely themselves to practice this element of critical pedagogy. If educators read the world of their students, they would find countless vehicles for moving forward their critical pedagogical agenda. Just such an opportunity presented itself to us as high school teachers in

Oakland when our students asked us to fill the coaching vacancy in the basketball program.

Before we discuss our use of critical pedagogy in the LWBP, we want briefly to emphasize the importance of educators identifying a vehicle for delivering the tenets of critical pedagogy. The sad fact about critical pedagogy in U.S. urban schools is that many educators well versed in critical pedagogical theory are unable to bridge that theory into practice. There are many reasons for this failure. The most common reason is the inability of teachers to capture the minds and hearts of their students. An educator's ability to develop vehicles for engaging students is an essential ingredient of being an effective critical pedagogue. In the case of the LWBP, we used sports. However, in our other work we have discussed popular culture (Morrell, 2004b; Duncan-Andrade, 2005c, 2007) and social science research methods (Duncan-Andrade, 2005b; Morrell, 2004a) as equally effective vehicles for providing students a program that combines some of their own interests with a critical and consistent focus. In short, there must be a programmatic vision and it must be something that students can believe in; it must provide hope and a sense that their investment will be rewarded.

Critical Pedagogy and Organic Intellectualism

Not all children learn at the same pace or in the same ways, even though schools mostly operate as if they do. Almost all schools in the United States group students on the basis of age, and they frequently sort them even further using faulty measurements of ability (Oakes, 1985). Once the sorting is done, students are taught from pre-programmed curricula that promote the same pacing and instructional methods for everyone. Educators mostly ignore or explain away the fact that this approach to teaching produces results that contradict our rhetoric that all children can learn. Even teachers deeply committed to the equity-oriented principles of critical pedagogy can end up reproducing trends of academic failure by reverting to time-honored traditions of one-size-fits-all instruction and assessment.

Gramsci (1971) contended that the inequitable outcome of schooling that results from such pedagogical practices should be attributed to social design rather than student inadequacies. For Gramsci, "all [people] are intellectuals ... but not all [people] have in society the function of intellectuals" (p. 9). He believed that each person has an organic intellectualism that results from his or her interactions with the world and that these interactions are almost always socially constrained by factors such as race, class, and gender. The fact that each person experiences the world differently means that each student comes to school with different forms of intellectualism. However, schools are often ill equipped to identify and cultivate a person's organic intellectualism. Instead, they end up sorting intellectuals from non-intellectuals through teaching methods that value the ability to acquire and reproduce information using specific formats within rigid timeframes. For this reason, most of what Gramsci saw as the organic intellectualism of humanity remains untapped in schools.

Gramsci's work suggests that many pedagogical practices in schools run counter to what we understand about cognitive development and educational psychology. It is widely agreed that students have considerable variations in their "zone of proximal development (ZPD)" (Vygotsky, 1978) and that ignoring this fact virtually guarantees that students who do not receive considerable additional support are doomed to fail in school. An effective implementation of critical pedagogy requires educators to disrupt pedagogical trends that ignore our most basic sensibilities about teaching and learning. Vygotsky's ZPD is particularly useful because it explains that each student has his or her own zone of development (social and academic) and is capable of moving through that zone if he or she is given support by someone who already understands the concepts in that ZPD.

For example, if Student A and Student B were in the same classroom learning about spelling, we could graphically represent the basic idea of ZPD (Figure 4.1). If the principles necessary for being a strong speller are represented linearly, then we can see two students in the same classroom at different places on that line of expertise. Student A enters the classroom knowing some basics about spelling, but she has not built up practice strategies to develop fully the fundamentals of good spelling. Her zone of proximal development begins at the point on the line that represents the level of skills she has already mastered well enough to teach to someone else and extends toward more advanced competencies in spelling. With assistance she can move through that zone (shaded in gray as ZPD) and become proficient at spelling. Student B comes to the group already having had strong training in spelling. She might have already moved through some parts of the ZPD that Student A still needs to work through. To be fully effective, the classroom pedagogy would need to provide a different set of opportunities for Student B, also known as differentiated instruction.

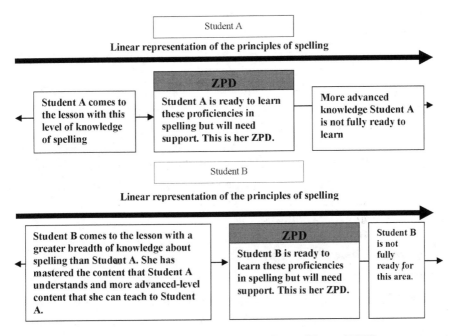

Figure 4.1. An Illustration of the Basic Idea of ZPD

In a classroom that begins instruction with the presumption the students have proficiency in spelling, Student A is likely to fall even further behind her classmates. The outcome of that increasing gap is predictably negative, and most issues of disengagement or classroom misbehavior can be attributed to a student's awareness of this widening gap. Another scenario is that the instructor identifies large numbers of students who, like Student A, are below spelling proficiency and modifies the curriculum to teach to the non-proficient speller. The outcome of this pedagogical adjustment is likely to be negative for Student B, who will find the class unchallenging and begin disengaging or seeking other stimuli, which will probably get her labeled as a behavior problem. A third scenario, one that incorporates pedagogical attention to the concept of the ZPD, could produce positive results for both Student A and Student B. In this scenario, Student B can be positioned to support Student A as she struggles to move through her ZPD. This would allow Student A to meet the challenges of the class and Student B to reinforce her excellent preparation and build pedagogical and leadership skills without feeling unchallenged in the class. This is an over-simplification. But it raises the point that there are ways to conceptualize classroom environments that properly address the inevitable variance in zones of proximal development.

Each student has sets of things he or she is ready to learn if someone helps, and there are also things outside of his or her ZPD that the student is not yet in a position to learn. Educators using the concept of the ZPD understand that there will be variance in each student's ZPD and that this variance is not neatly distributed on the basis of age. Therefore, effectively teaching all students requires educators to develop strategies for identifying a student's ZPD and then responding with the appropriate support for that student's particular needs. In most public schools, the only time this is formally required of educators is when students are referred to a Special Education program and given Individual Accommodation Plans (IAPs).

Identifying a Student's Organic Intellectualism

In the case of the LWBP we used three reflective meetings per student per year to identify each student's ZPD and her needs and goals for moving through that zone. The three meetings took place at the end of each summer (September), at the end of the basketball season (March), and at the end of the school year (July). Before each meeting, students prepared responses to questions dealing with basketball, school, and their future goals. The coaches also answered the questions on the basis of our evaluations and expectations of the student in each area. The questions were as follows:

Basketball
What are your strengths as a basketball player?
What are the areas you need to improve as a basketball player?

Academics
How would you describe yourself academically?
What are your strengths and weaknesses?
Why do you feel this way?

Future Goals
What do you want to accomplish this year as a player? How will you do it?
What do you want to accomplish this year as a team? How will you do it?
What do you want to accomplish this year as a student? How will you do it?

What are your long-term goals for yourself (five years, ten years, twenty years)? How will you accomplish them?

These meetings provided opportunities for the responses of the players and the coaches to be discussed and amended on the basis of dialogue. These discussions allowed us to identify areas where we under-estimated students and places where students were under-valuing their own potential. It was important that this was a collaborative process because our experience as teachers and coaches allowed us to identify potential in students that they often did not see in themselves. The discussions also gave us important insight into student strengths that we had overlooked. Students and coaches alike left these meetings with clear goals and concrete steps to achieve those goals, a process that one student pointed out is rarely experienced by students in urban schools:

> Ada (Class of 2001): You got me to think about where my life was going and what I wanted out of it. I know that most of the kids I knew never even thought about that at all. When I'd ask them stuff, they would just say, "I dunno." But you got me to think about my future. ... All the planning we do, it made me feel like I was together.

These meetings were part of a year-long process of self-reflection that helped participants focus their energies on specific goals. These evaluations were particularly helpful in providing us with a better of idea of what students expected from themselves. This powerful insight into the students' self-esteem allowed for the creation of individualized academic and athletic development plans. In turn, this meant more precise, personalized development that catered to the needs of each individual. These individualized plans included workouts tailored to the individual athletic goals of the participant and academic support geared toward the student's academic needs and goals.

The development of this structure for identifying zones of proximal development allowed us to appreciate each student's organic intellectualism more fully. We can take the cases of Ada and Lisa as an example. These two students came to the program at the same time but with very different skill sets. Ada entered the 9th grade with a reputation as a top athlete and a marginal student. Lisa entered the 9th grade with limited athletic preparation and mediocre academic achievement.

Over their four years in the LWBP, we used the ZPD model to develop individual plans for both students that accomplished two primary goals of effective pedagogy: they were positioned to contribute to the program from their areas of strength, and they received support relevant to their areas of most pressing academic, social, and athletic needs. For Ada, we designed an athletic program that challenged her to grow into one of the top athletes in the city. As Ada's athletic excellence matured through her development of self-discipline, poise under pressure, and work ethic, she began to transfer these skills organically toward her academic growth. This process was organic because she was learning these habits of mind through her choice to participate in the sport. Students like Ada who reflect habits of excellence in areas outside of the classroom rarely encounter educators who help them bridge these skills into the realm of academia. In the case of the LWBP, we recognized that Ada came to our program having already begun the organic development of habits of mind that are demanded of excellent students.

What was missing from the picture was a system for helping her build the bridge between athletic success and academic success. We provided Ada with daily academic support in the form of after-school and weekend tutoring by local college students, coaches, and teachers. We augmented this support with summer academic acceleration activities. As suggested in Ada's comments above, this support was all the more effective because it was coupled with ongoing dialogue that helped her bridge her athletic and academic potential. Over our four years together, her low academic self-esteem never completely went away. However, by her junior year she was making the honor roll and had found the confidence to take multiple Advanced Placement courses. After graduation she was admitted and enrolled at the University of San Francisco.

Had we attempted to replicate the strategies we used with Ada for Lisa, we would surely have failed, because Lisa did not experience similar success in athletics. Lisa had a rugged self-assuredness that resulted in her being well liked and respected, but before she joined the LWBP her charisma had not transferred into much athletic or academic success. We had to create opportunities for Lisa to contribute as an emotional leader on the team because her athletic skills never developed to the same level as those of other members of the program. In most athletic programs, she would have been cut from the team because of her lack of athleticism. However, we saw in Lisa the organic intellectualism of leadership, which included other key elements for academic success (risk taking, self-sacrifice, self-confidence). Lisa's self-confidence and tendency to be a risk taker allowed us to push her hard and fast academically.

We quickly enrolled her in some of the most challenging courses at the school and made sure to provide her with daily academic support so that she would experience success in those classes. Athletically, we remained patient with Lisa's slow gains, rewarding her for challenging others to work as hard as she did even though she did not receive the athletic notoriety that they received. Her rapid academic ascent made her one of the top students in the program and regularly placed her on the honor roll. Although we had other excellent students, we held her up as an example of academic growth, emphasizing that her achievements there were hard won. This position allowed her to take on a leadership role not available in most sports programs. Lisa became one of our most valuable tutors, particularly with younger students, because she understood the challenges of developing a new academic identity. After graduation she was admitted and enrolled at the University of California, Berkeley.

The application of critical pedagogy requires educators to challenge the existing one-size-fits-all pedagogical model. This requires an understanding that students enter schools with different zones of proximal development. These different levels of preparedness are tremendous opportunities for educators who are prepared and willing to diversify the strategies they use for motivation, instructional pedagogy, and academic and social support.

Critical Pedagogy and Critical Praxis

Successful sports programs are among the best places to study the effective use of praxis. Praxis can be defined as a thorough process of reflection where ideas are tested and experienced in the real world, followed by reflection, revision and reapplication of those ideas (Freire, 1970). Good coaches constantly reflect on their strategy, their performance, and the performance of their players to find places for improvement. The best programs videotape practices and games and scrutinize those videos regularly in hopes of uncovering areas for individual and team growth. Effective coaches regularly use these reflective tools to adjust their instructional methods to make sure that every player understands the team's strategy and that each player receives maximum preparation to carry out that strategy. They also regularly check in with players to assess their health and understanding of what is being taught and to identify areas (social and athletic) where a player might need additional support. Finally, coaches regularly dialogue with other coaches, players, and former players in search of critical feedback and advice for improvement. The teaching profession could greatly benefit from studying and adapting the way that the coaching profession uses praxis to improve their own instruction and performance.

Sadly, despite the proficiency of sports programs at using praxis for internal growth, they rarely engage in critical praxis. That requires engagement in, and reflection on, actions that aim to end injustice. In the LWBP we saw the challenge of critical praxis as the challenge to create a program that accomplished two things: consistent and sustainable achievement for all our students, and critical agency to respond to conditions of inequity that students saw in their immediate communities. We began with the understanding that we could not be effective if we asked students to do something we were not willing to do ourselves. We attempted to model critical praxis by being critically engaged as teachers in the school and as members of the Oakland community (we both lived within five minutes of the school). Issues of racial, social, and educational inequality were always at the forefront of our agenda as teachers and as coaches. These issues were the mainstay of our discussions with students, whether in the classroom, on rides home from practice, or between summer league games. We expressed, in no uncertain terms, that we taught and coached because we saw it as the most likely path to supporting a movement for radical social change. We modeled the reflective side of this critical praxis as students. We were both enrolled as graduate students, which allowed students to see us as lifelong learners, committed to the principles of social justice but not having all the answers. Students saw us reading, writing, and studying, challenging each other to think more deeply about issues of injustice. We shared with them our struggles as students, asked them for their advice and reflections, and brought them to our graduate classes as guests and presenters. Finally, we sought their opinion of our work as teachers and coaches in informal conversations throughout the year and with formal evaluations at the end of each semester. The importance of educators modeling critical praxis is under-emphasized in discussions on how to implement critical pedagogy effectively. In our case, modeling it illustrated the usefulness and impact of critical praxis and better positioned us to ask students to develop similar habits.

To help students in the LWBP develop critical praxis in their own lives, we developed a set of principles that each agreed to live by. These principles reflected habits of mind related to their desire to improve as students, as athletes, and as a team. The principles were a modified version of Pat Summitt's

"The Definite Dozen" (Summitt & Jenkins, 1998). Before a student could become a member of our program, she had to recite the Definite Dozen from memory and agree to uphold them. They were as follows:

Definite Dozen
"Discipline yourself so that no one else has to."

To stay in the program:
1. Be responsible (sit in the front rows in your classes)
2. Be respectful (treat people the way you want to be treated)
3. Be honest (leaders don't make excuses; they make improvements)
4. Be loyal (handle success like you handle failure)

To play here:
5. Work (every day, everywhere)
6. Play smart (correct your own mistakes)
7. Team before yourself (above all else, character matters)
8. Winning attitude (doubters never win; winners never doubt)

To be successful here:
9. Communicate (be coachable)
10. Accept your role (know your role and don't step out of it for personal glory)
11. Influence your opponent (make people leave their comfort zone)
12. Be a competitor (never, ever give up)

Students were reminded daily of the Definite Dozen and were consistently asked to self-assess their commitment and actualization of the principles as they related to the team and to their broader lives. For most of the students, this was the first time they had been asked to commit to a set of principles they could use as points of reflection for their personal and collective growth.

The Definite Dozen helped build three phases of self-development that Du Bois (as cited in Kincheloe, 2004, 60) saw as essential components of a worthy education: self-respect, self-realization, and self-consciousness.[2] To participate in the LWBP meant embracing a commitment to ask for and utilize support to achieve intellectual, social, and athletic excellence. For our part, we had to be sure that we maintained high levels of expectation, motivation, and support for all the students. In contrast to the traditionally low expectations of the school, the LWBP raised the bar, demanded that everyone in the program struggle to cross that bar, and refused to let anyone in the program succumb in that struggle.

In one of the end-of-year program evaluation surveys, several parents pointed out strong gains in the self-respect of their students:

> Melinda (parent): I've seen my daughter's sense of herself and responsibility to others grow. In this program she has been provided with a second family ... a group at school that I like her to spend time with. A real good group of friends that guide her right.

> Linda (parent): She has a place she feels she belongs. Academically she has never done better. She has friendships and seems to feel comfortable with herself. She seems more accessible than many teens—less rebellious and angry. The attention to team building has developed this.

As self-respect grows, so does self-realization. The concept of self-realization derives from a Sanskrit expression referring to knowledge based on experience, not mere intellectual knowledge. That is, the more the students value themselves, the more they are able to learn from their experiences, successes and failures. In most urban schools, students are taught to under-value or, worse, to devalue their own experiences. Without a strong sense of self-respect in the context of school and society, it is virtually impossible for a person to engage in the praxis of self-realization. The process of self-respect leading to self-realization is more likely to happen when students achieve hard-to-reach goals. The perseverance necessary to achieve hard-won success is more likely to happen when there are high doses of motivation (external and internal) and support.

In program evaluation interviews with six focal students at the end of the four-year study, each referred, in similar ways to Nancy's and Ada's comments here, to how unusual it was for a program to believe so fully in their potential:

> Nancy (Class of 2001): when things started going bad for me last year, all I had was this [LWBP] program. Every day I wondered if I was going to turn out just like my older sister and brother. My sister was really smart, but she still dropped out, and my brother was really good at baseball and he dropped out. But when I think about my teammates and this program and all ... how much it means to me, I want to keep fighting. I know I would have dropped out if it wasn't for this program. I just know it.

Ada (Class of 2001): The most helpful part of this program was the conversations that you had with me. When we would meet and we would talk about what you thought I could do, I really started to believe in myself. Sometimes, it felt like you believed in me more than I believed in me. This was a dramatic change for me. Before I didn't even see a reason for coming to school. I think because I didn't have any goals.

When students have self-respect and are allowed to value the self-realizations that emerge through their lived experiences, their self-consciousness is heightened. They recognize that awareness, and, for students who have felt the sting of being denied access to quality educational programs, this awareness has the potential to develop into critical consciousness. Sadly, this potential remains largely untapped because successful urban students are often encouraged to see their success as a way to escape the problems and suffering of ghetto life. Schools tend to teach that agency is about an individual's ability to pull himself or herself up by their bootstraps. Schools should focus instead on critical self-consciousness to develop students' confidence that they can use their agency to challenge inequities in their communities.

Our program also gave attention to developing students' sense of critical self-consciousness through shared readings such as *Savage Inequalities*, *Hagakure*, and *The Art of War*. We had formal and informal discussions about the readings and their relationship to conditions in Oakland schools, the students' communities, and global society. These opportunities helped students understand that they, together with other youth in their community, could be agents of change. Along these lines, the students in the LWBP developed a free basketball camp in the spring for elementary and middle school students. To spread the word about the camp, students distributed flyers in the community and returned to their elementary and middle schools to make presentations in the classrooms of their former teachers. Over three years the camp served more than 100 students for two full days, focusing largely on building self-confidence and strategies for coping with the challenges of adolescent life.

After the first camp, students decided more workshops were needed in the camp that addressed the challenges of urban adolescence. They identified two particular areas schools had never taught them that would have eased their transition into young adulthood. First, they felt they would have benefited from a crash course about the ins and outs of high school life. They called this workshop "The Secrets to High School Success." They also thought that they would have benefited from advice from other teens about nutrition, physical conditioning, sleep, drugs, alcohol, and sex. They called this workshop "Healthy Lifestyles." Students developed curricula for these two sessions by anticipating some of the challenges that the campers were already facing as young women of color in an urban center, and they gave strategies for overcoming those challenges and coping with defeats. They sought out advice and information from parents, teachers, other students, and the Alameda County Public Health Department so that their sessions would be informative and accurate. They also went through multiple drafts of the curricula for the workshops, using each other and us to fine-tune their plans. It is worth noting that these two sessions always received the highest ratings from the campers. As Mika notes in an excerpt from her interview, several of the players were so inspired by the impact they had as teachers at the camp that they began volunteering at a local YMCA summer camp to continue their work with youth:

> Mika: I started to think about how these kids were looking up to me and I thought about how we're always talking about doing more than just getting good grades and winning games. Every time I would go [to the YMCA], those kids would get so excited and jump around, like it was the greatest place in the world to them. It kinda made me want to go because I knew they wanted me to go. Then when I got Kendra and Lisa to go too, then it was even better because it was all of us doing something together.

This work with young people in the community became a key element of the critical praxis in the program. Each year students would make improvements to the camp on the basis of their experiences as teachers and in response to critical feedback they received from campers and parents. They also found ways to expand the impact of their work with youth by working at the YMCA summer camps, volunteering as coaches for youth basketball leagues, and speaking in classes at their former elementary and middle schools. Two other students started flag football and basketball teams on their blocks with elementary-age youngsters in their apartment complexes "so they can play outside and be safe instead of just sitting on their couch."

Critical Pedagogy and Counter-hegemony

If hegemony includes the process by which mainstream social, economic, and political inequalities are made to appear normal, then counter-hegemony should include critique of those inequities and actions to improve them. For

Gramsci (1971), this requires a dual platform made up of a "war of position" and a "war of movement" (pp. 238–239). The war of position is waged through efforts to gain access to voice and power in social institutions (education, law, government, health care) in order to normalize discussions of social and economic inequities that inspire revolutionary acts to change structural inequities. The war of movement occurs when victories in the war of position result in a widespread shift in social consciousness that leads to collective public action against inequity.

In the LWBP we engaged in the war of position by using our institutional capital (as teachers, coaches, and graduate students) to develop a counter-hegemonic education program that normalized self-respect, self-realization, and critical self-consciousness. We implemented this program using academic and social support structures that relied on the concepts of organic intellectualism (Gramsci, 1971) and the zone of proximal development (Vygotsky, 1978). These structures were victories in the war of position in that they used the institutional resources of school to provide equitable educational opportunity for our students. In urban schools, it is not hard to find instances of individual success, but these should not necessarily be considered counter-hegemonic or victories in the war of position. The achievement of outstanding individuals who use their success to escape the severe structural inequalities of poverty should not be considered counter-hegemonic. These isolated cases reinforce the dominant hegemony, which suggests that only an exceptional few can find success in urban schools and that success is partially defined by their ability to leave their community to join a more "successful" one. This is where the concept of the war of movement is helpful, because the traditional individualized model of success does not prioritize shifts in social consciousness that lead to collective public action against inequity. Quite the contrary, it contributes to social reproduction by reinforcing a survival-of-the-fittest paradigm that legitimizes inequitable opportunities and outcomes. To counter this traditional paradigm of success in urban schools, the LWBP emphasized the development of structures that supported success and collective consciousness for all its participants rather than a select few.

The approach we used can be regarded as counter-hegemonic in two ways. First, the program's consistently high achievement rate was counter-hegemonic to school and district cultures that normalized low achievement for most students. We ran the LWBP for six years (1996–2002), conducting a formal study of its impact over the four middle years (1997–2001). Over those four years, the team had a grade point average of 3.4, compared with a 2001 school-wide average of 1.6 for African Americans, 1.7 for Latinos, and 2.4 for Asian Americans. The most significant points of comparison for this measurement of achievement are the school-wide grade point averages of African American females (1.75) and our team grade point average of 3.4, because ten of the twelve participants were African American females (the program also had one Chicana and one Cambodian student). At the end of the four-year period of study, the program had 100% graduation and four-year college enrollment rates for all six of the participants who entered the program as 9th graders in 1997.[3] During that same period, the school had graduation rates of 53%, 47%, and 72%, and college eligibility rates of 9%, 9%, and 31% for African Americans, Latinos, and Asian Americans, respectively (California Department of Education, 2006).

We can also think about the methods used to achieve these results as counter-hegemonic. We worked hard to develop a counter-culture in the program, one that normalized excellence and collective achievement. We did this, in part, by raising students' awareness of the critical "double-consciousness" demanded of them if they were to become successful in school and the larger society. Du Bois (1903/1996) explained the idea of double-consciousness as the effect black people in America experience by having to struggle with two "warring ideals." Many urban youth of color experience this effect. On the one hand, they are "American" but never fully accepted as a group in a society that often portrays them as purveyors of social pathology and non-intellectual. They are also aware that they are connected to distinctive cultures (pan-African, pan-Latino, pan-Asian) but that living in the United States means they might never fully realize this identity. A critical double-consciousness is realized when a person faced with this internal battle is able to develop a critically conscious response to these conditions. Such a person is able to acquire the mechanical skills necessary to navigate oppressive social conditions and institutions and the critical skills to analyze and resist the hostility he or she endures and to develop a strong sense of self and community.

We sought to develop this critical double-consciousness in our students by helping them acquire the "master's tools" (Lorde, 1984) and the tools of "transformative resistance" (Solórzano & Delgado-Bernal, 2001). We paid special attention to providing academic support to students all year. Part of this support meant having explicit conversations with them about how to navigate the hostile dispositions and low expectations of some adults in the school. Lorde argues that the master's tools are the tools of oppression. She makes the point that oppressed people will not dismantle oppression by acquiring the tools of oppression and then using them to oppress others. Instead, the master's tools must be put to use to dismantle oppression. This message was explicit in our program. We insisted that students learn to negotiate their school environment effectively. However, there was also the expectation that as students acquired tools to navigate the institution of school they would share that knowledge with their peers.

We considered this sharing of their knowledge the application of Solórzano and Delgado-Bernal's concept of transformative resistance. These authors distinguish between forms of resistance that are conformist (self-serving) or self-defeating (self-destructive) and those that are transformative. Transformative resistance is the concept of a collective resistance that results in positive and transformational change for the individual and the community (2001, 319–320). Our students were able to resist the temptations of the model of individual achievement often promoted in schools and sports programs by finding ways to redistribute the knowledge they were acquiring. Part of this happened informally, as the older students would naturally develop mentoring relationships with younger students. It also happened formally through the program's year-round academic support program, which we called study table. In brief, study table was a mandatory tutorial session three times per week for two hours. In study table, students who displayed the skills to be successful were assigned younger players to mentor to ensure that they learned the habits and skills required to succeed at East Bay High. Students also shared their strategies for academic success in less formal ways with peers who were not in the program, and formally with younger children in the community through their development of the summer mini-camps.

Team sports are well positioned to develop young people's sense of collectivity and community when coaches emphasize the relationship between the individual and the team. In the LWBP, each student was responsible for her personal growth (social, academic, and athletic) and for contributing to the growth of the team in those same areas. They had, in effect, a double-duty in that they had to develop their own skills while also finding ways to use that growth to contribute to the growth of the team. A simple example illustrates this point. If one player worked hard to shoot the basketball better, the development of that skill would not necessarily benefit the team unless there was someone to screen the defender so that they could get open and someone to pass them the ball at the right time so that they could get their shot off. We often used such lessons about complementing each other for successful team play to challenge the individual achievement model promoted in school and the larger society. We also regularly talked with students about extending these principles of interdependency beyond the goal of athletic success and into other aspects of their lives (relationships, academic achievement, and community responsibility).

The impact of our emphasis on teamwork over individual achievement was reflected in the deep sense of community that students came to associate with the program. Lisa, like many of the students, described the program as an extension of her family:

> Lisa: This isn't really like a team to me. It's more like a family. You know if you ever need anything you can ask your teammates or your coach. They always have your back. If you are ever really in need or you're really down, someone is there. It's just like a real good support system, especially if you don't have any siblings or if you're not too close with your family. You have someone to lean on and support you, which most people don't have throughout high school. People say all the time to us that they wish they had friends like we have in this program. They ask me how we do it. I tell them we work hard at it.

Similarly, Saundra likened her teammates to sisters, saying that the program was the most significant part of her high school experience: "I had a team. This was the best thing that ever happened to me. If you go around the team, you have *so* many people you can talk to. They are like my sisters."

Like most tight-knit communities, we had our share of disagreements and conflicts. However, unlike many adolescent relationships that flame out in petty jealousy, conflicts were turned into opportunities for deeper friendships by the program's attention to the cultivation of community. It is counter-hegemonic to have that kind of closeness in an environment that rewards individual achievement and generally promotes a hostile culture (bars, over-crowding, intense police presence) that discourages positive emotional investment. Most high school students find a way to make friends anyway, and some of those friendships are lasting. What is rare is to have a school program that helps them cultivate those friendships and connects the power of those relationships to academic achievement and community consciousness.

What Should We Learn from This Program?

The success of the LWBP suggests that our approach warrants serious consideration for its implications in urban classrooms and schools. The space available here does not permit us to articulate fully the programmatic elements or the growth over time, but a book-length description of the LWBP is nearing completion (Duncan-Andrade, under contract). However, as this chapter has argued, core principles of critical pedagogy were used to guide the program, and these elements were fundamental to the program's success. What is important to re-emphasize here is that the success of the program was predicated on our ability to establish a counter-cultural community of practice with our students. That is, we established a programmatic culture and cultivated a set of community practices that were explicitly designed to counter the low expectations of the school and district. We accomplished this by first tapping into our students' love of basketball. This was our vehicle for developing a community based on the tenets of critical pedagogy. As we suggest in other chapters, classroom teachers can find and utilize various vehicles for engagement by working to understand the needs, concerns, and interests of students and then making those things starting points of the curriculum.

Once teachers have identified the vehicle(s) for engagement, it is critical that high expectations are established and that students are provided with consistent social and academic support to meet those expectations. This program highlights the importance of developing this support in such a way that it treats each student differently under the same set of rules. In other words, every student is held to standards of excellence that match his or her individual needs and abilities (ZPD), rather than every child being expected to reach the same level at the same time, as in a one-size-fits-all system.

Classroom teachers can also benefit from adopting our commitment to developing a sense of community and collective achievement over individualism. The nature of traditional schooling, with its emphasis on testing and grading, lends itself to a social system that emphasizes individual achievement. Teachers would do well to develop classroom cultures that emphasize collective learning and teamwork over strictly individual assignments and assessments. We recognize that it can be a struggle to develop a classroom culture where students act as a community because students typically come to the classroom with little school-based training on how to work collectively. Teachers must make an unwavering commitment to infuse their classroom culture with principles of collectivity. This means resisting the temptation to revert to the familiar comfort of individual assessment models when students are struggling with the concept of classroom as community.

Teachers should aim to develop classroom cultures that are counter-hegemonic in their outcomes and processes. This requires teachers to analyze critically and respond to school and classroom trends that promote deficit thinking and punishment. There is much to be learned here from our program's commitment to developing a critical double-consciousness in our students. As Delpit (1995) argues, it is crucial that urban teachers provide students with an explicit understanding of the rules and codes of power so that they can effectively navigate mainstream institutions. It is also vital that teachers prepare students to use those tools to engage in the process of transformative resistance (Solórzano & Delgado-Bernal, 2001). That is, teachers must help students envision ways that they can use their institutional success to transform conditions of inequity, rather than just for personal gain.

The success of such efforts will not come without self-reflection by students and teachers. Teachers should implement feedback structures that promote critical praxis by seeking consistent feedback from students, parents, and colleagues. They can learn from our program's regular meetings with students, where we reflected on their progress and their goals and received feedback from them on our work as educators. An essential element for the development of a culture of self-reflection is teachers' willingness to use students' feedback to improve their practice. This helps students feel that teachers are also participants in the community's practice of self-improvement, as opposed to traditional models, where students are the only ones being critiqued and asked to improve.

Notes

1. The names of participants are pseudonyms to protect their identities.
2. Psychologists distinguish between private self-consciousness and public self-consciousness. The former leads one to be acutely self-aware and introspective such that one is examining one's inner feelings and emotions. The latter bears more negative connotations as it refers to a preoccupation with how others view one. Du Bois refers to the development of private self-consciousness as a means to empowerment.
3. This was the first graduating class from the LWBP that was in the program for the full four years of high school. The following year, the program's 100 percent college enrollment continued, with another two seniors moving on to university.

5

Critical Pedagogy in a College Access Program for Students of Color

With assistance from Anthony Collatos

A team of district administrators and university-based researchers designed the South City High School Futures project to study and intervene in the pathways students of color follow through high school into higher education and the workplace. The project initially targeted a group of Latino and African American students just beginning 9th grade in a five-year study. These 9th-graders were chosen as relatively random representatives of a larger group of students (working-class African Americans and Latinos) who were not attaining college access in similar numbers to the wealthier white and Asian American students attending the same school. In fact, the African American and Latino 9th-graders at the school were just as likely to drop out of school as they were to graduate.

In addition to developing a body of scholarship pertaining to the pathways that high school students of diverse ethnic and socio-economic backgrounds commonly follow, the project team also designed a four-year intervention that they felt would take under-represented (and under-served) students through South City High and into four-year universities. Alongside this work with students, the South City High School Futures project team planned to support the efforts of educators at South City High School to develop more powerful and equitable models of learning that offered all students clear pathways to successful futures. The project thus sought to reshape students' lives, the work of one high school, and the understanding of the broader educational policy community.

As researchers and educators associated with the Futures project, we believed that apprenticing teens as critical sociologists of education would alert them to the structural inequality at their school while imparting the analytical and academic skills they needed to navigate South City High School more effectively as students, as members of marginalized ethnic and socio-economic groups, and as educational reformers working collaboratively with adults for equity and justice. The project had several core components.

The intervention with the students centered upon the South City Futures class, which was taught by the lead instructor (Collatos) through the Social Studies department and offered each of the four years of the program. The Futures class was originally designed to provide students with new ways of understanding how to achieve success in school, new skills in writing and social science research, and new roles to play in school and beyond. Its aim was to make students more conscious of—and capable of asserting control over—their own trajectories by engaging them in a study of the trajectories of other young people. Over the years of the project, however, the curricula evolved from a limited study of student trajectories into a series of large-scale interrelated studies dealing with educational inequality and the struggle for educational justice. This occurred largely as Futures students and teachers became increasingly frustrated with their own experiences and demanded that the research be used as a tool for social and educational change. As they matured as critical sociologists, the students also became advocates and activists for similarly situated students at their school and throughout the country. During their junior year, for instance, students studied factors preventing achievement for African American and Latina/o students at their school. During their senior year, students worked with the American Civil Liberties Union (ACLU) on a series of class action lawsuits against the State of California contesting inequitable educational conditions that low-income students and students of color were experiencing throughout the state. Attorneys visited the Futures class, and the students brainstormed ways they could gather and process information that might be helpful to those trying to understand how differently situated students experience schooling very differently, even sometimes while attending schools alongside very wealthy peers. In fact, the student research problematized the sole focus on between-school differences, as students rightly pointed out that students could receive very different educations within the same campus.

The Futures staff also sought to provide students with an authentic college experience that utilized the relative freedom of summer and the university space to develop research opportunities that were unavailable in the rigid structure of traditional schooling. In addition, the summer course provided the research team with the opportunity to demonstrate that the Futures students could produce college-level work within an appropriate teaching and learning context. Toward these multiple ends, the Critical Research and Writing seminar, held after the summers of their sophomore and junior years at a local research university, provided students with apprenticeships as researchers. The seminar was designed to give the students access to important research tools, to promote important academic skills, and to encourage them to take on significant new responsibilities. The seminar was also a space for the students to engage in critical research and social action relating to the sociology of education and youth access to civic life, the media, public space, and a livable wage in cities. During the summer seminars students generated research questions, designed and implemented research projects, analyzed data, wrote research papers, and presented these papers to audiences of academics, educators, community activists, and elected officials in their community[1].

As the students became more proficient at critical research, they were invited to give guest lectures to teacher educators, graduate students, practicing teachers, pre-service teachers, and educational researchers. The Futures students were also given several opportunities to interact with politicians and educational policymakers who were interested in their research. During the final two years of the project, the students traveled all over the western United States giving talks, presenting the findings of their research, and making recommendations for changes in classroom practices and educational policy. Students also presented their research to the annual meeting of the American Educational Research Association and the Sociology of Education Association.

Along with their changing participation came an increased commitment to and involvement in social action. Students participated in marches and rallies and joined and created organizations that were struggling for equity and access for urban youth. Many of the Futures students, along with the teachers and university faculty, wrestled with how to balance simultaneous commitments to critical research and social action.

In addition to the focus on research and academic skill development, a major portion of the project was devoted to college access. One thread of the Futures class curriculum encouraged students to study colleges and fill out the necessary forms for standardized tests, financial aid, scholarships, and applications. A parent component, Futures and Families, assisted parents in understanding the college admissions process and advocating for their children at South City High. The Futures project also took the students on several field trips to colleges around California, giving them the opportunity to sit in classes and talk with students, professors, and college counselors about the experience of attending a major university. During their senior year, several all-day college preparation workshops provided intensive support for writing essays, filling out applications, and searching for scholarships.

Collatos worked in the South City Futures project for all four years. He was the lead teacher at South City High School, a tenured member of the

Social Studies faculty, and a graduate student at a nearby university. Morrell co-taught the project classes for the final two years while employed as a researcher and instructor at the same university. Morrell also co-directed the research seminar for Futures students offered during the summers of 1999 and 2000. We feel it important to be explicit about our roles as active and interested project participants as well as researchers. These multiple roles do not conflict, as it often touted in traditional research. Rather, we are inspired by the growing numbers of critical qualitative researchers who see both roles as required for any researchers who are actively committed to social change and who seek to do work that is relevant to and inclusive of members of marginalized communities (Cammarota & Romero, 2006; Carspecken, 1996; Ginwright, Noguera, & Cammarota, 2006; Kincheloe & McLaren, 1998).

In the following section, we draw upon our experiences with the Futures class and the summer seminar to articulate a grounded theory of critical praxis in urban secondary education. In choosing to situate our work within grounded theory, we follow Strauss and Corbin (1999) in conducting research that does not begin with a particular theory in mind but rather seeks to build or generate theory through the analysis of data. In this method, data collection, analysis, and eventual theory stand in close proximity to one another, and the theory, emergent from the process,

> is more likely to resemble reality than is theory derived by putting together a series of concepts based on experience or solely through speculation (how one thinks things ought to work). Grounded theories, because they are drawn from data, are likely to offer insight, enhance understanding, and provide a meaningful guide to action. (p. 12)

We should also add that by pursuing grounded theory, we are following Freire himself, whose grounded theories of critical pedagogy emerged from his work with marginalized Brazilian peasants. With that in mind, we now turn to a discussion of critical pedagogy across the activity settings of the South City High School Futures project.

Critical Pedagogy in the South City High School Futures Project Class

As part of an agreement with South City High School, the Social Studies department granted Collatos permission to teach the Futures students in their Social Studies courses throughout their four years at the school. The only exception occurred during the students' junior year, when course conflicts prevented the collective scheduling of U.S. History. Instead, the students met during an A period (before school) for the school year in a special topics course dedicated to research. By their senior year, the students were once again combined for their Economics and American Government courses. Table 5.1 provides an overview of the course for the South City Futures students during the academic year as well as the summer sessions from their freshman through senior years.

Year	Project Class	Summer Research Seminar
9th (1997–1998)	Humanities	Introduction to Research Methods
10th (1998–1999)	World History/English	Introduction to the Sociology of Education
11th (1999–2000)	A-Period research seminar	Education and Youth Access: LA Youth and Convention 2000
12th (2000–2001)	U.S. Government/Economics	Graduation (no seminar)

Table 5.1. South City High Futures Project Classes
and Research Seminars

After Morrell joined the project in the spring of 1999, Collatos and Morrell worked very closely on the design and teaching of the project courses. Though Collatos remained the lead teacher, Morrell attended classes almost daily and the two assumed a team-teaching model with the students. The central research problem to be addressed by the A-period seminar concerned the alienation of African American and Latina/o students within South City High. The curriculum of the course consisted of examining demographic data and student narratives and discussing relevant social theory (Bourdieu, 1986; MacLeod, 1987) to help make sense of this alienation in non-deficit terminology while developing research projects aimed at contesting these realities. In early interviews, for instance, students attributed their failure and the failure of others like them to laziness or lack of ability rather than to structural or institutional constraints embracing what MacLeod (1987) terms the achievement ideology. Challenging these deficit narratives remained a primary goal of the adult researchers.

The South City Futures class attempted to enact critical pedagogy by invoking a liberating language with which to make sense of the realities associated with attending a high school that provided differential access and outcomes for students depending on their family income and their race. As critical educators, we worked to develop a collective language that was empowering in its critique of the current conditions for students of color and for its illumination of alternative pathways and alternative identities for these students associated with these new pathways that could allow them to engage the school without losing a sense of agency, progressivism, or cultural identity. This is significant because, for these students, evading or withdrawing from the high school was not a viable option; their only choice was to navigate South City High School even as they confronted the institution. It is also significant because this collective language simultaneously drew from critical social theory, from the examination of educational research, from the students' critical research projects, and from their collective analysis of their everyday conditions at South City High School.

The Futures class also attempted to enact critical pedagogy through the promotion of individual and socially transformational action. An example of this action is the major activity for the fall semester of the course in the junior year. Students worked on case studies that emerged from real experiences of African American and Latina/o students during their tenure at South City High School. Most of the cases required the students to design and implement a small research study to be conducted at South City High School. The students needed to collect and analyze data related to their respective research question and also to include in their research reports and presentations suggestions for action to confront or ameliorate the problem. For example, one study dealt with the unfair exclusion of many African American and Latina/o students, because of their over-representation in low-tracked classes, from a test of academic merit. A research team of two young women, both of whom had been excluded from the exam, collected data from teachers, other students, and the assistant principal. In their analysis, they found that the school's policies were not consistent with the intention of the exam; the school did not disseminate information to classes with higher concentrations of African American and Latina/o students even though the test was supposed to be open and available to anyone who was interested in taking it.

Enraged by the implications of the research, members of the South City Futures class encouraged their peers to take some form of action. Ultimately, these young women presented their report to the school principal, asking that the recommendation policy (for who was allowed to take the test) be changed. They were successful, as subsequent examinations were open to all students. Though a small victory, the change in testing policies exemplified to the students the possible connections between research and educational change and played a major role in changing the climate of the Futures class. From that point forward, the curriculum of the class was geared solely toward college access, educational research, and educational advocacy. As educators, we felt that students, as they conducted this research, learned about the barriers to college access for African American and Latina/o students at their school as they also learned the academic skills that might enhance their own college access and as they brainstormed methods of acting to expose and eliminate these barriers.

Throughout the Futures course, Collatos and Morrell played several roles that can be associated with a focus on critical pedagogy, including

- Providers of critical information: Collatos and Morrell introduced mediating artifacts such as school documents, academic achievement data, and academic texts that revealed the inequities in the school or facilitated the acquisition of conceptual language to explain various reasons for the school's inequities.
- Modelers of critical research: By conducting their own research with and beside the Futures students, Collatos and Morrell attempted to teach through action and encourage learning via legitimate peripheral participation in a research-focused community of practice (Lave & Wenger, 1991). In this way, critical pedagogy became the co-creation of counter-narratives through the manipulation of research tools and academic language in the cause of social justice and educational equity.
- Questioners, problem posers, and facilitators of critical dialogue: Collatos and Morrell also attempted to pose difficult questions, facilitate student discussions, and serve as resources during the data collection and analysis.

A significant challenge was dealing with student apathy, student fear, and student resistance in the context of the class. At times, prodding students meant telling students to get to work or directly confronting self-defeating resistance (Solórzano & Delgado-Bernal, 2001). These occasions often left sour tastes in our mouths; it seemed antithetical to our emancipatory missions to force or coerce students to engage in critical work. We struggled with an approach to students who verbalized that they did not want to participate in class assignments, even when these assignments emanated from students' interests and addressed students' concerns. To let them progress through the course without developing academic and critical literacies would have been unconscionable, but to use the threat of failing students to increase student productivity seemed equally unacceptable. We ultimately decided that we would have to develop strategies to positively motivate students while also providing the mentoring and supports that they needed to function at a high intellectual level. However, we were not above "getting on" students who were capable of more than they were producing. After all, our role as educators required us to demand excellence from students even when they were not demanding excellence from themselves.

A far more complex challenge emerged in conversations with students about how to deal with their offensive, alienating, or derogatory teachers. We could have promoted a sense of agency that would have had deleterious effects on the students' success at the school. Indeed, some of the more "critical" students were the victims of backlash pedagogy from certain teachers who saw them as insubordinate troublemakers (Morrell, 2004a). On the other hand, acquiescence was also a problem in that it encouraged students to accept dehumanizing conditions to gain a credential that could translate into increased economic capital.

As a viable compromise, we promoted what we called critical navigational skills or critical college access (Collatos, 2004). We advocated that the students learn to deconstruct the game and manipulate the "master's tools" as a form of critical pedagogy. It is important to heed Freire's concern that the oppressed, when acquiring power uncritically, can embrace the persona of the oppressors. However, we were also aware that it would be self-defeating, and even tragic, for critical educators to preclude postsecondary opportunities for the students to serve their own political purposes. Instead, we discussed the idea of gaining college access for community change and not for economic advancement. In other words, college stood as a gatekeeper to necessary credentials for professions as teaching, law, medicine, and business. It was also a place to gain much needed information about the world. Students could develop a narrative for college going that opposed and even resisted the idea of an American Dream, but there was no question that they needed to be prepared academically and socially to access college if, indeed, they decided to go.

In our work on the South City High School Futures project, we did not find easy answers; instead we became increasingly aware that the multiple aims of critical education could exist in dialectic tension with one another to produce positive results. Critical pedagogy cannot, out of convenience, evade the complexities associated with the structures and cultural practices of schools (Apple, 1990). Indeed, public schools are the ideal sites for critical praxis, given their central role in the socialization of citizens and their function as economic and social gatekeepers. Furthermore, critical educators cannot write off the demands of the K–12 educational system as bourgeois and self-serving. They must struggle, with students and their parents, to forge pathways that lead to an academic success that does not relinquish cultural identity or progressive ideals even as they work with equal diligence to dismantle a system that requires them to do so.

The Critical Research and Writing Seminar

The Critical Research and Writing seminar existed as a college-level course, offered during the summer session at West Coast University. Its stated goal was to teach students the craft of critical research to promote academic literacy, college readiness, and the tools to advocate for social change. The Futures students formed the entire cohort of the first seminar, offered during the summer of 1999. During the summer of 2000, they were joined by a larger group of teens attending other urban high schools throughout the area. These other students were not selected for academic performance or readiness for college-level writing. Instead, students were chosen based on their interest in issues related to the transformation of urban schools and communities.

The thirty or so student-participants attended all-day sessions for five weeks to earn a semester credit for a university course. As a part of the seminar, students were exposed to critical theory, cultural studies, educational sociology, legal history, social theory, and critical qualitative research methodology as they designed and conducted research related to issues of equity and access in urban schools and communities. In this way, the seminar sought to address these issues of access in terms of both course content and desired outcomes for its students. Over the two summers in which project students were involved, the seminar addressed the themes of language, youth culture, and transformational resistance in urban schools (1999), and youth access and the Democratic National Convention (2000). Futures participants and their peers from other schools presented their research from the seminar to university faculty, local and state politicians, teachers, community members, and parents. In addition, summer seminar research has been presented at regional and national conferences and has been featured by local and national media, including CNN.

Within the summer seminar space, we sought to create relationships between students and teachers and between students and the tools of critical research that simply were not possible in traditional classrooms, or even in the project class initially. We cut down the student-to-teacher ratio so that students were working in small groups with an experienced adult educator, an arrangement that encourages more dialogue and personalized interaction than didactic instruction. We also felt that the very creation of spaces for youth to participate fully in the critical research enterprise promoted the praxis that Freire and other theorists advocate. That is, youth-initiated research that begins with authentic inquiry into issues within the community and neighborhood schools and that brings together students, teachers, university researchers, and community workers to develop questions, collect data, and produce texts enables the students to oppose oppressive structures while also developing academic competencies and the ability to manipulate language and tools of power—namely, academic discourse and the academic research process.

Our conception of critical research was much influenced by Kincheloe and McLaren (1998), who identify new "standards" for critical scholarship (pp. 286–287). These authors promote humility as opposed to arrogance or assuredness, trustworthiness in lieu of validity, collective participation instead of individual authorship, and lived experience rather than predetermined methodological or theoretical approaches. We felt that creating an activity setting centered upon critical research and situating teachers within these settings with students would promote enabling pedagogical practices that drew upon and utilized the expertise of teachers while also allowing students to participate as they acted upon the world.

Over the course of their involvement with the seminar, Futures students explored many topics relevant to urban schools and communities, such as the impact of hip-hop culture on urban youth, student resistance, language practices in homes and schools, youth access to the media, discrepancies in school and community learning resources, and the declining minimum wage, to name a few. Furthermore, the students became advocates for the causes addressed in their research through presenting this work to university faculty, to local politicians and policymakers, to high school teachers, and to other high school students and taking leadership roles in activist and community organizations and school government.

As a way of illustrating the dialogic spaces and praxis of the seminar, we include a journal entry by one of the seminar participants that describes her experiences conducting critical research at the Democratic National Convention. Elena's reflections were recorded in a journal entry written just after the students and teachers finished sharing their thought about the research process and their growth as scholars and activists during the week of the convention:

> Elena: Today was a day of reflections. This week has been filled with many learning experiences and, at times, that can be overwhelming. There is always a need to take time to reflect and analyze, to learn and to grow. I found myself learning so much just from sitting in the circle today. Everyone had something of value to say. Hearing everyone's experiences and opinions has enriched my own experience here. I was not at every site all the time, but hearing the account of others has helped me live vicariously every part of the DNC.
>
> {I have gone through mixed feelings here this week. It began (I hate to admit), with cynicism. The Democracy Live! 2000 seemed like a complete farce, a joke[2]. But maybe that is the way TV is done. Then I experienced frustration at not being able to get into other parts of the Convention Center. I wanted to witness democracy inside those large halls.
>
> But I was not disappointed completely because I found democracy elsewhere. The speakers that visited us this week were all were fighting for equality in one way or another. They each had their way of approaching the issues that most concerned them. I discovered that there are people in this world who are really passionate and devoted to making this place better for everyone.
>
> Now I leave cynicism behind but not the anger of the first day. I will take that anger with me everywhere I go from now on, wherever that place may be. It is anger that leads to action, and action to changes. This place needs changes, and someone has to help achieve them. On this road, which is my life, I continue to walk ahead, going through doors and hoping to someday make positive changes. Someone I really admire said (something like this) "You go through doors in your life, and

through some doors you just can't go back." I think this seminar as a whole has been one giant door, and I know, I can never go back.

Elena's comments point toward the internal and external conversations promoted during the seminars. Included is a language of reflexivity, a language of awareness of one's self as agentive, that allows students a space to engage in action but also, through dialogue and journaling, to reflect upon that action. Elena struggles to make sense of her strong feelings of alienation from a society she must confront in her struggle for social change. She reflects upon the tremendous highs and lows associated with critical work. There are inspirational messages about the opportunity of working closely with like-minded students and teachers, but there are also the negative emotions that accompany confronting the ugly realities of an exclusionary society. Her resolution is similar to ours as educators, as she manifests a sadness coupled with resolve and a commitment to contributing to re-making the world.

Toward a Grounded Theory of Critical Pedagogy in College Access Programs

In moving toward our discussion of a grounded theory of critical pedagogy in urban secondary contexts, we would like to share why we believe critical pedagogy occurred in the South City High School Futures project. Of the thirty students involved in the Futures project, twenty-nine graduated high school and twenty-five gained acceptance to four-year universities. By the autumn semester after their high school graduation, seventeen had enrolled in four-year universities, six had enrolled in two-year colleges, two had enrolled in technical schools, four had entered the workplace, and one had joined the military. The Futures students had higher levels of matriculation, college acceptances, and college-going rates than comparable students attending South City High School during this same period (Collatos, 2004).

In addition to learning to navigate the structures of South City High School, the Futures students worked diligently to promote equity and access at their high school. Futures students participated in school government, they contested unfair testing practices, they met with individual content area departments to discuss curricular reforms related to their research projects and experiences in classes, and they spoke to incoming African American and Latina/o freshmen about their experiences at the school. The Futures students also fought against the school's efforts to add more ability groups and met with university researchers to craft a response to initiatives being discussed by the school board and the parent-teacher association, who were attempting to advocate for additional tracking structures to further segregate students at the school academically according to race and class.

The Futures students also participated in a variety of projects aimed at community transformation. Several participated in protests against derogatory portrayals of Mexican Americans in videogames, resulting in the recall of a fairly famous game at significant cost to the corporation that created and marketed it. Students marched to support the reinstatement of Affirmative Action in the University of California system, and they lobbied with the American Civil Liberties Union for students' rights to a fair and equitable education. These students also formed support organizations for young women and men of color at the campus and worked with community-based organizations dedicated to work for social justice.

Most important, the Futures students gained a set of academic tools, a critical language, and a sense of themselves as agents of change that allowed them to contest dehumanizing conditions and unjust practices. In addition to the individual academic achievement and the body of work produced through their critical research, students expressed their belief in themselves and their ability to change the world.

We do not shrug off the complex challenges associated with our attempts to enact a critical pedagogy as outlined throughout this chapter. Yet we feel compelled to articulate our grounded theory of critical pedagogy that has emerged from our collective experience with the South City High School Futures project. We highlight two components that we feel are useful to discussions of critical pedagogy in urban secondary contexts: critical pedagogy as facilitating critical navigational strategies and as demanding excellence from adolescents that they may not be able to demand from themselves.

Critical Pedagogy as Facilitating Critical Navigational Strategies

A critical pedagogy in urban secondary contexts has to account for the present reality in schools by attempting to promote critical navigational strategies for students and not just the language of deconstruction traditionally associated with American interpretations of critical pedagogy. It is imperative for critical educators in K–12 contexts to understand that having the ability or the language to deconstruct is not the same as having the ability to navigate dominant structures. While most critical educators would find odious a process that encouraged passive consumption of an oppressive curriculum, we can also agree that failing to acquire academic competencies and credentials is not a desirable outcome of education. In fact, it is only through these competencies and credentials that students will be fully equipped to contest structures of power. Teachers and students should not be made to feel guilty or to consider themselves "sellouts" for working within the system, especially as this concerns imparting the skills students need to navigate the very system that their educators, by definition, have already successfully navigated. Critical pedagogy can play a role in developing language and activity associated with this process that we have articulated as critical college access. These navigational skills will serve the students well throughout their lives because, whether we are talking about the world of work or the world of politics and advocacy, these students will not be able to divest from all institutions and practices that they find problematic.

Critical Pedagogy as Demanding Excellence from Teens

Even with our obvious need to promote student voice and student empowerment, critical educators of urban adolescents cannot abdicate our responsibility to nurture, to guide, to support, to cajole, to correct, and to demand from students what they may have been socialized not to demand from themselves. This may mean making students perform tasks and participate in activities that they see either as impossible or undesirable. At first glance, this may seem antithetical to the mission of critical pedagogy, which exists in direct opposition to teacher-dominated classrooms. However, even in a problem-posing education centered within student experiences and geared toward student action, teachers cannot lose sight of the fact that they are working with young adults who still need those with more experience in the academy and in life to help them learn how to participate in the world as responsible and critical citizens. These young people also need educators who possess enough cultural capital to help them acquire the language and tools of power, but, more than that, they require educators who love them enough to push them to their limits, to inspire in students the revolutionary and liberatory outcomes they could not previously have imagined given their prior experience in schools.

A goal of critical pedagogy is to help students have more power after the pedagogical encounter than they did before. Part of their power comes from their ability to engage texts and concepts academically that they could not previously have engaged. Part of their power also comes from having the confidence to participate in the world differently than they may have imagined. While dialogue is certainly an important part of this process, we argue that it is not possible to change skill sets and confidence outside of a context that is highly demanding and that puts students in a position to engage sophisticated academic content successfully. Educators must keep in mind that many students will never have seen or participated in a highly functioning and academically demanding learning environment and that it is wrong to rely on them to create on their own what they have never seen. Certainly student collaboration is essential, but adult educators will need to play a major role in changing the culture of mediocrity that unfortunately pervades many classrooms.

Just as it is not oxymoronic to mention critical pedagogy and academic excellence in the same sentence, it is not a contradiction in ideals to think of critical pedagogy and discipline simultaneously. In fact, Freire and Macedo (1987) remind us that to study demands discipline. To engage in reading as a revolutionary act is not a simple task, and it would be foolish to believe that young women and men can develop the necessary skill sets or confidence in themselves without strong leadership and support from the adult teachers in their lives. This is especially true in secondary education, where the average 9th-grader enters high school already having experienced more than 1,500 days of public schooling. During this tenure students develop (often negative) perceptions of their school, of schooling in general, and of themselves as (under-)literate beings. It takes a strong leadership to transform these attitudes and the practices that accompany them.

Even though the roles of teachers change dramatically in the context of critical pedagogy, the leadership demands placed on critical educators are not diminished in the slightest. Students still need adults with strong content knowledge, adults who understand learning theory and adolescent development, adults who understand the demands of secondary and postsecondary education, and adults who themselves possess academic and critical literacies. Most important, though, these students need adults who are strong motivators and who believe in them and their potential to become transformative intellectuals, adults who understand that they have faced difficulties in their lives but who will not give up on the students or allow them to give up on themselves. This means that situations arise when adult critical educators need to "get on" students, need to get them focused. We sometimes need to explain to them that the work they are used to handing in is not satisfactory. Sometimes we need to exhort them to hand in any work at all. After all, how "critical" is a critical classroom when students can talk the talk but no one is

handing in any homework, the grades haven't changed, and there are no de-
monstrable gains in academic achievement or skill development? It is from
physics that we learn that an object at rest remains at rest until some equal or
greater force acts upon it. When we consider the forces that we work against
as critical educators, it becomes obvious that we must be forceful and passionate ourselves. It doesn't necessarily mean that we become authoritarian,
but it definitely does not excuse us from playing powerful and explicit roles in
the lives of young adults, many of whom have been cheated out of an education long enough. A critical pedagogy can bring love, discipline, self-respect,
and academic rigor all at the same time. No one said it would be easy, but
the revolution of adolescent pedagogy will require no less.

By now, we hope that it is obvious that we believe that critical pedagogy
certainly can and should exist within urban secondary schools. We do not
believe that critical educators need to think of making choices between academic excellence and critical consciousness; indeed, we promote a critical
praxis that subsumes academic competencies, navigational strategies, critical
sensibilities, and collaborative action toward social change. Such critical
praxis, we argue, can lead to academic achievement, economic empowerment, and self and social transformation among populations currently being
alienated within America's public schools.

Notes

1. The summer seminar is addressed in further detail in Chapter 6. It is important to distinguish the initial seminar (1999), which featured only students from South City High
School, from the 2000 seminar, which comprised the incoming seniors of the South City
Futures project along with students from inner-city schools of Greater Los Angeles. After the graduation of the students in the South City Futures project, the seminar expanded to include students from throughout Greater Los Angeles.
2. Democracy Live! 2000 was a special cable television show developed to show how young
people were participating in the political process during the Democratic National Convention. Our seminar students were invited to participate as audience members during
one taping of this show.

6
Youth Participatory Action Research as Critical Pedagogy

For some time there has been excitement about the possibilities for critical pedagogy to inform practice in urban education. However, very little empirical work has been done that theorizes the possible translation of principles of critical pedagogy into practices, and even less work has been done that evaluates the outcomes of these practices in pushing forward the development of grounded theories of practice. The central premise of this book is that we need to examine critical pedagogy with urban youth. Erroneously, people have looked to theory to build theory instead of understanding that critical pedagogy began with practice to build theory. As a field, our attempts to develop theory from theory have left us essentially with a house built on sand. We need to develop sound theories of practice that can be implemented and evaluated through the use of critical lenses. That, essentially, has been our project over the past dozen years; as authors and educators we have endeavored to generate theories of praxis and to develop practices from these theories that inform greater theory and practice. We have labeled this project the development of grounded theories of praxis in critical pedagogy in urban contexts.

We have so far examined three instantiations of this grounded theory: critically teaching popular culture in English classrooms, using sport as a metaphor for personal and social development, and merging critical social theory and college access to create structures for academic achievement and collective action for educational justice. An additional manifestation of this theory concerns the positioning of urban youth as critical researchers and transformative intellectuals. In the next chapter we explore the connections between critical pedagogy and a pan-ethnic studies curriculum. We look at a program where young people were apprenticed as youth participatory action researchers. We begin with an examination of the foundations of youth participatory action research and principles common to youth participatory action research and critical pedagogy. The second portion of the chapter examines our summer seminar, a six-year intervention where youth attending urban schools become critical action researchers, and the outcomes of the seminar as they relate to academic skill development and action for social and educational justice. The final portion of the chapter draws upon these experiences with the summer seminar as we further our articulation of a grounded theory of critical pedagogy in urban contexts.

Critical pedagogy is often associated with the development of an intellectual identity, but the parameters of this identity are rarely discussed. Certainly, much-cited critical theorists such as Antonio Gramsci, Carter G. Woodson, and Paulo Freire have championed pedagogies that develop intellectuals among marginalized and oppressed classes of people, who have been largely positioned as passive knowledge consumers instead of empowered knowledge producers. For each population, however, the question of intellectual identity has to be re-addressed. What, for instance, does it mean for a young woman or man attending an urban secondary school to become an intellectual? Outside of academic performance indicators, how is this intellectualism measured? How is it manifested? We asked ourselves each of these questions as we designed our summer program for youth attending urban schools.

We surmised that one way to think about positioning urban youth as intellectuals was to place them front and center in the research process. When we think about the commentary of critical pedagogy (and critical theory writ large) on the process of inquiry, an implicit critique emerges concerning the "who" and the "why" of the research process. When we honor the principles of critical pedagogy while thinking about youth development and urban school reform, we are challenged to create ways to work with youth as collaborators in the research process. Instead of just doing research "on" young people, which makes them the objects of our research gaze, critical research holds the potential to reposition these young people as the subjects of their own research, research that matters to them and larger empirical questions that require their important, but often missing, perspective.

When we consider the problems we face in urban education, this process serves a two-fold need. First, we need more engaging pedagogies that draw upon youth experiences and perspectives to develop literacies of power. Second, we also need to include the voices and lenses of youth to help us further understand and intervene in the structural and cultural causes of urban educational failure. As educators and as advocates for educational justice, we must understand that youth are much-needed collaborators with valuable experiences and energy to add to our movements. We firmly believe that youth participatory action research can ultimately develop the academic capabilities of students and, equally important, that youth-initiated research can help adult researchers and advocates better to confront the seemingly intractable problems of urban education.

We began this program of apprenticing youth attending urban schools as participatory action researchers with three important research questions:

What are the overlaps between the principles of participatory action research and critical pedagogy? How might youth participatory action research push forward conversations about applications of critical pedagogy with urban youth?

What is youth participatory action research? How is it practiced? How is it taught? How can it function as a critical pedagogy when employed with adolescents attending urban schools?

What are the multiple outcomes associated with youth participatory action research as a critical pedagogical strategy with urban youth? Particularly, what are the outcomes associated with academic and critical literacy development? What are the outcomes associated with the development of empowered academic/intellectual identities? What are the outcomes associated with advocacy and action for social and educational justice?

It is clear that each of these questions ties back to our three major goals for critical pedagogy: academic achievement, empowered identity development, and action for social change. These three questions also tie back into our meta-question in that we are interested in the translation from critical pedagogical theory to urban educational practice. The examination of the intersections between youth participatory action research and critical pedagogy provides yet another example of what critical pedagogy might "look like" in urban educational practice. With that in mind we offer a brief background on the burgeoning movement known as participatory action research, especially as it pertains to the role of youth in the process of inquiry for social change.

What Is Participatory Action Research?

According to McIntyre (2000) three principles guide most participatory action research projects. The first is the collective investigation of a problem. This is significant because the focus of traditional research is often on individual scholarship. Although teams of university scholars may conduct research, it becomes important to distinguish an Albert Einstein or a James

Coleman from the pack. Indeed, when we academicians submit our works to be published, editors want a clear chain of authorship. Who is the *first* author on this piece, they want to know. Participatory action research, on the other hand, is from the outset a collective enterprise that involves participants who are generally excluded from the research process. Given its genesis or its desired outcomes, it is difficult to imagine how an isolated and distanced individual could conduct critical participatory action research. This leads into McIntyre's second principle: participatory action research relies on indigenous knowledge to understand and examine the problems that are of greatest concern to indigenous researchers.

In traditional research, indigenous populations, to the extent that they are involved at all, are generally positioned as the *objects* of research. They may be interviewed, videotaped, followed around, observed, examined, or tested. Their role is to provide information to experts who can then figure out how best to help them (or even understand them). Participatory action research involves these populations as *subjects* and partners in the research process. Within the framework of youth participatory action research, it is perfectly logical (even mandatory) that parents, teachers, students, and community members be positioned as researchers and valuable contributors toward the collective intellectual enterprise. While the focus of this chapter is on students as researchers, it is important to consider that the larger goal of participatory action research is to include multiple populations that are often excluded from the formal research process. In that vein, this work itself exists as an example of participatory action research. Both authors began this work as classroom teachers who felt they had something to share about the pedagogical practices in their classrooms. At that time neither of us had any formal credentials or any official "business" conducting research in our classrooms and sharing that work with professionals. However, we were ideally positioned to do the work because we were in the classroom every day. Participatory action research is valuable because it brings in populations that are often alienated within the traditional research paradigm, but it is also important because these populations often have the best vantage point and the greatest vested interest in the work itself.

McIntyre's third principle is that participatory action research involves the desire to take individual or collective action to deal with the stated problem. Indeed, some may say that "action" is the operative word that really distinguishes participatory action research from other paradigms of inquiry.

While most traditional researchers would claim that all research is conducted to make the world a better place, the process of traditional research is often separated from action in the world at large. Generally, the research process ends when the last pieces of data are analyzed and published in scholarly journals or books. If an award-winning sociologist, for example, articulates the causes of urban poverty, no one expects that sociologist to actually wipe out urban poverty. That is someone else's job. With participatory action research, on the other hand, the collective action is a part of the process. This is not just research intended to understand problems; it is a research process designed to intervene in problems, to make them go away. Given the positionality of the researchers, again, this makes sense. Researchers who are daily experiencing injustice are highly motivated to end that injustice, and, to the extent that participatory action research can help in this regard, they become motivated researchers as well.

Participants in the action research process become researchers about their daily lives in hopes of developing realistic solutions for dealing with the problems that they believe need to be addressed. In the project discussed in this chapter, for example, students worked to develop realistic solutions to the structural and cultural barriers to academic achievement in the urban schools they attended. By assuming active and full participation in the research process, people have the opportunity to collect and analyze meaningful data themselves; even more, they possess the ability to utilize the information they collect and analyze to mobilize, organize, and implement individual or collective action.

Clearly there are critics of participatory action research in the educational field. Purists claim that action research is biased, that the "lay" researchers are untrained, and that the methods of participatory research are unsound. As conservative forces seek to eliminate all qualitative educational research (National Research Council, 2005), participatory action research is lumped together with a whole array of "soft" and unsound methodological approaches that only hinder educational progress in our country. For these reasons participatory action research is not prevalent in our leading journals, it is rarely taught in our leading postsecondary institutions, and it is rarely cited in conversations about educational policy that are supposedly informed by the latest research.

Despite these obstacles, some of us are foolish enough to believe that we can and should engage in research that changes the world and that we should involve citizens in this process (Denzin, 1997). We draw upon Latin American movements in critical social science research (Morrow & Torres, 1995) as we design studies and interventions that allow us to confront directly many of the challenges we now face in new-century urban schools. As authors and as committed action researchers, we also saw a direct connection between this burgeoning movement and our practice of critical pedagogy. Thus, we worked to develop a practice of participatory action research with urban youth as part of our critical pedagogical project.

This chapter now transitions to the examination of critical pedagogy in a summer research seminar where urban teens, teachers, and parents were apprenticed as critical participatory action researchers of urban and educational inequality. Much of the philosophy of pedagogy and initial practice builds on the principles and practices of the South City High School Futures project. Indeed, there was a great deal of initial overlap between the Futures project and the then fledgling summer seminar. The first cohort of the summer seminar (which convened in 1999) was composed entirely of students from the Futures project, and in the second seminar nearly half of the students were also members of the South City High Futures project. Moreover, the leaders of the seminar (including Morrell, who co-directed the project for its entire six years, and Duncan-Andrade, who worked with the seminar for three years) were also participants in the Futures project. Even though there was significant overlap in leadership, initial student-participants, and initial conceptual framing, the seminar has always existed as a separate and independent entity.

One reason the pedagogy was different is because it came largely after the completion of the South City High School Futures project, allowing us to translate our learning from that program into the continual development and redevelopment of the seminar space. Part of this development included wresting ourselves away from the time and logistical constraints of the K–12 classroom, which is not conducive at all to the research process. Even more, however, we needed to wrest ourselves away from the ideological constraints placed on us as lifelong educators who had also been students in the K–12 school system. In past projects we had pushed the boundaries of curriculum and sought to empower students through the texts that they read and the way they talked about those texts. The critical research process, however, challenged everything we thought we knew about the relationships between teachers and students and between students and their social worlds. As we began to learn about the possibilities of participatory action research, we also began to rethink the ways that teachers and students could work together in a pedagogic space. We wanted to brainstorm ways that this could work in the classroom, but to do that we felt we needed to create a separate space to carry out the critical research projects. With that purpose, we created what became known simply as the "summer seminar."

The summer seminar exists literally and ideologically outside of the space of schools, which allows for a different (and more empowering) set of relations between teachers and students, between students and texts, and between students and their world, since the seminar largely centers around critical research in local community contexts. We instituted features in our design that were more in line with our developing sense of learning theory and with our theories of pedagogy. We had students working together in small research teams with the assistance of group leaders, who were usually teachers from the local schools. We developed a progression in the curriculum that moved from exposure to concepts, to the design of a research study, to the actual research process itself. We mixed the learning spaces of the seminar to include large-group lectures, small-group planning sessions, field work, and other forms of data collection, and we brought in leaders from local community-based organizations and parents to work with the students.

The work of the seminar is problem posing in every respect. The central activity entails students posing problems from their real world and using critical research skills to investigate and then intervene in those problems. In this vein, the seminar project serves as an exemplar of Freirean praxis—that is, the students are learning to combine the intellectual nature of the research process with real action upon and against the dominant world that threatens to constrain their existence. This model for instruction also draws heavily upon Freire's (1998) conceptions of popular cultural notebooks, in which he and other educators made direct references to the lived experiences of the people they were teaching as they were trying to develop both their traditional literacies and their critical sensibilities. It is important that we expand our notion of popular culture as a set of lived experiences and local cultural practices that can be used to acquire dominant literacies and thus to contest hegemony (Morrell, 2004b). Popular culture does not just inhere in films, music CDs, and television shows; popular culture really occurs in the people's everyday experiences as they navigate the postindustrial world. Often these experiences are co-opted by culture industries into products such as films and television shows, but the actual popular cultural production occurs before this co-optation, or, at the very least, the spaces of production are more contested than it seems when we simply look toward the products sponsored by the culture industries (Storey, 1998). This is important when considering the applications of a pedagogy of popular culture to critical work with urban youth. It is within this larger framework of popular cultural production that we situate our participatory action research with urban youth.

We now explain in more detail the conception, substance, and history of the summer research seminar. We then analyze the philosophy and praxis of pedagogy across a variety of activity settings, including large-group discussions, reading pedagogy, research skills development, the pedagogy of the field, data analysis and write-up, and the pedagogy of presentation and distribution. The heart of the chapter situates the work of the summer seminar within a larger context of participatory action research. From this vantage point we examine the work of the students and their personal transformations as they become critical researchers. We conclude the chapter with consideration of how youth participatory action research informs a grounded theory of urban critical pedagogy along with consideration of what needs to happen in our field to increase the proliferation of youth participatory action research as a sanctioned educational practice.

Six Summers of Critical Research

In 1999, several colleagues at UCLA's Institute for Democracy, Education, and Access (IDEA), including Morrell, developed a summer seminar at the University of California, Los Angeles. The seminar brought together students, teachers, and parents from urban schools and communities to design and carry out critical participatory action research projects pertaining to issues of immediate concern to these schools and communities. As part of the format of each seminar, the students worked together in groups of four or five in research teams led by teachers from local schools. They read important works in social theory, critical pedagogy, the history of urban education, the sociology of education, and methods of critical educational research; they developed research questions, read relevant scholarly literature, collected qualitative and quantitative data, analyzed data, and created research reports; and they presented these reports to multiple audiences consisting of university faculty, policymakers, and, on occasion to regional and national conferences of educational researchers and practitioners. Students also wrote individual papers in which they contemplated the practical applications of their research to the issues in their own schools and communities.

The seminar had multiple goals, but two emerge as primary. We wanted to use the seminar space to help students acquire the language and tools they need to function within the academy, what we have called "academic literacy" (Morrell, 2004a). Traditionally, the student populations that we worked with had not been well represented within colleges and universities throughout the state. In fact, we deliberately selected students who attended some of the lowest-performing high schools in the state. We wanted to demonstrate to the schools and universities that dismissed these students that the students were indeed capable of college-level work. At the same time, we wanted to use the context of critical, community-based research to help the students gain the literacy tools they would need to be successful at these universities. As advocates for social and educational justice, we believed firmly that all of our interventions needed to develop students' academic competencies. As we have argued repeatedly throughout this text, there is no educational justice without the development of strong academic skills among populations that have been historically underserved by our educational system.

A second goal of the seminar relates to the research itself. We held the sincere belief that teachers, students, and parents were the most legitimate collaborators in the kind of community-based praxis-oriented research that we ourselves were interested in. In other words, the research studies were not merely a context for literacy learning; the products themselves were important to the struggle for educational justice within the teacher education program, with the local districts and the greater metropolitan area, and even statewide. The student-participants and their work would influence policy and practice across all of these settings.

During the six consecutive summers between 1999 and 2004, the research seminar convened at UCLA. The thirty or so student-participants (all incoming high school seniors and all drawn from local Los Angeles–area high schools) attended all-day sessions for five weeks and, as a result of their participation and successful completion of the course requirements, earned four quarter credits of university coursework. As a part of the seminar curricula, students were exposed to critical theory, cultural studies, educational sociology, legal history, social theory, and critical qualitative research methodology as they designed and conducted research projects that investigated issues of equity and access in urban schools and communities. In this way, the seminar sought to address these issues of access in terms of both course content and desired outcomes for its students. That is, the seminar research worked to expose and intervene in structures that prevented equity and access as the seminar itself worked to develop skills and provide credit that would lead to increased access for the students who participated. Over the six years of the seminar, for instance, the overwhelming majority of our students did seek postsecondary educational opportunities, and several returned to the seminar as university undergraduates to mentor subsequent cohorts. We now offer a summary of the content of the six summer sessions.

Our inaugural seminar, held in the summer of 1999, focused on the themes of "Language, Youth Culture, and Transformational Resistance in Urban Schools." The twenty students who participated were divided into four research groups that investigated the positive and negative impacts of hip-hop music and culture on urban teens and the potential of hip-hop music and culture to transform high school literacy curricula; the different (transformational and self-defeating) manifestations of student resistance in urban schools; the correlation between teachers' attitudes toward students' home languages and student academic achievement; and the differences between home and school attitudes toward what constitutes a well-educated citizen in the African American and Latino communities.

Given that Los Angeles hosted the Democratic National Convention (DNC) in 2000, and given that a major goal of the seminars is to develop critical civic engagement, our 2000 summer seminar focused on "Youth Access and the Democratic National Convention." As seminar directors we were able to obtain limited access to the convention activities, providing the opportunity for the students to participate in the event as researchers and as interested community citizens. In their dual roles, the students attended formal meetings associated with the DNC, spoke with delegates and media personnel, listened to progressive elements of the party who were critical of the convention, interviewed local community residents, visited the headquarters of convention protesters, met with elected officials, and participated in organized protests. In response to the seminar theme, we probed the DNC to explore provocative political, social, and educational issues around which students formulated research questions, collected and analyzed data, and presented their findings to a panel of university faculty and community activists. In the context of the DNC, we were concerned with urban youth access to the political process, but we were also concerned with the relationship between educational equity and political access. Given these interests and concerns, the research teams investigated youth access across five domains: the media, a livable wage, community learning resources, learning resources in schools, and civic engagement.

In the run-up to our third seminar in the summer of 2001, a series of legal actions filed against the State of California for educational inequities encouraged discussions between legal advocates, community-based organizations, and university researchers. Within these discussions, the various constituents became concerned with a fundamental question: What does every student in the State of California deserve in his/her educational experience? This questioning led to the development of a draft document entitled the *Educational Bill of Rights*, which became the chosen theme for the summer of 2001. In addition to the concerns reflected in the legal actions and conversations with local constituencies, recent polls had shown that education remained the number one priority for most Californians. Regardless of political affiliation and belief, most citizens recognized the importance of a quality education to social, economic, and political empowerment. That being said, most citizens, particularly those affiliated with the urban poor, realized that not all children in California have fair and equal access to a quality education. As educators and researchers, we clearly understood that educational access is often determined by one's race, class, and geography, and, as a result, great disparities can exist within a "public" school system that unfairly disadvantages the poor, those located in urban or rural environments, and those attending schools where the majority of students hail from racially marginalized groups. Our reading of the allocation of educational resources and the educational achievement data confirmed this hypothesis. To examine and challenge these inequities, the seminar convened to articulate an *Educational Bill of Rights* that outlines the basic entitlements of all students in California. The students selected for this seminar, along with university faculty and community leaders, developed research projects that examined these rights in the context of urban schools across Los Angeles. The seminar sought to answer the following questions:

What does every student in California deserve?

What inequalities arise in the experiences of California's students?

Why do these inequalities arise? (What is our explanation for the inequality?)

What can youth do? How can they use research to play a part in legal advocacy?

The 2002 summer seminar focused on "Equity and Access in California's Public Schools." The central question was how students (and parents) could contribute information about school conditions to the state-mandated School Accountability Report Cards (SARCs)?[1] This question embodies three sub-questions: What are the conditions of learning in urban schools across Los Angeles? How can students access and contribute information about these conditions? How can students, working in conjunction with parents and community advocates, pressure their schools and districts to include student-generated data in the official SARCs?

The seminar divided students into four student research teams, each focused on one core condition of schooling—quality teachers, a rigorous curriculum, adequate learning materials, and a positive physical and social environment. Under the guidance of teachers, the research teams conducted field research in several Los Angeles–area schools. The students explored various research and pedagogic tools for gathering and representing these data (GIS mapping, audiotape recording, video and still digital photography, and theatre of the oppressed). The research teams were asked to report both results and methods so that their example might guide other students and teachers. Throughout the five-week seminar, the students also interviewed and met with educational researchers, community organizers, parent advocates, school administrators, civil rights attorneys, and elected officials to investigate how student research might become a standard part of the SARC process. On the final day of the seminar, the research teams presented their findings, methods, and analysis of the politics of implementation to a public audience of UCLA faculty, civil rights attorneys, educators, community advocates, and parents

In the summer of 2003 the seminar focused on "Oral Histories of the Educational Experiences in Post-*Brown* Los Angeles from 1954 to 2003." Young people who attend substandard schools for many years generally understand that they have been given a raw deal. They know that teachers are supposed to be well prepared and care for their students. They know that water fountains should work and bathrooms should be open and safe. They know that they should receive their textbooks when the semester begins. And they know that none of these conditions exists at their schools. Yet, because these students have not been educated about how such conditions came into being, they do not have a language to explain why their schools are the way they are and how they might be different.

We felt that students attending under-performing schools needed a sense of history to understand that the present is not inevitable and the future is open to creation. Toward this end, we decided to create a space for young people to learn about the educational history in their city through apprenticing as critical public historians. Young people forge their deepest understandings through practice. When students make public history—conducting interviews, examining historical records, analyzing census data—they see what it means to construct a historical narrative. The process lets them look at how people's lived experience is shaped by and in turn shapes structural conditions in the economy and legal system. As young people place themselves and their families in this historical narrative, they forge a deeper understanding of who they are and the society they live in. And when this history calls on them to study people like themselves who have joined the struggle for education on equal terms, they begin to imagine an identity as historical agents. By writing public history, young people, we felt, would come to see themselves as *authors* of the future. Each research team focused on one of the post-*Brown* decades in Los Angeles and collected oral history interviews from participants in Los Angeles schools. They juxtaposed these interviews with census data, educational achievement data, media artifacts, and high school yearbook analyses to paint a portrait of life for students of color in Los Angeles schools over the past half-century.

In the summer of 2004, the seminar focused on "Urban Youth, Political Participation, and Educational Reform." Students explored what it means for urban youth to participate powerfully in civic life, how urban youth can learn to participate in such ways, and what civic lessons young people now learn in and outside of urban schools. The students, who were placed into small research teams, talked with youth, educators, community leaders, and elected officials about issues facing young people in the local community, how young people should participate in civic life, and what skills are needed for such participation. Each team conducted research at a high school site and a community center in a local neighborhood. The teams also developed research tools for examining civic education in a school, including survey instruments, interview and focus group questions (or protocols), and rubrics for examining books and curricula.

In each seminar students produced individual texts and group texts. These texts ranged from standard written documents to iMovies and Power-Point presentations. Individually, students produced 1,500–2,000-word essays dealing with their journeys to becoming critical researchers and the implications of their seminar work for engagement in their schools and communities. Student research teams produced PowerPoint presentations, research reports, and a public presentation, which showcased the tools that they developed along with their research findings. The students also produced iMovie documentaries (in the summers of 2003 and 2004) and materials for an electronic journal targeted toward urban teachers and parents. Student-participants presented their research from the seminar to university faculty, local and state politicians, teachers, community members, and parents and at regional and national conferences such as the annual meeting of the American Educational Research Association (AERA), the Sociology of Education Association, and the California Association of Teachers of English.

Now we move to an analysis of the seminar's underlying pedagogical principles and its academic and social outcomes. First, we discuss the importance of positioning urban youth as critical sociologists and public intellectuals. Next, we talk about the city as a context for teaching learning focusing on the seminar's explicit pedagogy of the city. We also address the explicit pedagogy of distribution. That is, we did not focus only on the production of research artifacts; an important component of the critical pedagogy was to find or create meaningful opportunities for the students to distribute their work products. We then discuss the role of participatory action research in developing academic and critical literacies and young people with strong activist/intellectual identities, and we examine the role of participatory action research in bringing about social and educational change.

Becoming Critical Sociologists

Our initial goals in the seminar included orienting the students to the world of social science research, explicating a critical perspective on social science research, and positioning the students as critical social science researchers. It became necessary, then, to create a context where urban adolescents could become proficient and prolific readers of complex social science texts. For example, the initial two weeks of the seminar involved reading seminal texts in urban sociology and the sociology of education such as Jean Anyon's

(1981) "Social Class and School Knowledge," Jeannie Oakes's (1985) *Keeping Track: How Schools Structure Inequality*, the reproduction theory of Bourdieu (1990) and MacLeod (1987), and the critical social theory of Paulo Freire (1970), to name a few (Table 6.1).

---

1. Introduction to Social Theory

Sanchez, Sonia. (2004). Poem for July 4, 1994. In D. Menkart, A.D. Murray, & J. L View (Eds.), *Putting the movement back into civil rights teaching.* Washington, DC: Teaching for Change.

Freire, P. (1997). First letter: Reading the word/reading the world. In *Teachers as cultural workers: Letters to those who dare to teach* (pp. 17–26). Boulder, CO: Westview.

Oakes, J., & M. Lipton. (1999). *Teaching to change the world.* Boston: McGraw-Hill. Chapter 1, pp. 3–33.

MacLeod, J. (1987). Social reproduction in theoretical perspective. In *Ain't no making it: Aspirations and attainment in a low-income neighborhood.* Boulder, CO: Westview.

Finn, P. (1999). *Literacy with an attitude: Educating working class children in their own self interest.* New York: SUNY Press. Pp. 53–56, Finn presents MacLeod; pp. 9–26, Finn presents Anyon.

Anyon, J. (1981). Social class and school knowledge. *Curriculum Inquiry, 1,* 3–4.

Sólorzano, D., & D. Bernal. (2001). Examining transformational resistance through a critical race and LatCrit theory framework: Chicana and Chicano students in an urban context. *Urban Education, 36* (3), 308–342.

Noguera, P., & A. Akom. (2000). Disparities demystified. *The Nation,* June 5, 29–31.

Morrell, E. (2004). *Linking literacy and popular culture.* Norwood, MA: Christopher-Gordon. Pp. 91–101.

Table 6.1. Reading List from 2004 Summer Seminar

The practices of the seminar included basic reading comprehension, vocabulary development, and the synthesis of ideas. We developed activities where we explored "how" to read, even as we were learning the "what" of critical sociology (Table 6.2). As one might expect to find in a postsecondary seminar, we learned how to break down a piece, how to engage a text actively, and how to wrestle with meaning when terms seem obscure or difficult to access. Students began to interrogate and ultimately appropriate terms such as "social reproduction," "praxis," "ideology," and "structural inequality." They developed the language and instincts of critical sociologists as they gained confidence as competent readers and writers of academic texts in general.

What Will Be Asked of You as a Participant?

- **Participation in seminar.** Students will be asked to read legal briefs, educational research, and social theory. Instructors will call upon students to discuss the relationship between these readings and ongoing research projects.
- **Participation in research study team.** Each student will participate in a five-member student research team examining the methods of assessment and the politics of implementation related to one educational right. Students will be responsible for defining a research question, surveying related literature, developing a research design, collecting and analyzing data, writing a group report, and making a public presentation of the research.
- **Preparation of critical texts.** One of the goals of the seminar is to increase the production of critical texts, that is, texts that serve to inform common citizens in their struggles against inequities in dominant institutions such as schools. Toward this end, all seminar participants will write daily about issues related to critical research, social justice, access to quality urban schools, and youth civic engagement. The course instructors will lead a series of exercises that will culminate in the completion of an individual critical text in addition to a group research project. Following are some examples of critical texts:

  o   an article for IDEA's online journal Teaching to Change LA
  o   a letter to the editor of a local newspaper
  o   a letter to the principal, faculty member, or school board member addressing critical issues relating to urban schools
  o   a letter to a member of a community service organization
  o   a brochure, pamphlet, or Web page related to social justice

- **Preparation of critical research tools.** As part of the research process, you will develop interview protocols, surveys, maps, guidelines for textual analysis, and observational protocols. We will ask you to share these tools with educational researchers, policymakers, teachers, and other students who are interested in conducting research on youth civic engagement.
- **Preparation and presentation of final research project.** Student research teams will produce a final project that will be presented to a UCLA faculty panel. These projects will synthesize the group's findings, offer policy recommendations, and lay out a plan for future research. Each member of the student research team will be responsible for a substantial piece of the group's written project.
- **Preparation of PowerPoint presentation.** Student research teams will create a PowerPoint presentation to accompany the research report. The PowerPoint presentations will be presented on August 6 in the faculty center.

Table 6.2. Description of Seminar Activities

Through the initial seminar discussion and activities the students learned to read the world through the lens of critical sociology as they applied this language to their explanations of the contemporary conditions in their schools and communities. Even more, however, they learned to see themselves as legitimate critical researchers. An important component of critical sociology is to do critical sociology. Where a university undergraduate course would be satisfied with students grasping the difficult content of the discipline, this served only as our launching point for students to engage in designing and conducting their own original research projects.

We did not want students only to be exposed to critical social science research and theory; we also wanted them to become critical social science theorists and researchers. This meant that the students needed to conduct their own research. Becoming critical sociologists means that one needs to do the work of critical sociology. This seems logical until one examines the current structure of secondary schooling. Rarely does enrolling in a social science course translate into developing proficiency at doing social science per se. Students enrolled in history courses, for example, rarely engage in any historical research. We felt that the best strategy for generating active involvement among the students included allowing them to participate in the process of activist research. This process, we felt, would foster the development of core academic competencies as well as a different set of relationships between the students, their schools, and their communities. It would also change the students' relationship to the research process and the products of academic research. Toward these ends, the seminar led up to the designing of local, community-based research projects that included methods used by social scientists (participant observation, interviews, surveys, database analysis, visual sociology, oral history).

Part of helping students to become readers of the word and world in the Freirean sense entailed using the language and tools of critical sociology to give them lenses through which to read their world. This is important in moving forward from folk sociologies and deficit theories of social reproduction toward informed analyses both of the sophisticated mechanisms of social reproduction and of the grounded theories of critical praxis. Students read complex works by Freire, Oakes, Anyon, MacLeod, and others (readings of the word). It is important to mention the overlaps between academic literacies involved in reading traditional texts and the Freirean principles of reading the world. Of course, there are other texts (non-academic and non-print ones) that a critical sociologist must read, which would include a reading of the world. Supplementary to critical reading is a critical re-writing of the world that involves designing research projects and collecting and analyzing data. Preparation for this process included introducing the students to the tradition of social science research from a critical perspective. Our critical pedagogy of youth participatory action research involved conceptual reading and the development of critical methodological tools.

The Pedagogy of the City

A significant portion of seminar time involved fieldwork in neighborhoods and schools around the city of Los Angeles. The fieldwork was a prerequisite for completing the projects that the students developed; youth participatory action research is necessarily going to entail having young people out and about in their schools and communities. It is simply not possible to conduct transformative participatory action research projects *solely* within the four walls of the classroom. We knew from the outset that we wanted students to spend significant portions of the seminar learning about the various neighborhoods and communities that comprised "inner-city" Los Angeles. We were thus deliberate about introducing students to new neighborhoods in a segmented and often fragmented city. Los Angeles, we felt, held a geographical and political coherence only to politicians and mapmakers. The real Los Angeles that we knew consisted of a patchwork of self-contained neighborhoods, frequently divided by race and class. Students inhabiting the Eastside neighborhoods, for instance, might have very little experience in the neighborhoods of South Central or Watts. Equally, students from the largely African American neighborhoods of South Central LA would not often travel east of the Los Angeles River toward neighborhoods that are almost exclusively Latino. Very few of the students from South or East Los Angeles would have spent any significant time on the Westside or in the San Fernando Valley. To give students a broader perspective of their city and a sense of ownership over their city, we deliberately created activities that would take each student into several different neighborhoods in addition to their own. We also divided up the student-researchers in such as way that each team would include a representative level of residential and racial/ethnic diversity (all would have been classified as coming from poor or working-class families).

As seminar educators, we were also interested in changing the nature of the relationship between students and members of the city infrastructure (superintendents, police, local media personalities, parents, alumni of local schools). Usually students experience their schools and communities in passive ways: they are the recipients of schooling and community services, they are protected and served or punished by police, and they are written about in local media outlets. We wanted the students to develop respectful and agentive relationships with the adults in their city—both those who held traditional leadership positions and those who were directly or indirectly associated with knowledge production in or about the communities and neighborhoods. An important component of the pedagogy of the city entailed putting young people in touch with onsite and district-level administrators, practicing teachers, prominent members of community-based organizations, civil servants (police, judges, attorneys), citizens, and members of the local and regional media. We intentionally scheduled field trips to public parks, malls, libraries, schools, law offices, and public events that would be heavily attended by police and members of the media.

Each of these activities served a larger purpose of changing the way that students looked at the city and participated in civil life in Los Angeles. We wanted the students to understand the plurality and diversity of their city, but we also wanted them to gain an understanding of the similarities of experiences among citizens who might be classified differently or might be seen initially not to have much in common. For example, students attending a predominantly African American school in South Central LA would ideally be able to identify with the struggles of their peers attending schools in Boyle Heights and unincorporated East Los Angeles.

In addition, we wanted students to develop a vested interest in advocating on behalf of all the marginalized groups in the city. Students came together across many lines of difference to speak with a common voice about what concerned them in their city and the city's schools, and also they were able to speak to what gave them cause for hope. This coalition building is important to bridge some of the divides that exist between marginalized communities in our city; it is also fundamental to the development of our students as citizen-advocates who are able to bring people together in causes of social justice.

Finally, we wanted students to envision themselves as being able to play more powerful roles in advocating for equity and justice in their city, so the seminar sought to create contexts that would allow them to learn about becoming critical researchers as they also participated in meaningful ways in exposing and ameliorating oppressive conditions in their schools and communities.

Our work as educators entailed creating the conditions that would allow the students to be able to experience the city. This included developing relationships with school personnel, city and neighborhood leaders, community-based organizations, and a cadre of parents and volunteer workers who could help to transport young students around a city as expansive as Los Angeles. The capital component to critical pedagogy included working with public transportation agencies to acquire monthly passes and tokens that would allow students and teachers to use public transportation to navigate the city efficiently throughout the research process.

Critical Pedagogy and the Praxis of Distribution

Once the students became invested in their participatory action research projects, an important component of our work as critical educators entailed locating and developing meaningful sites of exchange for the student research. There were several reasons for this focus. We knew that, to the extent that the young people were placed in positions where they were treated as intellectuals, they would also begin to see themselves as intellectuals. We also knew that, given that the young people worked so diligently on projects of social import, they deserved to have these projects shared with greater publics who would be able to benefit from or act upon this knowledge. Thus, we invited to our final presentations audiences that included university faculty members, classroom teachers, members of community-based organizations, media personnel, and elected officials and their staffs, along with peers, parents, and family members. Each of these populations had something to contribute to the experiences of our student presenters, and each of these authentic audience participants had something to gain from the research that the students had to present.

Following the presentations we arranged several physical, virtual, and print outlets that allowed the student research groups to distribute their findings. The university institute published an online journal that was frequently accessed by local teachers and students as well as researchers and policymakers from around the country, and students were encouraged to revise their individual and group projects for inclusion. We arranged for students to present their work to graduate seminars, to teacher education courses, and at regional and national educational research conferences such as the American

Educational Research Association, the Sociology of Education Association, and the California Association of Teachers of English. Many students created their own channels of distribution in their own schools and communities. Several students created presentations for their peers or faculty meetings on campus, students ran for school office on platforms that were bolstered by their summer seminar research, students lobbied school district personnel for policy changes on the basis of their research, and students contributed editorial and journalistic pieces to their school publications.

We argue that the distribution of youth participatory action research serves important pragmatic and pedagogical purposes. First, disseminating information to authentic audiences provides a rich, intellectually rigorous, and inspirational context for students to develop superior products. It was not necessary to tell the students to revise their work or to rehearse their presentations when they knew they would be speaking to an audience of several hundred people or if they knew that their films, PowerPoint presentations, and research reports would be accessed virtually by thousands of people (quite literally: the online journal received approximately 1 million hits during 2000–2006).

Furthermore, developing sites for information distribution allowed us as critical educators to position young people as scholars and intellectuals. Often when students "present" to adults the purpose is either to demonstrate a competency or to entertain, or the adults serve simply as external validation for the hard work of the students. These are all worthy reasons for young people to share their work with adults. Rarely, though, are young people placed in the position of experts with information that can *inform* adult audience members. It was important to us that our students felt as if they were bringing important information that contributed to ongoing conversations between researchers and advocates for social and educational justice. Student research teams brought data, analysis, and recommendations based on their findings that were meant to assist adults in their struggles to reform urban schools. The legitimacy and the relevance of these exchanges between adults and students further reified the students as researchers and as public intellectuals.

Youth Participatory Action Research and Academic and Social Development

As we stated in Chapter 1, any critical pedagogy in urban education must simultaneously address academic, social, and identity development. Leaving any of these three goals out of the equation robs students of the education that will enable them to act powerfully upon the world as informed and affirmed agents. We have already discussed at length the impact of the youth participatory research on identity development. We would now like to elaborate the relationship between a critical pedagogy of youth participatory action research and academic skill development. We start with a quotation from the final research report of the hip-hop research project from the 2000 summer seminar:

> We also found that the average student owned 10–15 hip-hop compact discs, several students own more than 20 compact discs and some own 5–10 compact discs or less. The average student watches 3–5 hours of hip-hop videos a week on television and listening on the radio. Several students watch 10 hours of hip-hop videos a week and a few students watch an hour or an hour and a half. With this abundance of information, we found that the average student believes that hip-hop music has an extreme influence on teens.
>
> The students we interviewed and surveyed in the Los Angeles area believe hip-hop is so widely listened to for a myriad of reasons. The most popular reason was that they like it. The second most noted reason was that the students could relate with the music. It has to do with everyday things they have to go through. Students gave responses such as: "Hip-Hop is an expression of the soul that everyone can relate to because it combines so many art forms," and "they talk about whet teens are experiencing in life, so the teens feel a connection with the music."

This short passage from a twenty-page research report (reports ranged from twenty-five to forty pages) reveals the extent to which the students appropriated the tools and language of social science research. To understand the impact of hip-hop culture on their peers, students created interview protocols and distributed a survey. They were able to quantify the very strong attachment that most of their peers had to hip-hop culture and to identify the ambivalence that many teens felt toward a culture that they thought represented their feelings to a certain extent but also glorified ways of being in the world that were dangerous (i.e., violence and drug use) and demeaning (i.e., sexism in lyrics and videos). To prepare themselves to engage in this level of research, students also had to become readers of social theory texts and texts related to social science research methods. Over the course of the six summers of the seminar, every group produced a research report and presentation that contained at least this level of investigation and analysis.

In addition to increasing students' academic skill development across multiple core content areas, participatory action research also increased student motivation and student engagement in intellectual work. We documented this increased motivation throughout the work of the summer seminar in several ways. First, the students volunteered their evenings and weekends to continue the work of their projects. Faced with the time constraints of the seminar, students volunteered to conduct further research on their own time. Students borrowed our equipment to conduct interviews over the weekends, and they often asked whether they could stay late to finish projects. During the final week of preparation, it was not uncommon for students to remain after for several hours to complete data analysis or to rehearse their final presentations. On one night in particular, the final evening of preparation for the 2004 presentations, the entire cohort remained until 10 o'clock in the evening working on their research projects. Volunteers and university staff remained to help students with final edits on their research reports and short films, and the instructors ordered pizza for the entire group. As we look back on a dozen years of working with young people, watching the commitment of time and the energy and enthusiasm of a group of young people stands out as one of our more special moments of teaching.

Students also demonstrated their motivation by being more willing to take writing to extra drafts before submitting to external audiences, and they used the extra time and energy to create documents, documentaries, and presentations that were of a very high caliber. Our analysis of the quality of student work has been confirmed by interviews with practicing social scientists, who also spoke to the power and quality of the students' projects. In terms of sheer numbers, the twenty-five-page research reports and the notebooks, which averaged about a hundred pages written over five weeks, testify to the amount of work that students were willing to invest into the completion of these research projects. In addition, in interviews, students admit to being more interested and engaged in academic/intellectual work as a result of working collaboratively on these participatory action research projects.

A big challenge we face in adolescent education concerns motivation and engagement. Academic achievement (or under-achievement) is not always a question of skills; many times it is a question of motivation. After years of being told what they cannot do and years of attending oppressive schools, many students quite unsurprisingly decide not to continue to engage in school. We must understand that fact if we are going to be effective with all adolescents, not just in urban education. We must understand the logic of their disinvestment, rather than just pathologize youth. One of the things we look for in our analysis of data is evidence of student engagement. We can see examples of engagement in the work from and the student commentary on the summer seminars. Students, in becoming participatory action researchers, are more likely to want to read complex and relevant texts, they are more likely to exert energy in the data collection and data analysis phase when they are conducting research that matters to their own lives and the lives of people they care about, and they are more likely to want to take their products through this process because they want their work to be solid, rigorous, and valuable to the process of remaking the world. We conclude this section with another excerpt from a research group report, written in the summer of 2002:

> **From Learning Resource Group 2002**
> The differences are exposed. The demands are voiced. Like the Chicano, Black, and Women's civil rights movements before us, we are engulfed in social and educational reform. We demand equity and the preservation [of] our civil rights. We demand that all our schools in urban and suburban communities be taught equally and be provided with the same quality educational resources. Otherwise, how are working-class people supposed to become an active part of society? Cesar Chavez once said, "Once social change begins, it cannot be reversed. You cannot un-educate the person who has learned to read. You cannot humiliate the person who feels pride. And you cannot oppress the people who are not afraid anymore." We are educated, full of pride, and united by a common goal for social change. We cannot be uneducated nor can we be humiliated. We are no longer afraid.

This is the summary paragraph from a prior seminar report where students focused on educational rights. It demonstrates the clarity and passion of the research groups, and it also demonstrates how they become powerful writers through this process of engaging in critical research. Finally, the quotation shows the willingness of the students to embrace the identities of action researchers and public intellectuals. The students implicate themselves in the process of working to change the conditions that they call out in the report. They further identify themselves as possessing the skills (academic content) and social awareness needed to engage in the struggle for educational, social, and racial justice. Everything we could possibly want for young people vis-à-vis their public educational experience is contained in this one quotation, and it largely comes from creating contexts that allow for a critical pedagogy of youth participatory action research.

Implications for Critical Pedagogy and Urban Education

It is possible to draw on the principles of critical pedagogy to develop curricula and practices that are effective with urban youth. First, it is important to restate that we cannot separate critical pedagogy with urban youth from the development of academic literacy skills. One of our goals has to be the transmission of skills that help students to navigate professional and civic life; we must also acknowledge that there are too many sophisticated literacy skills required for true praxis. If these students are going to wear the mantle of the struggle for social and educational justice, if they are going to produce knowledge that forces us to look at our world differently, and if they are going to motivate people to act as collectives for social change, they will need to be able to read, write, and speak at high levels. As educators, we need to do a better job of linking academic skills to our ideal model of the public intellectuals that we want our students to become.

Given that schools and classrooms remain our primary sites of engagement with young people, we must do a better job of promoting youth participatory action research as a pedagogical approach across the K–12 spectrum. We talk more about this in the concluding chapter, but our research (Rogers, Morrell, & Enyedy, 2007) shows that when students are involved in action research projects, they also learn valuable skills and tools across the major content areas.

In addition, there needs to be more focus on the principles and applications of participatory action research in teacher education programs, in professional development seminars, and in master's degree programs for practicing teachers so that they can have the confidence and the expertise they need to help students with these most important projects. Given that most educators have little training in traditional research methods, their lack of expertise can limit their ability to work effectively with youth on local action research projects. Once schools accept the premise that participatory action research is a form of empowering critical pedagogy, they can also begin to reconfigure the skill sets that teachers need to be effective. Changing the nature of instruction or changing the ideology of effective practice has direct implications for what it means to teach. We must acknowledge that for every change we advocate in the classroom, we are also implicitly recommending a change in the preparation of new teachers and changes for experienced teachers as well. That said, if we want critical educators to work with youth on participatory action' research projects, we will need to figure out ways to help them do this.

In his work with a large East Coast urban school district, for example, Morrell developed a three-day seminar with interested teachers where they reviewed the principles of action research, read about what other students and teachers had done, and designed their own curricula to incorporate these principles. This working group and Morrell met monthly, often visiting each other's classrooms and refining their research projects with their respective classes. At the end of the year, each of the classes involved presented one of its action research projects to an audience of teachers, community leaders, and school and district leaders. In more than one instance, the issues raised by students (dropout rates, tardy policies, school discipline, etc.) were taken on by the appropriate authorities and these students themselves became involved in thinking about possible solutions to the problems they had investigated. In the relatively short period of an academic school year, teachers with no prior experience in participatory action research were able to develop concrete projects with a diverse array of students across a range of academic abilities. It all began with exposing teachers to the possibilities of participatory research as an instantiation of critical pedagogy and developing their own skills as researchers.

As critical pedagogy is defined largely by its outcomes for identity development and social change, it becomes the responsibilities of urban teachers and administrators to seek out more venues for the distribution of youth participatory action research. By its very definition, action research needs to lead to transformative action; teachers and students need opportunities to act upon the knowledge that they produce during the research process. This means that they need ample opportunities to share their work with the appropriate audiences, be they other teachers and students, district-level leaders, policymakers, or the community at large. We also know from our prior research (Morrell & Rogers, 2007) that students develop greater confidence in themselves as intellectuals and activists when they are affirmed in these identities through their public presentations. With the Futures project and with the summer seminar, we sought out opportunities for the young people to present their research. We created an end-of-seminar conference, we arranged for students to speak at professional and academic conferences, we brought them into graduate seminars at the university, and we negotiated access to department meetings at individual school sites. In the East Coast project alluded to in the previous paragraph, students expressed increased motivation after presenting their work to school and district-level officials.

Finally, we need more empirical research on youth participatory research as a legitimate instantiation of critical pedagogy. In the spirit of this book, we urge critical educators across the K–12 educational spectrum, and across all major content areas, to initiate and document their action research projects with urban youth. We further challenge book publishers, series editors, journal editors, and organizers of professional conferences to provide ample space for educators who do this invaluable research to share their work. There should be whole book series, special issues of journals, and working conferences dedicated to the investigation of the practical applications of participatory action research to urban education. The high visibility of these events as well as the sheer quantity of critical studies that could be produced would ideally impact public awareness as well as shape educational policy.

The next generation of critical scholarship will need to push the theoretical parameters of our work as the scholarship of prior generations has done. To develop a complete grounded theory of critical pedagogy in urban education, we will need many more examples of the possibilities and dilemmas that accompany the transition from theory to practice. What we have provided in this book are powerful examples of what this practice might look like in traditional and out-of-school interactions with urban youth. With a call for additional work in this regard, we now turn toward our fifth case, which considers the intersections between critical pedagogy and ethnic studies in urban education.

Note

1. The state mandates that each school develop and provide an SARC that includes required elements (e.g., standardized test scores, teacher certification information) but may be supplemented with locally generated information.

7
Pan-ethnic Studies

Many connections have been made in educational research between academic failure, educational inequality, and race in American schools. These investigations have looked at schooling inequalities (Anyon, 1997; Darling-Hammond, 1998; Kozol, 1991; Noguera, 2003), tracking and teacher preparation (Oakes, 1985; Oakes & Lipton, 2001), and critical literacy (Delpit, 1995; Freire & Macedo, 1987; Lee, 2004), among other issues. The research has been crucial in linking these issues to deeper structural problems such as under-qualified teachers (Akom, 2003; Delpit, 1995; Oakes & Lipton, 2001), teacher shortages (Darling-Hammond, 1998; Kozol, 1991; Oakes & Lipton, 2001), and funding inequalities (Anyon, 1997; Kozol, 1991; Meier, 1995).

These studies have laid important groundwork for the documentation of urban educational inequality and U.S. educational disinvestment in places where people of color reside. However, given intolerably low academic achievement in urban schools that serve predominantly students of color (Council of the Great City Schools, 2007), there is a growing need to highlight, examine, and understand the practices and strategies that actually work in these schools, specifically those that are simultaneously focused on educational and racial justice. We call these "counter-narratives" because they are stories that challenge narratives that normalize failure in urban schools and pay special attention to the conditions of inequity.

Research that exposes the level of inequity (educational, social, political, and economic) in this country and throughout the world should be ramped up. The selfish exploitation and hoarding of resources cannot be tolerated in any civilized society. However, an exclusive emphasis on an exposé of suffering can lead to hopelessness as this type of work rarely presents much in terms of practice-based solutions and often paints the picture that collective agency under such conditions is impossible. While we continue to expose the "savage inequalities" (Kozol, 1991) of urban schools and communities, we must also pay attention to the effective pedagogy that goes on there in order to demystify and normalize it. Toward this end, this chapter draws from research in ethnic studies, critical, social, and post-colonial theories, and empirical research on the experiences of racially and ethnically marginalized groups in urban schools to theorize a critical pan-ethnic studies approach to research and pedagogy.

The Discourse(s) of Ethnic Studies

In our work over the years, we have drawn from disparate fields such as critical pedagogy, various ethnic studies fields, civil rights historiography, anticolonial and post-colonial discourses, multicultural education, critical race theory, and youth popular culture to develop a theory of empowering practice upon which the curricula and pedagogies discussed in previous chapters have been based. We wanted to honor how ethnic studies are traditionally defined, but in thinking about the foundation of "critical pan-ethnic studies" as a pedagogy of urban education, we were driven to consider other fields of study as well. It is important to consider that all of these fields have dealt with studying or intervening in the conditions of people of color in local, national, and global contexts (including schools). They offer an interesting array of possibilities when we consider the purpose of education, the structural barriers to access, important knowledge bases indigenous to youth and their communities, and methods of investigating the past and present for ethnic minorities in the United States.

Critical Pedagogy

Critical pedagogy remains a foundation of our scholarship, even as it pertains to our developing model of critical pan-ethnic studies in urban education. This is primarily because critical pedagogy, in the Freirean sense, begins with the problem of dehumanization and seeks, through dialogue and praxis, to develop an individual who is able to participate in the transformation of society. Critical pan-ethnic studies have to begin with the relationship between racialization in U.S. society and the dehumanization of students of color attending urban schools. The pedagogical encounter needs to draw students' attention to this dehumanization as it also works toward the development of racially conscious individuals who are able to participate within larger movements for racial and educational justice.

Traditional Ethnic Studies

Africana, African American, Asian American, Caribbean, Chicano, Latin American, Raza, Native American, and pan-Asian studies also inform our framework. As a group, these fields of ethnic studies offer important historical insight into the ways that colonizing and imperialist governments have engaged indigenous and non-white populations over the past 500 years. Even more, these fields offer important insight into the histories, legacies, and cultures of communities that are often lost in U.S. educational narratives of Western progress and Western values. Narratives of ethnic studies do not necessarily have to be at odds with the Western educational paradigm, but they do provide information that is sorely lacking from traditional education. These fields of cultural studies also contain counter-narratives of resistance against colonial oppression that explicitly critique the ideas of passive compliance with or acceptance of colonial expansion. Finally, these fields offer explicit critiques of dominant epistemologies as they force us to rethink how we have come to know what it is we believe and even to question the paradigms of knowledge production that determine our concepts of truth, science, and scholarship.

Social Historiography

The new social history has radically expanded the range of subjects available for historical study. What the French call "marginals"—the poor, the sick, the insane, the lame and halt, the criminal—have become a central focus of many such historians, as have social institutions and social groups that previous historians had all but ignored—the family, the school, the prison, the hospital, women, gays, lesbians, transsexuals, immigrants, and people of color. Social history has re-written political history as well, shifting emphasis from great men and their deeds to the institutions and networks that make politics possible—clans, clientage and patronage systems, voting blocs, political parties, and so on (Howell & Prevenier, 2001, 14).

None of us understands fully how to use what we know of the past to shape a more just present. But we can be sure that social analysis is lacking when history does not somehow make it clear that ordinary, flawed, everyday sorts of human beings frequently manage to make extraordinary contributions to social change. History that does not make it easier for people to see in themselves, and in those around them, the potential for controlling their lives takes us in the wrong direction (Payne, 1995, 440).

Payne's 1995 study *I've Got the Light of Freedom* is an example of social history, one that he calls "civil rights historiography." This method is explicitly critical of top-down research that ignores the local struggles of everyday actors. Social history reminds us that these actors are the foundation of any understanding of radical social movements. This becomes increasingly important in a study of revolutionary movements. Our contention is that the most important lessons for educators today come from a thorough investigation of how others, positioned similarly, participated in collectives that ultimately led to massive social transformations. For these reasons, social historiography focuses on the work of the people (students, teachers, journalists, radio deejays, workers, upstart political parties) rather than solely on the macro-politics and deeds of great leaders. These contexts and individuals are important to the story, no doubt, but they are not to be studied to the exclusion of people working at the ground level.

Anti-colonial and Post-colonial Discourse

Although colonization happened differently in different parts of the world, all colonial interchanges involved the settlement of European people in new lands, generally inhabited by indigenous peoples, for the cultivation of land and development of products that would be of service in Europe. Loomba (1998) comments:

> The process of "forming a community" in the new land necessarily meant unforming or reforming the communities that existed there already, and involved a wide range of practices including trade, plunder, negotiation, warfare, genocide, enslavement, and rebellion. (p. 2)

Throughout the centuries, colonialism has been maintained by force, including torture, maiming, and even murder (James, 1938/2001), but it is also maintained largely by the domination of ideas—particularly in the industrial age, when many of the formal structures of oppression, such as slavery, have been officially disbanded. Antonio Gramsci (1971) talks about how industrial capitalist societies use hegemony instead of force to maintain inequitable power relations, shaping the consent of the oppressed toward their oppressive conditions. According to Gramsci, schools existed as the primary site of cultural education, for better or worse. Gramsci's educational project targeted schools and teachers in the development of a revolutionary proletarian culture that he hoped would counter the dominant culture of his time (see Chapter 2 for a more detailed explanation of Gramsci's ideas). Edward Said (1978) made connections between the work of Gramsci and Foucault (1995) and the emergent field of colonial studies by examining how Western powers had used dominant discourses of schooling and the media to maintain oppressive narratives of the colonized subject.

It is important to acknowledge, however, that the indigenous peoples who found themselves bombarded with European imperialism did not accept their colonization without resistance. To underscore this point we quote at length from Ashcroft, Griffiths, and Tiffin (1995):

European imperialism took various forms in different times and places and proceeded through conscious planning and contingent occurrences. As a result of this complex development something occurred for which the plan of imperial expansion had not bargained: the immensely prestigious and powerful imperial culture found itself appropriated in projects and counter-colonial resistance which drew upon the many indigenous local and hybrid processes of self determination to defy, erode, and sometimes supplant the prodigious power of imperial cultural knowledge. Postcolonial literatures are a result of this interaction between imperial culture and the complex of indigenous cultural practices. As a consequence, postcolonial theory has existed for a long time before that particular name was used to describe it. (p. 1)

As these authors point out, as soon as colonialism became an economic, cultural, and political reality, anti-colonial and post-colonial ruptures in thought and action occurred among "colonized" peoples. Educators who understand the long history of resistance to oppression in communities of color are better positioned to develop anti-colonial pedagogy. In so doing, they extend traditions of resistance by oppressed peoples.

Anti-racist Pedagogy

Any anti-racist pedagogy must acknowledge white privilege (McIntosh, 1988) and the widespread existence of racism in society (hooks, 2003). An anti-racist pedagogy needs also to challenge dominant narratives about race and the institutions (e.g., schools and the media) that construct them (Nieto, 1992; Zinn, 1995) while also developing among students and practitioners the skills to locate and produce critical information to be used in the reconstruction of empowering ethnic counter-narratives.

In addition, an anti-racist pedagogy needs to reduce prejudice (Banks, 2001) among members of dominant ethnic and racial groups. One strategy for accomplishing this end is to create a curriculum that centers and honors the works and lives of non-white people (Nieto, 1992). This, in and of itself, however, is not enough. We contend that an anti-racist pedagogy ultimately strives to create humanized agents who advocate for racial equity and justice (Freire, 1970). For this reason, it must be *dialogic*; it should engender conversations among students and between students and the social world. It must also be *humanizing, celebrating* the humanity in those who are "Othered" (Fanon, 1967). Finally, it must be *praxis-oriented*; it should promote reflective action upon (and against) a racially unjust world.

Foundations of a Critical Pan-ethnic Studies (CPES) in Urban Education

Drawing on this collective framework and our own experience as educators and scholars, we offer a preliminary model of critical pan-ethnic studies in urban education that has informed our work with students of color. "Critical" implies praxis (Freire, 1970), the dialectical intersection between theory and action. "Pan-ethnic" implies not merely a question of class but rather a collective multi-ethnic struggle and the centrality of race and ethnicity to transformational work in U.S. education. The word "studies" implies subjectivity and engaged research, the process of critical inquiry and knowledge production with (and about) populations who have been marginalized in dominant discourses and institutions.

CPES involves teachers and students coming together to investigate racial injustice as they collaborate to eradicate it. The work is pedagogical in that it develops young people's intellectual capabilities and racial identities, but it is also pragmatic in that it is rooted in struggles for change. Most notably, the focus is on praxis, or using theory to inform transformative action, which in this study translates into student knowledge production, literacy development, academic advancement, ethnic empowerment, and commitment to social change. It is also noteworthy that the focus is on the collective struggle for racial and economic justice that includes members of all ethnic groups while still holding race and ethnicity as central to understanding power and privilege in society.

CPES and Research Methodologies: Whose Principles and for What Construction?

The current debate over what constitutes legitimate educational research has been heavily influenced by the 2001 No Child Left Behind Act (NCLB) and the Education Sciences Reform Act of 2002. These two policies helped establish the Federal Institute of Education Sciences, which purports to "reflect the intent of the President and Congress to advance the field of education research, making it more rigorous in support of evidence-based education [by] identifying and implementing educational practices supported by rigorous evidence" (U.S. Department of Education, 2005).

NCLB's direction for educational research seems logical and in the best interests of schools and the research community. However, upon deeper examination, this direction for educational research steers us down a dangerous road—one that Emerson (1841) cautions us against:

> There is a time in every man's education when he arrives at the conviction that envy is ignorance; that imitation is suicide; that he must take himself for better, for worse, as his portion; that though the wide universe is full of good, no kernel of nourishing corn can come to him but through his toil bestowed on that plot of ground which is given to him to till.

The road that educational researchers must walk is not the road taken by other disciplines. If we lose sight of this fact, we will find ourselves on someone else's path, using someone else's map, perpetually lost in someone else's field. However, if we can draw from the successful strategies of other disciplines to create our own path, our work will nourish our field as well as inform the work of others. This demands of us the recognition that just as success for educational practitioners is predicated upon the development of caring relationships with students, so educational research should be grounded in authentically caring relationships.

Valenzuela's (1999) articulation of the concept of *cariño*, or caring, as a central tenet of good teaching seems to have passed over the heads of many educational researchers working in poor and non-white urban schools. Too often, their research agendas take no responsibility for improving the quality of services at research sites and have even less commitment to improving the lives of the people who reside in those communities. The challenge to the educational research community is to rethink the merits of business-as-usual research agendas, now disguised under more progressive and convoluted titles such as "No Child Left Behind." This calls for educational researchers to develop lines of questioning and data collection methods that foreground *cariño* rather than striving to simplify data acquisition.

Cariño is often translated as "caring," "affection," or "love," but much is lost in this translation. *Cariño* is more a concept than a word. It is the foundation of meaningful relationships—often the only thing left to give in families raising children on substandard wages. Valenzuela (1999) describes *cariño* in the context of schooling as "authentic caring," a concept distinctly different from what she calls "aesthetic caring." She explains that schools serving poor and working-class Latino children often fail to develop reciprocal relationships whereby children are authentically cared for and in turn open themselves up to care about school. Drawing from the literature on caring in schools (Gilligan, 1982; Noddings, 1992; Prillaman & Eaker, 1994), Valenzuela (1999) argues that "schools are structured around an aesthetic caring whose essence lies in "an attention to things and ideas" (p. 22). This leads to a culture of false caring, one where the most powerful members of the relationship define themselves as caring despite the fact that the recipients of their so-called caring do not perceive it as such. Ultimately, aesthetic caring results in pragmatic relationships between school officials and students, straining the teaching and learning process.

Not far removed from aesthetic caring is the technocratic jargon of educational discourse that encourages an "impersonal and objective language, including such terms as goals, strategies, and standardized curricula, that is used in decisions made by one group for another" (Valenzuela, 1999, 22). This discourse is largely shaped by educational research agendas that view "authentic caring" as an afterthought. At their worst, these agendas promote scientific objectivity that frowns upon overt discussions of caring in an effort to mirror more traditional forms of research.

Authentic Caring in Educational Research

Some researchers are rethinking educational research by emphasizing reciprocal relationships with schools, leading to deeper commitments for researchers to the school's and community's welfare (Duncan-Andrade, 2007; Noguera, 2003; Morrell, 2004a). These researchers understand that each school has its own set of stakeholders and material conditions and that this requires research methodologies that recognize such differences. Rather than aiming to develop a model that can be overlaid on any school, a pan-ethnic studies educational research approach focuses on forming relationships that pay attention to the special needs of a school. This focus on relationships translates into a greater emphasis on producing real change in the schools where the research is taking place.

The value of this type of critical research is its focus on empowering individuals as agents of meaningful, sustainable change. The direct aim of this type of research agenda is positively to impact the material conditions of those involved with the study; it is an approach to research that gives more than it receives. McLaren and Giarelli (1995) call this action research, contrasting it with policy studies whose aim is to provide "useful," expert knowledge for institutional planning. They argue that action research leads "not to bureaucratic directives, but, more important, to the possibility for emancipatory change" (p. 17) because of its emphasis on reflexive and shared study.

Smith (1999) makes a similar argument for "decolonizing" research paradigms that focus more directly on improving immediate circumstances. This de-emphasizes the traditional method of searching for empirical truths that can be rigidly implemented on a large scale. Instead, it seeks to democratize the tools of research and knowledge creation (see also Kincheloe & McLaren, 1998). In this way, researchers imbue a sense of hope and promise, one that is directly tied to the study participants' sense of themselves as capable agents of change. Beyond a heightened awareness of the capacity to change, this kind of research develops a set of tools for participants that can be used and reused in continually improving whatever is most in need of attention. This is particularly noteworthy because traditional research methods leave these tools in the hands of the researchers; when the researcher leaves, so do the research tools and, to a large extent, so does the sense of agency.

Research agendas committed to collaboration with participants as colleagues rather than subjects can result in richer studies. This approach reduces dependency-based colonial models of knowledge production that have historically reproduced the status quo. With the insertion of multiple voices into the conversation, the process of identifying problems and researching solutions becomes more democratic. This research program also provides for individual and structural reflexivity that can serve as a mechanism for ongoing feedback and adaptation when new issues arise that need research. Perhaps most important, it recognizes the complexity of each set of conditions and encourages a sensibility toward local agency and control for developing solutions to local problems. This is not to say that sites cannot learn from the research of others; this is not a subtractive model or a zero-sum game. Instead, this is an additive model of educational research, one that suggests that sweeping policy amendments will not be sufficient to bring about the local attention to change that is necessary in institutions such as schools. What is necessary is a combination of progressive policy and more attention to localized research that allows for broad policies to be efficacious and relevant locally.

Examples of CPES Research Projects

THUG LIFE Pedagogy: Pedagogy of Indignation, Challenge, and Change

This section describes the first year (2005–2006) of a three-year research project carried out by Duncan-Andrade at a small public high school in east Oakland, California. I began this project with the sense that it was my duty as an educator to provide direct service to the young people in my community. This commitment to impact in a positive manner the lives of people involved in the research is what we mean when we talk about research agendas that foreground *cariño*. While we expect the impact of such research to extend beyond the daily effect on the participants, this goal comes second to the expectation that the project will have a measurable impact on the participants.

In an effort to pursue this research agenda, I began teaching a cohort of thirty high school students for three years (from their 10th-grade year through graduation). This project, now entering its third year, combines an effort to study and improve my classroom practice with provision of access to CPES pedagogy for young people. The broader goal is to use this research to provide other urban educators with grounded research on effective critical pedagogical strategies and to give them some explanation about why those approaches work. To advance these efforts to stimulate dialogue about critical pedagogy, I have used this research to develop an iteration of Freire's *Pedagogy of Indignation* (2004). As Ana Maria Araújo Freire states in the book's prologue, the title was chosen as a counterbalance to Paulo Freire's other writings. where he articulates his commitment to pursuing and promoting pedagogy that is imbued with hope, love, *conscientização*, and freedom. He has said many times over that we cannot be pedagogues with these traits if we are not indignant about the existence of conditions of oppression. Likewise, he cautioned us to balance our anger against an awareness that the future is not predetermined; anger should be partnered with critical hope that we have the capacity (and responsibility) to act to change oppressive conditions.

This research project investigates the use of pedagogy that directly responds to the social conditions facing youth in communities such as east Oakland, where graduation rates for Latino and black students are below 50%, college eligibility rates are below 10%, and seemingly intractable poverty and violence exist. In contrast, in the city of Piedmont, Oakland's immediate neighbor, graduation rates are more than 95%, college eligibility rates are more than 85%, the median income is $146,000 (Oakland's is $44,000), and violent crime is virtually non-existent. Freire's sagacious advice to critical pedagogues is that we must develop pedagogy that balances indignation over these inequitable conditions with critical hope that our work will change them. This is what I call THUG LIFE pedagogy.

I borrow the term THUG LIFE from Tupac Shakur. I realize, and am critical of the fact, that some of the messages delivered by Tupac were highly problematic. However, I also am aware that even after his death in 1996,

Tupac remains wildly popular among young oppressed peoples around the globe. To be sure, the music and poetry that Tupac used as a medium to deliver his message are key to his popularity. But I am convinced that the longevity and extent of his popularity are the result of the portion of his work that speaks to the righteous indignation that festers in almost every person who detests injustice. Only twenty-five at his death, Tupac had just begun the development of a theory of humanization for oppressed peoples that drew from their indignation. He argued that oppressed people needed to search within themselves and their communities for freedom and that this required adults to pay special attention to children born into a society that hates them. For Tupac, hate that is passed on to children through the cycle of social inequity destroys communities. He gave his theory an acronym, THUG LIFE (The Hate U Gave Little Infants Fucks Everyone), a deliberate appropriation of a phrase that has associations with the racist stereotype of urban men of color as street thugs. In an interview, Tupac explained:

> By "thug" I mean, not criminal or someone that beats you over the head. I mean the underdog. The person that had nothing and succeeds, he's a thug because he overcame all obstacles. It doesn't have anything to do with the dictionary's version of "thug." To me "thug" is my pride, not being someone that goes against the law, not being someone that takes, but being someone that has nothing, and even though I have nothing and there's no home for me to go to, my head is up high. My chest is out. I walk tall. I talk loud. I'm being strong. ... We gonna start slowly but surely taking our communities back. Regulate our community. Organize. We need to start taking care of our own. We gotta start somewhere, and I don't know about anything else, but this, to me, is a start. (Lazin, 2003)

Much like Tupac, I believe that the hatred/rage/hostility/indignation that result from any group of people systematically being denied their right to food, clothing, shelter, education, and justice will ultimately cause a society to implode. Likewise, properly channeled, those legitimate feelings can be developed into the courage to act and fundamentally change the direction of a society, even in the face of the broader society's cowardice. In fact, the necessary courage dramatically and justly to alter the direction of an empire might be found only among those who suffer under its oppressive weight. This is the type of young person a THUG LIFE pedagogy aims to nurture.

Urban Sociology at Northeast Community High School. The class where I began implementing and researching this pedagogical approach was a 10th-grade urban sociology class with thirty students—thirteen of them African American (eight girls and six boys) and sixteen Latinos (ten girls and six boys). The class was de-tracked, although given the context of academic achievement described earlier, the overwhelming majority of the students in the class would be considered low achievers. The school was on a block schedule, which meant that our class met three times a week for ninety minutes. The core curriculum for the spring semester was a project called "Doc Ur Block." This project was split into three segments, guided by the five stages of critical praxis discussed in the section on Paulo Freire in Chapter 2.

Segment 1: Identifying and Analyzing a Problem. The first two phases took about eight weeks. I introduced several key sociological terms using readings (see reading list in the appendix), lectures, films (*The Matrix* and *Bus 174*), and discussion. The core ideas included hegemony, through Gramsci (see reading list) and films such as *Bus 174* (Padilha & Lacerda, 2002) and *The Matrix* (Wachowski & Wachowski, 1999); counter-hegemony, through Freire, the speeches of Malcolm X, Lolita Lebrón's life, Sólorzano and Delgado-Bernal (see reading list), and hip-hop artists such as Immortal Technique, GOODIE MOB, and Tupac; habitus, through Bourdieu and *The Matrix*.

Next, the class developed a list of influential elements of youth popular culture that they could analyze using those terms. The list included television shows, movies, music, fast food, snack food, advertisements, videogames, fashion, and sports. Students were then placed in groups of five according to the neighborhoods where they lived, so that when they later went into the community as a research team they would already have experience working together. Each group chose a guiding sociological term to add to the list of three core terms above. These were sociological terms that we had discussed in class or that students had investigated on their own, such as "social degradation" or "social reproduction." In their groups, students used their selected term and the three core terms to conduct a sociological analysis of the various forms of popular culture that they and their peers interact with regularly. We did some initial modeling of this with the class, after which the students spent a week doing their own research and analysis.

After their study, students used PowerPoint to develop twenty-five-minute research presentations to explain the presence or absence of the four sociological terms in the popular culture they studied. These presentations were attended by members of the school community, including teachers, administrators, students who were not in the class, community members, and parents. The presentations consisted of a literature review, in which they explained the terms they had learned to the audience. This forced them to rephrase much of the academic language traditionally used to explain sociological phenomena so that people without their level of training in sociology could understand their work. After the literature review, students presented examples from their research to reveal the existence of these sociological phenomena in popular culture and to explain their analysis of the community impact.

Segment 2: Planning and Implementing through Street Sociology. This segment prepared students to move their research on sociological terms to their community. We spent a week-and-a-half giving students basic training in qualitative research methods. We began by introducing them to an adapted version of Burawoy's (1998)"extended case method." Burawoy's approach has the ethnographic researcher conduct the following four steps: examine existing theory, enter the field as a participant-observer, document counter-instances of the theory, and reconstruct theory on the basis of those observations. We adapted Burawoy's approach by putting the tools of study, research, and theory construction into the hands of the students themselves (Buroway's "natives"), rather than keeping them in the hands of the university researcher.

Each research group used their lived experience and studies of social theory and popular culture to develop a hypothesis about what they would see when they studied their community. The idea here was that they would take the prevailing logic about their community (dysfunctional, pathological, resource poor, disenfranchised, hopeless, hostile), including their own notions, and investigate whether these assumptions were borne out in fact or whether there was significant evidence to counter these opinions.

To prepare the class to carry out the extended case method in the community, students received a week of training on basic ethnographic research tools:

- digital video and still photography
- observational field notes
- formal and informal interviews
- basic surveys
- artifact collection

Students practiced these techniques with each other and around the school and then hit the streets of their community over the next three weeks to collect data. We would take out two groups, one group at a time, during lunch and then again after school. Each group had at least one video camera and one still camera to gather visual evidence and to conduct interviews. Groups were largely self-directed during their field research. They told us where they wanted to go, and they decided how to split themselves up.

Segment 3: Evaluating—Data Analysis and Research Conference. After the field research, the next four weeks were spent analyzing the data and preparing for a research conference that would once again be attended by key stakeholders in the school community. The groups had to prepare three main products for the conference: a twenty-minute PowerPoint presentation, an eight- to ten-minute "Blocumentary" film, and a twelve- to fifteen-page research report. The division of labor for these products was the decision of the research group. The minimum requirements for each of the products were as follows:

- The PowerPoint presentation needed to have slides covering their literature review of social theoretical terms, research methods, hypothesis, findings, and reconstructed theory.
- The research report needed to have sections covering the same topics as the PowerPoint.
- The "Blocumentary" film needed to have visual examples of the social theoretical terms, counter-instances, and reconstructed theory.

Implications of a THUG LIFE Pedagogy. Gramsci (1971) wrote that "all [people] are intellectuals, one could therefore say; but not all [people] have in the society the function of intellectuals" (p. 9). He went on to argue that schools are often the social institution used to validate this unnatural division in a society, one where an individual is cast as either *Homo sapiens* (one who thinks/works with his or her mind) or *Homo faber* (one who labors/works with his or her hands). A pan-ethnic studies approach to educational research demands a methodology steeped in *cariño* for the people and the community where the work is being done. Such an approach should deconstruct the division between thinker and worker and replace it with a paradigm that values the intellectual potential in all people. This was also Tupac's dream—that those who had the least would reclaim their humanity through self-determination.

The Doc Ur Block project was a commitment to those principles of humanization by providing young people an education that prepares them to analyze their world critically. It put tools of critical thinking, research, and intellectual production in the hands of young people so that they could counter-narrate pathological stories of their families and communities. Along the way, many students discovered that they too had come to believe the dominant discourse about their community and had lost sight of the countless indicators of hope and strength that are present on their blocks everyday. As one example of this budding awareness, Assata made the following comments while presenting her group's research at the American Educational Research Association's national conference:

> To be completely honest ... we didn't think we were going to see any counter-hegemony in our community because we believed the hegemony just like everybody else. That's why our key data, the stuff we just [presented], is so important because it proves us wrong about our own community.

This project did not attempt to shelter students from the harsh reality of urban life. In fact, while one group was conducting an interview on the block, they witnessed the shooting of a high-school-age student and chose to include the footage of the incident in their film. When they returned to the classroom to reconstruct their theory, they developed the term "habitus of hopelessness" to describe these types of self-defeating actions by community members. However, the project also allowed them to find counter-instances to negative responses to the conditions of oppression in the community. That same group called this the "agency of hope." In fact, every group reconstructed social theory to capture the strength and self-determination that they witnessed. Assata's group used the term "counter-hegemony" to describe the hopefulness they saw from people in their community, which she also explained during their presentation:

> We found people like Mike Rubio, the director of Youth Uprising [a youth community center in east Oakland that fights for social justice], and we asked him:
> "Would you build another Youth Uprising in Oakland?"
> "No," he said, "I would build fifty more and that's just in Oakland. This idea should be replicated throughout the country and world."
> He does not promote individualism; instead, he provides a sense of community for the youth in Oakland. In addition, we found counter-hegemony in everyday people on the street. We interviewed Tiffany, an African American female in her twenties who teaches hip-hop classes throughout the Bay area. She goes against the degradation of women in the media. She also shows women that they have the

agency to resist degradation. And although women are degraded by the media's use
of hip-hop she uses the same institution to be counter-hegemonic.

So what's really missing from our community? The media would say hope, desire, and dedication to change. But our data proves otherwise. As you can see, 59%
of the people we surveyed said they would open up a youth center that fights for justice. So hope, desire, and dedication isn't what's missing from our community. Instead, it's the funding to support our community.

So what are the implications of this study? We found that people outside our
community use the four cultural institutions, school, media, religion, and family, to
tell our stories, and as a result, black and brown youth are degraded by much of the
dominant hegemony. We also found that there is room to resist through counter-
narratives and counter-hegemony. Black and brown people controlling and producing their own stories, this is a counter-narrative. The importance of this is that these
are truthful stories about Oakland, and this will lead to counter-hegemony. It will
influence other people to tell their own stories, and this is counter-hegemonic.

After Assata's analysis, her research partner Malcolm concluded their
conference presentation by explaining "diffusion theory." This was the theory
they reconstructed on the basis of their research and their belief that counter-
hegemonic practices can be expanded by everyday people. In front of a stand-
ing-room-only audience of more than 150 graduate students and professors,
Malcolm shared this as the group's theory of change:

When you affect many people you have power, and when you have power people listen. When you get people to listen to you, you get people to understand you because
they wouldn't be listening to you for nothing right? ... Y'all know how a rumor will
pass, right? Y'all know how long it takes to pass a rumor to twenty people? It can
pass in thirty seconds. So, my knowledge, and what my group is telling y'all ... If
y'all talk to your students about the knowledge you soaked up today, that you understand today, at least 1,000 more people out there can understand. By talking to your
family, your students, your friends, just five of 'em, not twenty or thirty, just five of
'em. That five can tell five more, one of them five can tell five more, five more, five
more, and it adds up and next thing you know 20,000 people can know. And 20,000
people can change stuff. If 20,000 people get together not just in Oakland, California, not just in Houston, not just in Chicago, not just in Florida, not just in New
York, everybody, this whole United States, we can take it farther than the United
States. We can take it to Africa. We can take it to Asia, pass our knowledge down,
and everybody can know. So basically that's what the diffusion theory means. It can
be done. Ain't nothing impossible. Nothing.

Groups also developed the terms "popular materialism," "counter-
habitus," and "agency of hope." These reconstructed theories exemplified
high-level intellectual production, but they were also examples of hopefulness

that are mostly absent from our communities and from the lives of urban youth. The real value of this project rests in the way it helped students re-envision their communities and their roles in creating and contributing to counter-narratives that promote hope and self-determination.

Students as Critical Public Historians

In the second case discussed here, Morrell examines a summer research program (described in Chapter 6) where high school students attending schools in Greater Los Angeles learned to conduct critical historical research pertaining to the educational experiences of students of color who had attended city schools over the previous fifty years. Morrell examines the student work as an example of youth-initiated praxis. He also looks at the work as an example of student literacy development, of student-initiated research, and of the intersections between critical pedagogy, public history, and pan-ethnic studies.

In July and August 2003, thirty students attending high schools in various neighborhoods of urban Los Angeles participated in a six-week seminar in which they developed research projects that studied the educational experiences of people of color who attended LA schools in the post-*Brown* era (each of the five groups studied one post-*Brown* decade). Students collected oral history interviews, examined statistical databases, and researched other historical artifacts such as yearbooks, newspaper articles, and photographs. As a result of their involvement, students created research reports, Power-Point presentations, and short films that documented life in Los Angeles schools for students of color during the post-*Brown* decades.

Figures 7.1 and 7.2 are examples of how students used geographic information systems (GIS) software to document the rapid changes in Los Angeles' population during the 1950s and 1960s. As neighborhoods became more integrated, students of color began to experience more overt forms of segregation within and between schools as district administrators worked to keep the merging groups apart. Many students interviewed by the 1950s and 1960s groups spoke to the racial tensions present in their schools and communities during that time. Others spoke to the ways that students of various ethnicities came together during that period to exist in relative racial harmony. Unfortunately, by the late 1970s, there were very few white students left in many of these communities, and schools have been largely segregated since. However, in their research, the students were able to collect meaningful demographic data that helped to create an important counter-narrative of schooling for students of color in the city.

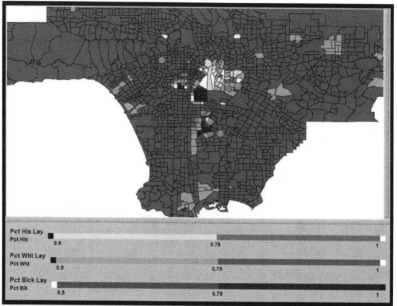

Figure 7.1. Census Tracts by Ethnicity in Los Angeles in 1950
Source: 2003 Summer Seminar Student Research Report

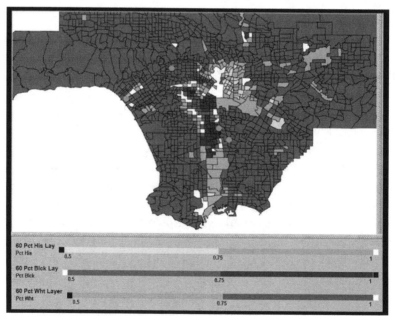

Figure 7.2. Census Tracts by Ethnicity in Los Angeles in 1960
Source: 2003 Summer Seminar Student Research Report

The students also used qualitative methods, particularly in the oral history methodology, to collect the narratives of various participants in Los Angeles public schools during the half-century following *Brown*. In this way, the students were inhabiting an emergent research tradition in history and ethnic studies employed by scholars such as Ronald Takaki and Charles Payne, who were critical of top-down approaches to historical research that omitted the voices of everyday people who had experienced history and who also contributed to history. Although the students were interviewing anyone who had experienced LA schools in the post-*Brown* era, they were especially interested in students of color who had participated in the numerous movements for social and educational justice in the neighborhoods, communities, and schools of Los Angeles. The traditional political historians and sociologists who studied education in the city ignored many of the students' actions over the years. Two quotes taken from oral history interviews that the students conducted for their research are appropriate:

> In wealthier neighborhoods, a quality education is a human right, in low-income neighborhoods students have to fight for a good education, let alone take advantage of it.

> Violence was a way of life at Downtown High School; we would always hear gunshots around the neighborhood and for us it became more like roadside traffic. Due to this, students became more accepting of violence, as we were more susceptible to violent activities.

These excerpts reveal the power of being able to testify to one's experiences as well as the power of researchers who are able to capture and record these testimonies. We found that adults were more than willing to talk to the youth researchers about their experiences. Our youth were invited into community centers and the homes as well as other sacred spaces of their elders, some of whom had experienced life in many of the same schools that our students were now attending. The elders viewed the interviews as opportunities finally to share their stories; they also used these interactions to communicate directly with the next generation about the importance of education. Every interview that Morrell witnessed contained some element of cultural transmission, where the adult stepped out of the role of interviewee and assumed the role of cultural expert and elder. And in those moments they almost always talked to the students about the suffering and advocacy that had occurred in the past to ensure that they would have the right to become educated. These encounters were powerful for all parties involved.

Outcomes. Many important outcomes are associated with this summer intervention with teens of color. First and foremost, the seminar intervention allowed these students to develop a different relationship to history, to historical research, and to narratives surrounding ethnicity, culture, and education in their city. For example, students of color created history in that they added scholarly research to the historical archives (elements of their work were archived at a local historical library, and their research reports were presented to multiple audiences of residents, policymakers, and leaders in the city). They also became involved in history-making research. They were history-making agents in the sense that youth are rarely positioned as the cultivators and collectors of their neighborhood and cultural histories. They were also history-making agents in terms of the substance and methodology of the research itself.

Through this process, they articulated the foundation of a new research method, what became known to them as critical public history. We say that these methods are new because the subjects of the research are everyday people and their struggles for resistance against inequitable educational conditions. Rather than tell the historical narrative from an examination of policy documents, students interviewed former youth participants in Los Angeles schooling; they looked at high school yearbooks and other personal artifacts such as newspapers and magazine articles (Figure 7.3). When the students did analyze policy and quantitative data, they did so through a critical lens that focused on issues of race and class and inequality. For instance, when students studied census and educational attainment data, they developed the hypotheses that the increase in the Latino population in certain sections of the city had led to decreased attention to the educational needs of students. That is, as the population of the neighborhoods began to change in the 1960s and 1970s, public attitudes toward those schools began to change for the worse.

The scholarship is critical public history also because the positioning of youth as historians and intellectuals fundamentally challenges the perspective of who is normally able to do this kind of work. It is significant that youth, and youth of color at that, were conducting oral history interviews and excavating narratives of the experiences of youth of color in their city schools over a fifty-year period. As the inheritors of an impoverished and inequitable set of educational conditions, these students have a different relationship to the historical knowledge that they collect and analyze because this historical knowledge also shapes their present relationship to their schools and society. In this way, the process of engaging in critical public history creates tools and narratives of resistance and transformation for those involved. In this case, the incoming high school seniors were able to reposition themselves in relationship to their own histories and to their school system, and they were able to share valuable information with community organizations, academicians, parents, peers, and policymakers who were all actively involved in the struggles for educational, social, and racial justice in their city and in their schools.

Yearbook Analysis Protocol

School _____

Year_____

Ethnicity of Students

	Sample page #: ____ Total # of students on page: ____ Grade level of these students: ____		Sample page #: Total # of students on page: ____ Grade level of these students: ____	
	number	percent	number	percent
African American				
Asian				
Hispanic/Latino/ Spanish Surname				
Native American				
White (Non-Hispanic)				
Other				

Ethnicity of Teachers

	Total # of teachers: ____	
	number	percent
African American		
Asian		
Hispanic/Latino/ Spanish Surname		
Native American		
White (Non-Hispanic)		
Other		

Estimated Dropout Rate

year	# of freshmen	year (4 years later)	# of seniors	estimated dropouts	
				#	%

Figure 7.3. Yearbook Analysis Protocol Used by Student Historians

Through this process, the students were able to obtain information that complicated their view of race relations in their city and in their schools. For example, the historical narratives of integration and racial equity were not as one-sided as many imagined. The students actually found historical periods when certain Los Angeles schools were more integrated than they are today. And they found examples where students of color were more involved in the fabric of school life in multiethnic schools than they are in the present. The students also found that there was no tale of unequivocal hatred or unlimited progress in their city schools. They found examples, such as when the white students of a particular Westside school walked out in protest at the internment of their Japanese classmates during World War II, where students of different racial backgrounds stood together in solidarity against racist, imperialist policies. Students found many other disconfirming narratives of agency, resistance, and harmony in the Los Angeles public schools, causing them to question the source and intent of the narratives they had grown up with.

Students developed sophisticated research skills. They learned how to conduct oral history interviews, they learned how to develop and analyze surveys, they learned how to access historical archives, they learned how to access large quantitative databases, and they learned the art of documentary filmmaking. Students also developed sophisticated literacy skills such as note taking, the collection of field notes, the ability to read social theoretical literature and educational research, the ability to write literature reviews, and, ultimately, the ability to create extensive research reports and personal critical memoirs that were, at once, critical life histories and exemplars of social and cultural analysis.

Here we briefly mention some of the social, historical, political, and academic outcomes associated with the students' development as critical public historians. This example of critical pan-ethnic studies in practice addresses both the need to develop academic skills and competencies in urban youth and the need of members of marginalized ethnic groups and communities to develop their knowledge base about important narratives of struggle and resistance.

Recommendations for Education. To move toward this pan-ethnic framework in education, we make the following recommendations for classroom teachers, school administrators, teacher educators, and educational researchers:

- Focus on student production of knowledge (rather than consumption of knowledge).
- Focus on collective agency.
- Create opportunities for students to be public intellectuals.
- Develop a pedagogy of the city (and community).
- Prioritize cariño in pedagogies and research methodologies.

The creation of legitimate space for pan-ethnic studies in K–12 education will also require the inclusion of stand-alone courses in ethnic studies and urban sociology courses such as the one we have discussed here. The principles and practices of pan-ethnic studies must intersect with traditional K–12 content areas such as English, social studies, math, and science, as we see in the Los Angeles project. School districts have met this challenge in places such as Tucson Unified, where they have implemented a K–12 ethnic studies program. The Mexican-American/Raza studies program, in particular, has had a dramatic impact on the engagement and achievement of its participants, owing largely to its development of Raza studies classes that provide students with pedagogy that meets all of the recommendations listed above (Cammarota & Romero, 2006). The issue we face as educators seems to be less about know-how and more about our courage and commitment to meet this challenge.

Appendix A

10th-Grade Urban Sociology
Course Reader
Table of Contents

Technique, I. (2001). Poverty of philosophy. On *Revolutionary*, Vol. 1 [CD]. New York: Viper Records.

Gramsci, A. (1999). Intellectuals and hegemony. In C. Lemert (Ed.), *Social theory: The multicultural and classic readings* (pp. 259–261). Boulder, CO: Westview. [Reprinted from *Selections from the Prison Notebooks*, New York: International Publishers, 1971.]

Bourdieu, P. (1999). Structure, habitus, practices. In C. Lemert (Ed.), *Social theory: The multicultural and classic readings* (pp. 441–446). Boulder, CO: Westview. [Reprinted from *The logic of practice*, Stanford: Stanford University Press, 1990.]

Malcolm X. (1965). A message to the grass roots. In G. Breitman (Ed.), *Malcolm X Speaks* (pp. 3–17). New York: Grove Press.

Malcolm X. (1965). To Mississippi youth. In G. Breitman (Ed.), *Malcolm X Speaks* (pp. 137-146). New York: Grove Press.

Freire, P. (1970). *Pedagogy of the Oppressed.* Ch.1 & 2 (pp. 43–86). New York: Continuum.

Sólorzano, D., & D. Delgado-Bernal. (2001). Examining transformational resistance through a critical race and LatCrit theory framework: Chicana and Chicano students in an urban context. *Urban Education,* 36 (3), 308–342.

8
Critical Pedagogy in an Age of Standards

In our penultimate chapter we revisit the conclusions from the case studies to consider the interrelation between critical pedagogy in urban education and the debates over standards that currently plague the nation. We begin by acknowledging the current moment in education as important, albeit misguided. Although standards and standardized tests have been used largely to label and to constrain curricula and pedagogies, members of the public have a right to expect that educators and the educational establishment will adequately educate their children. When we fail to do so, and when we lose the public trust, politicians are able to push through legislation such as No Child Left Behind (NCLB). The public has recently reconsidered its endorsement of this legislation, and it behooves us as critical educators to separate the legitimate reasons for their critique from our legitimate critiques of the nature of standards discourse and the harmful outcomes for teaching and learning associated with the culture (or, better yet, regime) of testing that has followed in the wake of NCLB.

We want to state explicitly that this is not a chapter about standardized tests, which we generally find indefensible in the ways that they have taken over the public discourse about educational attainment and the ways in which they have invaded school curricula and actually changed how many teachers approach the profession (McNeil, 2000). Students are being tested with increased frequency, and the tests are being given greater weight than ever before, even though what they actually purport to assess is very limited (Kohn, 2000). Members of the public and politicians seem fixated with the idea of objectified tests, even though the tests, given the biases of the creators and the idiosyncrasies of the students and the conditions, are not objective measures. Standardized tests are to be interrogated and critiqued, not accepted unquestioningly, and even though students are stuck with them for the present moment, we do not have to acquiesce quietly; compliance doesn't have to be complicity. If students are to be tested and judged on the basis of their performance on tests, we remain constant in our assertions that critical pedagogy is the best approach to test preparation in that students are developing important skills that will allow them to perform on the tests as they also develop the language to critique the structure and nature of the tests that they must take if they are to make it successfully through the K–12 system.

That being said, we also endeavor to make important distinctions between standardized tests and disciplinary standards, which oftentimes do have a logic for educators. Disciplinary standards are not unproblematic; the movement toward standardization can limit individuality, cultural diversity, and creativity for students and teachers and run counter to our goals of providing access to an authentic citizenship education (Meier, 2000). These standards, however, do have at least some basis in the learning and demonstration of discipline-specific tasks and, at their best, describe processes for information consumption and production that are important for young people to acquire. We do, for instance, want our youth to understand culture, time, and geography. We want our future parents, leaders, and professionals to be exposed to a wide range of literature, and we want them to be able to write across multiple genres. We want activist citizens who are able to reason mathematically and problem solve. In the remaining sections of this chapter we show how a critical pedagogy of urban education helps to meet many of the legitimate standards across disciplines, paying particular attention to the frameworks provided by organizations in English/language arts, social studies, and mathematics. We conclude by considering how a critical pedagogy of education may help us to re-think the language we employ to talk about standards and the measures we use to evaluate student learning.

The Standards Question

Everyone, from both the left and the right, is talking about standards these days. Although they cannot agree on anything else in education, it seems that both sides can agree on the need for standards. Their reasons for the convergence are varied, but it is important to acknowledge them all. For one, there is a fundamental disappointment with public education and a pervasive belief that schools are not doing what they should to educate the population of the future. This belief is held by rich and poor alike. If the participants in education feel as though they are getting a raw deal, it behooves educators to listen. The public grows weary with teachers' unions calling for strikes when the students attend dilapidated schools with outdated textbooks, if any. Voting members of the public strike back at requests for tax increases and bonds when they perceive their money is going down the tube. This end of the public, worried about future pensions, qualified workers, or even the economic prospects for their descendants, look at standards and tests as checks on a dysfunctional system, a way of holding the adults in the system accountable for educating children. Without them, they feel, school personnel would be comfortable with the same mediocre results. How can we blame a large segment of our public for feeling this way?

There is another segment of the public that views the schools as hotbeds of liberalism and liberal discourse. They see schools as unloading a liberal dogma on unsuspecting youth rather than teaching the three Rs. These people claim that schools are supposed to be politically neutral places that teach students skills, not ideologies. And to the extent that schools teach ideologies, they should be pro-American. Many members of the voting public view schools as anti-religion, anti-white, anti-Republican, or even anti-American. They openly lament the fact that the National Education Association endorses Democratic presidents and they cry foul when studies show that the overwhelming majority of professors in postsecondary education self-identify as liberals. They also see the political education as detracting from the mission at hand, which is to teach the students the academic skills they need to contribute to the global marketplace. These members of the public envision standards as a way to keep liberal educators in line, to ensure that they leave their politics at home and stick to the business of educating children.

Regardless of how we might counter either of these viewpoints, it is important to acknowledge the large consensus on the need for standards. While the public may be growing weary with an over-dependence on standardized tests, the call for externally imposed guidelines on the practice of teaching and the measurement of learning is undeniable. As educators, the notion that the public feels that they are more interested in student achievement than we are should trouble us. This bears acknowledging, even if we fail to agree with the public assessment of urban public education. The external conversations about standards are a testament both to the increasing importance of public education and to the public's waning faith in that public education system. And while we may offer our own critiques of their critiques, we owe it to those we educate to pause and ask ourselves whether we are doing all we can to educate all children. In addition, we need to seek out ways to demonstrate student learning to the students themselves and to larger publics in ways that restore confidence among both populations. And, of course, we feel strongly that critical pedagogy should not be seen as antithetical to these goals; rather, we see the outcomes associated with critical pedagogy as consonant with our vision of the educated citizen.

This chapter, then, is not a diatribe against standards and their proponents, nor is it a blind stamp for the status quo. It is a reflection, using critical theory and critical pedagogy, on the past, present, and possible future of

standards and measures of student learning and achievement. Regardless of
how we feel about current standards, we need to understand how important
they are to important constituents in education, the most important of whom
are the students themselves. They do not have the leisure of deciding
whether they agree with education standards, because they are evaluated
against them for better or worse. The standards are the gatekeeper that
stands between them and their future. Most of these students adopt a pragmatic approach to the standards; they figure out what is asked of them and
they attempt to do it or head for the door. Unless they navigate the standards, though, they cannot successfully navigate the K–12 educational system, nor can they access higher education in any meaningful way. For this
reason, they need to be understood by critical pedagogues working within
urban education. Unfortunately, critical pedagogy has been extremely silent
on the pragmatic end of the standards question. This chapter aims to break
that silence. We also aim to contribute to conversations about finding alternative ways to measure student performance that are consistent with our vi-
sions of critical education.

Critical Pedagogy and Academic Standards

We began this book by acknowledging the myriad ways that schools serving
low-income students fail to provide them with an adequate education. We
then proposed that a critical approach to education would allow educators to
engage students academically, intellectually, and socially. We would be re-
miss, then, to evade the issue of standards in education. Our entire approach
has been one that puts forth critical pedagogy as the backbone of educational
interventions that go above and beyond the standards. In the preceding five
chapters, we outlined projects that challenged students to read the word and
the world and to use their intellectual capabilities to act upon the world in
empowering ways. In Chapter 3, for instance, students applied critical lenses
to analyze literature, and they became writers of expository texts and poems.
In Chapter 4 members of a women's basketball team used their interest in
athletics to learn academic concepts and to struggle for social justice in their
schools and communities. In Chapter 5, a college access program apprenticed students of color as scholars and activists and provided a context for a
civic education that included academic rigor and social action. In Chapter 6,
a summer seminar challenged students to read social theory, to develop
mixed-method research projects, to write research reports, and to present

their findings to a public audience that included experts and community leaders. And, in Chapter 7, students became public historians and created their own counter-narratives of the experiences of youth of color in the city schools in the half-century following the *Brown v. Board of Education* decision. Each of these interventions focused explicitly on developing the core academic competencies and the confidence and motivation needed to navigate educational standards successfully. We accessed the disciplinary standards of the National Council of Teachers of English (NCTE), the National Council of Teachers of Mathematics (NCTM), and the National Council for the Social Studies (NCSS) to demonstrate how the projects we describe intersect with the disciplinary goals of these three organizations.

National Council for the Social Studies

The NCSS (http://www.socialstudies.org) identifies ten thematic strands that should form the basis of any social studies standards (Table 8.1). A close analysis of these strands shows that a critical pedagogical framework closely parallels the goals that social studies educators have for students. For example, strand 1 requires that social studies programs include experiences that provide for the study of culture and diversity. In each of the summer seminars, in the Futures project, and in the sociology course at Northeast Community High School, students studied cultural practices in their local experiences. These students were also able to understand the relationships between culture and power, and they were also able to make recommendations for how educators could utilize non-school cultural practices in homes and communities to make connections with academic content. Through this process of studying culture in local contexts, students acquired skills as ethnographers and engaged in high levels of reading and writing. The students collected quantitative data that revealed the demographics of the community; they also collected interview data, field notes, digital photographs, and digital video footage.

Strand 2 requires that social studies programs include experiences that provide for the study of the ways human beings view themselves over time. Our 2003 summer seminar required students to collect the viewpoints of participants in city schools over a fifty-year period. These students also studied census data that revealed changing population patterns in the city over this same period. By engaging in critical work aimed at educational equity and justice, these students gained a sophisticated historical understanding of life in Los Angeles for young people of color in the last half of the twentieth century. We could go on, but it is obvious how critical work can prepare students to study culture, history, society, and change while also helping them see themselves as informed intellectuals and agents of change. Finally, critical projects can help young people to develop as readers, writers, and speakers as they collect, analyze, and present information to multiple audiences through multiple genres. We say more about the reading and writing development of our students when we examine the curriculum frameworks for the English language arts.

1. *Culture.* Social studies programs should include experiences that provide for the study of culture and cultural diversity.
2. *Time, Continuity, and Change.* Social studies programs should include experiences that provide for the study of the ways human beings view themselves in and over time.
3. *People, Places, and Environments.* Social studies programs should include experiences that provide for the study of people, places, and environments.
4. *Individual Development and Identity.* Social studies programs should include experiences that provide for the study of individual development and identity.
5. *Individuals, Groups, and Institutions.* Social studies programs should include experiences that provide for the study of interactions among individuals, groups, and institutions.
6. *Power, Authority, and Governance.* Social studies programs should include experiences that provide for the study of how people create and change structures of power, authority, and governance.
7. *Production, Distribution, and Consumption.* Social studies programs should include experiences that provide for the study of how people organize for the production, distribution, and consumption of goods and services.
8. *Science, Technology, and Society.* Social studies programs should include experiences that provide for the study of relationships among science, technology, and society.
9. *Global Connections.* Social studies programs should include experiences that provide for the study of global connections and interdependence.
10. *Civic Ideals and Practices.* Social studies programs should include experiences that provide for the study of the ideals, principles, and practices of citizenship in a democratic republic.

Table 8.1. NCSS Thematic Strands
Source: http://www.socialstudies.org

National Council of Teachers of English

In a similar vein, the NCTE offers a dozen standards that should form the core of K–12 English/language arts programs (Table 8.2). We paid attention to these standards as we developed our curricula in our East Bay High School English class and in our various interventions across the Futures project, the summer seminar, and the sociology course at Northeast City High School. Like Freire, we believed that any reading of the word would be informed and strengthened by a reading of the world. We also believed that an ability to re-write the world was essential to true revolutionary praxis in our information age. Furthermore, we understood that students needed strong literacy skills to navigate the world of secondary and post-secondary education effectively. For all of these purposes, we wanted to be able to articulate the numerous overlaps between the practice of critical pedagogy and the development of disciplinary proficiency in the English language arts.

We discuss briefly a few intersections that become obvious from an overview of the standards. Standards 1 and 2 require students to read a wide range of print and non-print texts to come to an understanding of the human experience and to respond to the needs and demands of society. In the process of acquiring a critical perspective on the development of Western society, our English students read classical texts such as Homer's *Odyssey* and Shakespeare's *Othello*, in addition to contemporary texts such as *Native Son* and popular texts such as Francis Ford Coppola's *Godfather* films. In preparing to become critical sociologists, our seminar students read graduate-level texts in the sociology of education.

Standards 5, 11, and 12 deal with students as writers for public consumption and as members of a variety of literate communities. In all of our interventions, there were ample opportunities for students to write across a variety of genres for multiple private and public purposes. In the context of critical analyses, community-based research, and advocacy for social justice, students wrote journal entries, field notes, lecture notes, reading notes, essays, poems, interview protocols, surveys, PowerPoint slides, and research reports, to name a few. Students took many of these public documents though multiple stages of the writing process from brainstorming to revision, and many of these documents were published in legitimate outlets ranging from online archives, to newspapers, to poetry anthologies, to peer-reviewed academic journals and book chapters. In addition, students used their new media skills to create digital documentaries that have been aired on numerous Web sites and in public presentations.

1. Students read a wide range of print and non-print texts to build an understanding of texts, of themselves, and of the cultures of the United States and the world; to acquire new information; to respond to the needs and demands of society and the workplace; and for personal fulfillment. Among these texts are fiction and non-fiction, classic and contemporary works.
2. Students read a wide range of literature from many periods in many genres to build an understanding of the many dimensions (e.g., philosophical, ethical, aesthetic) of human experience.
3. Students apply a wide range of strategies to comprehend, interpret, evaluate, and appreciate texts. They draw on their prior experience, their interactions with other readers and writers, their knowledge of word meaning and of other texts, their word identification strategies, and their understanding of textual features (e.g., sound-letter correspondence, sentence structure, context, graphics).
4. Students adjust their use of spoken, written, and visual language (e.g., conventions, style, vocabulary) to communicate effectively with a variety of audiences and for different purposes.
5. Students employ a wide range of strategies as they write and use different writing process elements appropriately to communicate with different audiences for a variety of purposes.
6. Students apply knowledge of language structure, language conventions (e.g., spelling and punctuation), media techniques, figurative language, and genre to create, critique, and discuss print and non-print texts.
7. Students conduct research on issues and interests by generating ideas and questions, and by posing problems. They gather, evaluate, and synthesize data from a variety of sources (e.g., print and non-print texts, artifacts, people) to communicate their discoveries in ways that suit their purpose and audience.
8. Students use a variety of technological and information resources (e.g., libraries, databases, computer networks, video) to gather and synthesize information and to create and communicate knowledge.
9. Students develop an understanding of and respect for diversity in language use, patterns, and dialects across cultures, ethnic groups, geographic regions, and social roles.
10. Students whose first language is not English make use of their first language to develop competency in the English language arts and to develop understanding of content across the curriculum.
11. Students participate as knowledgeable, reflective, creative, and critical members of a variety of literacy communities.
12. Students use spoken, written, and visual language to accomplish their own purposes (e.g., for learning, enjoyment, persuasion, and the exchange of information).

Table 8.2. NCTE Standards for the English Language Arts
Source: http://www.ncte.org/about/over/standards/110846.htm

National Council of Teachers of Mathematics

Although much of our early work focused on the correlations between critical pedagogy and academic literacy development, our work in schools alerted us to the abysmal performance of students of color in mathematics (U.S. Department of Education, 2005). We knew it was important to begin to explore connections between critical pedagogy and the development of mathematical competencies. At the same time, our own research interests convinced us of the importance of critical quantitative work to the goals of educational equity and access. Given this convergence of interests and desires, we made a concerted effort to include mathematical reasoning and quantitative research in the work of the seminars. Students began to incorporate survey research, census data, educational attainment data, and GIS programming, which required them to plot data into regional and neighborhood maps. A study performed by an educational psychologist (Rogers, Morrell, & Enyedy, 2007) revealed that the GIS mapping increased the students' ability to reason mathematically.

In addition, the quantitative and statistical database research offered opportunities for the students to develop their problem-solving and processing abilities (Tables 8.3 and 8.4). When we were researching educational attainment in Los Angeles schools, for instance, students developed many questions that required them to increase their mathematical proficiency. Students became interested in dropout rates, in test scores, and in correlations between income levels and educational outcomes in local neighborhoods. Moreover, students wanted to ascertain their peers' opinions on a variety of educational issues, so they created annual surveys that they distributed to high school students around the city. The data from the surveys (usually in the neighborhood of 500 sets) were inputted, and the students were given reports that they could manipulate for their research ends. Students presented analyses from the surveys and statistical databases via maps, charts, tables, and graphs that facilitated communication of their findings to a number of different audiences.

Instructional programs from pre-kindergarten through grade 12 should enable all students to:
Build new mathematical knowledge through problem solving;
Solve problems that arise in mathematics and in other contexts;
Apply and adapt a variety of appropriate strategies to solve problems;
Monitor and reflect on the process of mathematical problem solving.

Table 8.3. Problem-Solving Standards for Grades 9–12
Source: http://standards.nctm.org/document/chapter7/prob.htm

Problem Solving. Solving problems is not only a goal of learning mathematics but also a major means of doing so. It is an integral part of mathematics, not an isolated piece of the mathematics program. Students require frequent opportunities to formulate, grapple with, and solve complex problems that involve a significant amount of effort. They are to be encouraged to reflect on their thinking during the problem-solving process so that they can apply and adapt the strategies they develop to other problems and in other contexts. By solving mathematical problems, students acquire ways of thinking, habits of persistence and curiosity, and confidence in unfamiliar situations that serve them well outside the mathematics classroom.

Reasoning and Proof. Mathematical reasoning and proof offer powerful ways of developing and expressing insights about a wide range of phenomena. People who reason and think analytically tend to note patterns, structure, or regularities in both real-world and mathematical situations. They ask if those patterns are accidental or if they occur for a reason. They make and investigate mathematical conjectures. They develop and evaluate mathematical arguments and proofs, which are formal ways of expressing particular kinds of reasoning and justification. By exploring phenomena, justifying results, and using mathematical conjectures in all content areas and—with different expectations of sophistication at all grade levels, students should see and expect that mathematics makes sense.

Communication. Mathematical communication is a way of sharing ideas and clarifying understanding. Through communication, ideas become objects of reflection, refinement, discussion, and amendment. When students are challenged to communicate the results of their thinking to others orally or in writing, they learn to be clear, convincing, and precise in their use of mathematical language. Explanations should include mathematical arguments and rationales, not just procedural descriptions or summaries. Listening to others' explanations gives students opportunities to develop their own understandings. Conversations in which mathematical ideas are explored from multiple perspectives help the participants sharpen their thinking and make connections.

Connections. Mathematics is not a collection of separate strands or standards, even though it is often partitioned and presented in this manner. Rather, mathematics is an integrated field of study. When students connect mathematical ideas, their understanding is deeper and more lasting, and they come to view mathematics as a coherent whole. They see mathematical connections in the rich interplay among mathematical topics, in contexts that relate mathematics to other subjects, and in their own interests and experience. Through instruction that emphasizes the interrelatedness of mathematical ideas, students learn not only mathematics but also about the utility of mathematics.

Representations. Mathematical ideas can be represented in a variety of ways: pictures, concrete materials, tables, graphs, number and letter symbols, spreadsheet displays, and so on. The ways in which mathematical ideas are represented is fundamental to how people understand and use those ideas. Many of the representations we now take for granted are the result of a process of cultural refinement that took place over many years. When students gain access to mathematical representations and the ideas they express and when they can create representations to capture mathematical concepts or relationships, they acquire a set of tools that significantly expand their capacity to model and interpret physical, social, and mathematical phenomena.

Table 8.4. NCTM Process Standards
Source: http://www.nctm.org/uploadedFiles/Math_Standards/12752_exec_pssm.pdf

Standards in Context

Although we have endeavored to make a pragmatic argument in this chapter that critical pedagogy can contribute to the achievement of disciplinary standards, we do not want to excuse the circumstances within which students are educated, nor do we want to adhere blindly to the logic of the standards in the core disciplines. As critical educators, we must remain vigilant against the inherent racism embedded within the standards as well as the structural conditions that limit the opportunities of certain students, who are still held accountable for the same standards. Students who attend schools without adequate facilities, without credentialed teachers or rigorous courses, are still held to the same scrutiny as students who have received everything that money can buy. We also need to remain vigilant against the institutional racism prevalent in schools that contributes to a sense of alienation as well as outcomes such as the stereotype threat, where students who have been marginalized within a system underperform on high-stakes assignments out of fear of how they will be perceived by those in power. These are real issues that require real solutions. The bottom line, however, is that if critical pedagogy provided urban students with better skills and greater confidence, as well as a sense of humanity, they would perform better than they do on educational standards and standardized assessments.

Rethinking Standards in an Age of Critical Pedagogy

Critical educators involved in the current educational system must often play the role of radical pragmatists. Much of what needs to be done requires us to wear the pragmatic hat. It is not possible, for instance, to ignore the practical realities associated with the culture of testing and standards. For this reason, we have devoted a significant portion of this chapter to the myriad ways that critical pedagogy may help to improve students' abilities to meet disciplinary standards and perform on standardized tests. We showed how students' reading and writing fit into disciplinary conversations, and we also showed how work that explicitly seeks to develop culturally affirmed identities would help students as they prepare for standardized exams.

However, we cannot close this chapter without returning to more radical endeavors. Even as we prepare students for the educational system that is, we have a responsibility to work to make the educational system what it could be. Part of that transformation, we argue, includes radically rethinking the ways that we "test" students and the ways that we allow them to demonstrate relevant knowledge. Even further, critical educators need to wear their radical hats as they enter into conversations about what that relevant knowledge should be. How, for instance, do we insert forms of knowledge that cannot be easily quantified, such as humanity, or tolerance, or knowledge of self, or are we satisfied if students possess the requisite literacy and numeracy skills even if they are selfish, racist, sexist, and close-minded or frightened, insecure, and ashamed of everything that defines them when they leave campus? If we are not satisfied with the prospect that we may be educating skilled, yet fragmented, human beings, then we need to find ways to transform our guidelines and our measures.

How, then, can critical educators help the larger public to rethink the discourse of standards? First, we need to ask a set of questions that will allow us to be explicit about what we want from our students. After involving our students in critical pedagogical interventions, what do we want them to know? How would we expect these students to be able to demonstrate what they know? What do we want our schools to accomplish? To what ends? At what costs? Answering these questions may reveal some inconsistencies between what we claim to want for our schools and our children and the practices we advocate through the standards we accede to. Even for those who support a completely corporate logic, one that propounds the idea of schools being training grounds for the workplace, we would have to ask ourselves what kinds of skills one needs to be an effective worker in today's marketplace. What we are seeing now is the need for workers who are creative, who are able to think for themselves, who are able to adapt to new situations, and who are able to work with diverse teams to accomplish collective ends. At present, very few of these skills and dispositions are even valued in the standards as they are laid out. What we care about now is what we can measure best, discrete skills and the accrual of discrete facts.

A critical pedagogy of urban education would tend toward narrative and formative assessments in lieu of so much attention being paid only to standardized summative assessments. Assessments are most valuable when they are informal and immediate and when they allow the students opportunities for revision and improvement. Assessments that are final prognoses, sent months later in the form of a percentile, do little to help students to learn.

A critical pedagogy of urban education would also lead to more emphasis on critical inquiry over discrete knowledge of facts and would encourage the development of processes associated with intellectual activity. This debate is as old as Deweyan progressivism and the beginning or public education. Dewey (1990) and his supporters believed that the entire curriculum could be centered on following students' inquiry into the natural world. Rather than have them learn science from a textbook, kids could "do science." Rather than look for history in a book, they could perform historical research. Rather than read only existing plays, they could write, produce, and perform their own plays (or even screenplays). A critical pedagogy of urban education would push us toward fundamentally changing the ethos of K–12 education from one of knowledge consumption to one of knowledge production. We would argue that students would be positioned to learn all of the important skills they need within the context of exploring things that are important to them in their community and within the larger society. There would be room for the study of classical and historical texts within this framework, but there would also be room for educational praxis.

Production, Performance, Service

In rethinking standards and measures, we can turn to the real world for models that may be helpful. How, for instance, do we expect people in the real world to demonstrate knowledge and competence? Although tests play some role in the world of work, most people do not demonstrate their knowledge or competency via paper-and-pencil tests. Most people are asked to do something authentic, or else they have their work evaluated by those knowledgeable enough to make a decision as to the relative merits of the work. The summer seminar model fits nicely within this real-world application, as the student-participants had their work informed at every level by practicing sociologists who were able to provide expert feedback and guidance. The students demonstrated their knowledge through presentations and papers that were very much like those that professional social science researchers produce for their own conferences and journals.

When we consider the overuse of standardized tests in schools in the context of how people are evaluated in their life after school, it does not make a whole lot of sense. Think, for instance, about how tests would work in determining a quality filmmaker or dancer? What test could Gandhi, Ella Baker, or Martin Luther King Jr. have taken to demonstrate that they were revolutionary leaders? Better we draw from these real-world examples to think about production, performance, and service as measures of student achievement. The human population thrived for millennia before the advent of the standardized test, and we'll do fine after these tests have gone. In the interim, we can work together to develop "acceptable" standards of production, performance, and service across the disciplines and grade levels in ways that fit with the goals of critical pedagogy and the demands of the public. What parent wouldn't be proud to know that their daughter had created a literacy program for young children? Who wouldn't be convinced of scientific knowledge after attending a student-run conference on environmental pollution in major metropolitan cities?

Students should be writing books, plays, poems, research reports, and investigative journalism. They should be gathering historical data and conducting and scoring surveys. They should be accessing census data and other large statistical databases. They should be designing cars and homes that run on cleaner fuel. They should be developing computer software; they should be creating advertisement campaigns for drug awareness, for environmental conservation, for anti-racism, and for peace on earth. Students should start this work in the early elementary grades, and it should continue from school into the world of work and citizenship. And we, as educators and researchers, need to be ready to show how the students are learning everything they need to in the context of undertaking meaningful, life-affirming work. All of this could be accomplished, we believe, without the use of most of the standardized tests that currently occupy so much of our thinking.

9
Toward a Grounded Theory of Praxis

The final chapter in a book of this length customarily wraps up the arguments made in earlier chapters, but concluding an argument on a subject as loaded as critical pedagogy is no small task. At the outset, we stated our charge as one that would move from theory to practice and return to theory. We have not engaged in a definitive study of critical pedagogy in urban education. Rather, we have provided several examples of practices with urban youth (successful practices, we think) that built on our interpretations of the critical pedagogy theories to which we have been exposed. In the process, we feel as though we have generated some core principles of a grounded theory of critical pedagogy with urban youth that we hope will inform policy, practice, teacher development, and future research in critical pedagogy.

We now highlight several key principles that have emerged during our extensive work. We have alluded to some of these principles in earlier chapters, and they all relate to ideas in the work of others, but they bear repeating here in our concluding chapter. From the core principles we shift our discussion to the implications of this latest instantiation of our approach to critical pedagogy for the development of educational policy, educational practice, and future urban educators. We conclude the chapter by situating the work of critical pedagogy within a larger context of social movements. One cannot examine and become intimate with the problems of urban schools across our country without also becoming aware that the answers are much broader than simply improving the academic achievement of a subset of students. Simply put, we will not be able to solve our serious social ills without some sort of major social transformation. That said, urban schools exist as important sites of intervention, and the work of urban educators can certainly contribute to these larger movements. It is with these considerations that we hope to leave our readers.

Informing Practice: Core Principles of the Art of Critical Pedagogy

To implement critical pedagogy in urban contexts, it is vital that educators identify and articulate to students the vehicle for delivering critical pedagogy (critical research, critical media literacy, etc.). This vehicle must be intriguing enough to generate student engagement and relevant enough to warrant student investment. In short, educators must be able to explain to students, in a compelling way, why they should invest in the project. This explanation should answer the common student question, Why is this important to me in this moment and in my future life and the future life of my community? Vehicles for implementing critical pedagogy should draw from culturally relevant material that builds on students' existing knowledge base (i.e., popular culture, language, culture, history). These efforts should foreground and value student knowledge as legitimate and intellectual. From there, critical pedagogues can and should build bridges into other forms of knowledge that will give students access to the codes that allow them to crack into, extract resources from, and change dominant institutions.

After identifying the vehicle, educators should create a critical counter-culture in their classrooms and programs. This should be a culture that mounts a deliberate attack on any and all forms of low expectations and social, political, and economic exploitation, replacing them with a culture of excellence and justice. These efforts should begin by confronting the immediate material conditions of the community where the teaching is taking place. However, the developing counter-culture should also work to connect the local struggle for freedom to larger state, national, and global struggles over similar issues.

Critical pedagogues should also create opportunities for students to use what they are learning in ways that directly impact their lives. Such efforts should also prepare students to develop common goals and ready them to work collectively toward them. This means developing a curriculum and pedagogy that address the material concerns of students and their communities (education, housing, justice, jobs, etc.) and that permit and encourage students to use what they are learning to act upon those concerns.

In addition, critical pedagogy should offer opportunities for students to reflect on what they have learned, to evaluate their work, and to move forward with their work on the basis of the knowledge gained from that reflection. This requires educators to use individualized assessment programs that evaluate student efforts on the basis of their own growth, such as the learning assessment and growth program suggested by Vygotsky's (1978) "zone of proximal development" (see description in Chapter 4). Such a program requires educators to connect smaller projects to larger ones, so that students feel that each project builds on the others and that the skills and knowledge they are developing are creating an intellectual momentum that will allow them to get stronger by drawing on what they have already learned.

Implications for Policy

Policymakers must find the courage to commit resources to addressing the challenges facing urban schools. Everyone knows that school funding policies are unequal and inadequate in every state in the country. If our society did not have this social compact around unequal funding, then people would not make entire life choices on the basis of access to school districts, and realtors would not be able to use public schools as selling points. An equal-opportunity society would provide every child with the exact same opportunity. That would require us to provide more to children who have fewer resources, which would mean that schools serving poor children would receive substantially more than schools serving wealthy children. Some will argue that this already happens because urban schools receive additional funding (i.e., Title 1). But any honest examination of school funding reveals that wealthy parents more than make up for that funding gap with the social and economic capital that they provide to their local schools. We do not believe that families should be punished for contributing to the education of their children. However, we do believe that it is dishonest to allow that to happen and then call the system equal. If we want an equal system, then every school should be provided with equal resources, no matter where those resources come from.

A policy for truly equal funding would be step in the right direction. However, we do not believe that the ultimate goal is an equal education for all. Instead, as we argued in our opening chapter, to be a truly great society we must have an equitable educational system. The importance of the distinction between equal and equitable warrants repeating here. An equal education system believes that everyone should get the same education—we are a far cry from even this seemingly simple principle. An equitable education believes that people should receive an education specific to their needs, as defined by their circumstances. If we were to reach the point where we had an equal education system, we would certainly have to admit that people of privilege (economic, racial, political, social) will, more often than not, provide their children with advantages beyond the institution of school that cannot be matched by those without privilege. Although we would be in a better place as a society if schools were at least equal, the inequalities of this system would still provide a moral challenge to our society.

An equitable school system would partially address this moral challenge. In such a school system, the institution would provide service on the basis of

the specific needs (social, economic, linguistic, political) of the people being
served. This would not mean less or more, but different, such that the resources and the pedagogy would match the specific needs of the community.
This is equity, the heartbeat of critical pedagogy. It is a movement away from
educational practices that primarily measure student achievement on the basis of assimilation into white middle-class norms. Let us be clear. The ability
of a student to read, write, and do arithmetic at the highest levels is *not* what
we are referring to as white middle-class norms. We are referring to the fact
that our current educational system uses curriculum, pedagogy, and measurements of these skills that center around white middle-class epistemologies. Thus, the path to acquiring those skills is associated with the belief that
they must be applied in the service of the existing power structure (economic,
social, and political). There are always a few students who see the trade-off as
worthwhile and even fewer who see the system for what it is and consciously
maintain a critical double-consciousness (see Chapter 2). But, for most, our
existing system translates into poor students of color choosing between two
distinct cultural worlds: that of their family and community and that of the
existing power structure. No educational system in a multi-cultural democratic society should force large portions of its children to make such a choice.
An equitable education system would nurture students' own cultural identities and promote the use of their school success in the service of their communities.

Policymakers will not resolve this dilemma simply by committing more
resources to schools. They also need to develop policy that addresses the
need for more effective school evaluation tools if they are to support schools
to meet the specific needs of the students and communities they serve. Any
successful organization recognizes that its potential to improve begins with
its ability to self-evaluate honestly and accurately. In the case of schools, such
an assessment tool must give all service providers an evaluation of their performance on the basis of three primary measures: feedback from clients (students, parents, community), quantifiable growth (assessment scores, grades,
attendance, qualifications), and feedback from colleagues (teachers, administrators, support staff). Many schools and districts have attempted to create
evaluation tools that they call "school report cards." The failure of these report cards to provide meaningful feedback for school improvement is due to
the fact that they do not give teachers and school leaders qualitative feedback. They provide copious amounts of quantitative data (test scores, suspen-

sion rates, teacher credentials, etc.), which can be used to identify problem areas. But without systematic input from clients, efforts to address those problem areas are equivalent to throwing darts in the dark. Any organization worth its weight knows that it must invest heavily in self-evaluation that prioritizes honest feedback from the clients it serves. We can theorize a variety of reasons for why schools do not do this, and we can also find numerous schools that do have systems for feedback. We also know that the schools least likely to have such a system are schools that serve poor children of color and that the schools most likely to have such a system are schools that serve children from wealthy families. The fact of the matter is that policymakers rarely make a concerted effort to create opportunities for poor communities to contribute to the dialogue about how they can best be served by public institutions. A meaningful urban school improvement policy must address this need for a more meaningful evaluation tool.

The problem facing policymakers is that policy often results in the implementation of a one-size-fits-all program. This approach will inevitably be ineffectual for the majority of schools. What policymakers should be thinking about are dynamic policies, such that each school can apply the policy to evaluate and react to its own needs. Such policies would allow for school report cards that solicit evaluations of all elements of a school (teacher quality, school climate and discipline, facilities, health and nutrition, student achievement, parent involvement, programs) from the clients and the participants (support staff, teachers, and administrators) themselves. That evaluation tool would give teachers and school leaders direct feedback from students and families so that they would know what they need to work on to address the gaps revealed by test scores. It would also give school leaders direct feedback from their staff on areas that would improve the adult culture (an area of school improvement that is largely ignored). Schools could use such information to give classroom teachers targeted support in the areas where they are struggling the most, rather than pursuing school-wide professional development that will meet the needs of only a few. It would also give site administrators feedback about necessary improvements to the physical condition of the school, school culture, and school staffing, which would allow leaders to make informed decisions based on the needs of the clients and staff.

We are adamant that policymakers should work to dramatically increase the resources allotted to schools. However, in the absence of policy that supports a comprehensive school evaluation tool, the allocation of those resources will not meet the needs of many students and families. This absence of tools for self-reflection, the most basic tenet of critical pedagogy, prevents schools from improving. It is important to recognize that a more effective evaluation tool is not out of reach. In fact, the template for such a tool is in place with the existing school report cards. However, until those report cards provide meaningful feedback to individual service providers, such that they are aware of the specific likes, needs, and desires of the clients they are serving, school improvement efforts will almost certainly fail to enhance significantly the quality of education that is provided.

In addition, policymakers should be pursuing strategic models that incorporate research and development around quality instruction specific to urban schools. Policy should support major investments into research that explores the work of teachers who are effective in schools where most of their colleagues are failing. There is not enough support for the work of effective urban teachers, and there is even less research aimed at understanding the core principles behind their effectiveness. This dearth of research into effective urban teaching leads to a vicious cycle of poorly informed recruitment, credential program training, and professional development for urban teachers.

Implications for Urban Teacher Preparation and Development

Teacher education programs have long been under siege as weak interventions that do little to change the pre-existing beliefs that teachers bring with them from their own experiences as students. Furthermore, programs have been attacked for being soft, for admitting under-qualified students, for not demanding enough from pre-service teachers, and for making the credentialing process essentially pro forma. In 2004, Congress lambasted teacher education programs for not being able to measure their own effectiveness. A lack of systematic research on the impacts of teacher education programs on the performance of teachers adds fuel to the conservative congressional fire.

Conservative outsiders, however, are not the only ones attacking teacher education. A recent report published by Arthur Levine, *Educating School Teachers* (2006), claims that more than half of the teachers who graduate from teacher education programs feel as though they have not been adequately prepared. In urban contexts the situation is even more dire; top universities have committed to creating teacher education programs that focus on the preparation of teachers for urban contexts, but even after several years of such programs no noticeable changes in academic performance can be identified (National Center for Education Statistics, 2007).

All of this talk about the failure of teacher education is happening at a time when we are clinging more tightly than ever to a culture of standards and standardized tests. Schools that are unable to demonstrate gains in achievement or adequately yearly progress run the risk of being closed or taken over by the state. In a sense, with all of the rigid external requirements via mandatory testing and scripted curricula, these schools already have been taken over. Our experience while visiting many schools and working with pre-service teachers at several universities reveals a sense of apathy, defeat, and cynicism that enters into the conversations of teachers before they even set foot into urban classrooms.

Given these tremendous challenges, one may wonder whether there is any hope at all for a focus on critical pedagogy in teacher development. When all of the focus is on rigor and achievement, critical pedagogy may seem like a hard sell to pre-service and practicing teachers and to the universities and districts that regulate teacher development. We argue the contrary. Given the tremendous challenges and alienation from the process of policy decision making, and even curriculum, teachers now, more than at any other time, need something to believe in. They need to feel empowered as agents of change inside and outside of schools. Current regimes of power dismiss and de-intellectualize teaching populations, at least in part because the beliefs of teachers often run counter to the interests of those in power. Urban parents, students, and community members are distrustful of teachers in the aggregate because they are associated with institutions that have not proven willing or able to educate youth adequately. While teachers may never be able to convince those in power of their worth or their intellect, they can ally with students and members of communities to demand educational reform. Such allegiances can begin mending bridges that have been broken for far too long.

We would argue that the current political climate has unwittingly created ideal conditions for teachers in urban schools to reposition themselves as critical pedagogues and to develop practices that are empowering of themselves and their students. When coercion is public, encompassing, and dehumanizing at once, it creates conditions for radical social change, and conditions could not be more amenable to fomenting this change than they are right now. Teachers are angry, they are hurt, and they are ready to resist policies that they know hurt the children they interact with on a daily basis.

Arguing that the conditions exist for preparing urban teachers to become critical pedagogues is important, but it does not move us closer to preparing a generation of teachers for this undertaking. As a field of professionals, our faith has wavered in our ability to affect the dispositions and practices of the teachers that we, as university educators, are charged to prepare. Whole volumes of literature speak to the challenges: the social class and race of pre-service teachers, the lack of sufficient time to prepare these teachers, the power of their own socialization into classroom life, antagonistic and dysfunctional environments in the schools where they will work, and the limitations of scripted curricula. Each of these has been offered to us as teacher educators as an advance explanation for why the teachers we teach will not be effective once they set foot in the classrooms. We cannot afford to believe this any longer. If we continue to articulate reasons for our ineffectiveness, we will lose the right, as teacher educators, to influence the next generation of (a few million) teachers. It behooves us, then, to think for a moment about the implications of our teaching and research for the preparation of the next generation of teachers in urban schools.

Teaching Teachers about Critical Pedagogy

Teacher educators must pay closer attention to the pedagogy we use to prepare students to be critical pedagogues. We are finding that a growing number of new teachers have been exposed to critical pedagogy in their teacher training programs and that many of them find it valuable. Sadly, most people who use critical pedagogy to train teachers, particularly Freire's version, do little to help new teachers interpret its relevance for urban K–12 classrooms in this country. Many teacher educators fail to mention the fact that Freire's analysis emerged primarily from his experience working with adults. It seems critically important to us that teachers understand Freire's pedagogical recommendations, particularly his critique of the banking model of education, as an analysis of work he did with adults. He was working with students who chose to come to his classroom. We are working with students who are mandated, under threat of legal repercussions, to come. He was working with students who had the wisdom that comes from surviving and subsisting into adulthood in a society that marginalized them. We are working with children who, like any children, have not had the lived experience of adults to guide their decision making and therefore need a more deliberately structured and disciplined environment.

Sadly, the result of this de-contextualized teaching of critical pedagogy is often two more forms of oppressive pedagogy that we must battle. The first of these is a pedagogy guided by fear. Many teachers are so afraid of being labeled as oppressive (read racist) that they shy away from their responsibility as the adult and educational leader in the classroom. They shirk their duty to exercise authority for fear of being authoritarian, which results in classrooms that lack structure and discipline under the guise of being non-oppressive and democratic. As teachers, they are exactly like the parents Freire describes in the first letter of *Pedagogy of Indignation*, complacent authorities who think of themselves as champions of freedom but find themselves vexed by the "tyranny of freedom." Far too many of these teachers, who may consider themselves to be well meaning, use democratic sensibilities and social justice leanings to defer to students on decisions that are the responsibility of the teacher. In so doing, they fail to establish themselves as a legitimate adult authority with a clear plan for the direction of their students. Inevitably, when the class has spiraled out of control and the teacher decides to hold the young people to some random rule of discipline, the requisite respect of the students is gone. The two most common results of this situation are equally bad. Either students refuse to recognize the authority of the teacher to the point that the teacher gives up on the class or the teacher shifts to the role of uncompromising dictator, regains some semblance of control, and then interprets the authoritarian approach to be the most effective one with urban youth.

Of course, it is usually students and families who get blamed for this, and the archetype of the unruly ghetto child unable or unwilling to stake a claim to her or his education is reified. Insert into this scenario the culture of poverty "experts" who situate the problems with students and their families. Their solution is a "pedagogy of poverty" (Haberman, 2006): "back to basics" drill-and-kill scripted literacy, social studies, and mathematics lessons; zero-tolerance discipline policies; high-stakes testing; one-size-fits-all standards-based instruction; and phenomenally expensive all-inclusive in-service programs for teachers. The latter are particularly disturbing because they are designed by people from outside urban communities to help teachers understand the "culture of poverty" that vexes urban communities. Ruby Payne's *aha! Process*, the most widely sold of these programs, claims that teachers should teach their students to examine individuals who have attained prosperity to learn the hidden rules of wealth creation. Payne's program argues that teachers should be trained to "provide a window of escape for individuals who are intent on improving their economic lot" (*aha! Process*, 2007, 4). There are numerous problems with Payne's program, not the least of which are the absence of critiques of historical and present-day racial and structural inequities, weakly supported empirical claims, and the use of a cultural deficit perspective (Gorski, 2006; Ng & Rury, 2006). The program also promotes a model of achievement that is individualistic, escapist, and based on wealth accumulation rather than on critical thinking and social change (Gorski, 2006). Year after year, these kinds of regressive pedagogical methods produce identically low test scores and achievement patterns, along with questions from teachers wondering how critical pedagogy might help break the pattern: Does critical pedagogy mean that we are no longer supposed to prepare students to do well on tests? Does it mean that we should throw out state and national standards? Does it mean that college is unimportant? Does it mean that we should not be preparing young people to enter the economy? What does this look like in a classroom? Won't I lose my job if I teach these things?

These questions reflect the second outcome of misinterpretations of critical pedagogy—pedagogical decisions guided by the false dichotomy of critical pedagogy or academic rigor. Teachers trained as critical pedagogues sometimes believe they must choose between academically rigorous teaching and teaching for social justice. This false binary is largely the result of the pedagogy of poverty, where teachers are trained to believe that an academically rigorous pedagogy does not have time for critically investigating the material conditions of society. Instead, an academically rigorous pedagogy focuses on skill development to prepare students to score well on state and national achievement tests—most of which are norm-referenced tests and tend to be more useful (and accurate) as predictors of parent income than intellect (see http://www.fairtest.org as a critical resource on testing).

We find that many teachers believe in the value of a critical and socially just pedagogy, at least on a theoretical level. But under the pressure facing their students to perform on a battery of tests by which their ability as teachers will be judged, they find much more job security in teaching to the test (learn to earn) than teaching students to think critically (learn for freedom). The bitter irony of it all is that even when they teach to the test, their students usually end up not doing any better.

To caution teachers against buying into this dichotomy, teacher educators would do well to introduce their students to the first letter in Freire's last book, *Pedagogy of Indignation*, in which he writes:

> The progressive educator does not allow herself any doubt with respect to the right boys and girls from the masses, *the people*, have to know the same mathematics, physics, or biology that boys and girls from the "happier parts" of town learn. At the same time, she never accepts that the teaching of any discipline whatsoever could take place divorced from a critical analysis of how society works. (2004, 20)

The disciplined classroom environment, producing the academic rigor and critical social awareness of which Freire speaks, is the foundation on which any effective pedagogy is built. There is no binary; you cannot have critical pedagogy without academic rigor, and you cannot be academically rigorous without drawing from critical pedagogy. Ultimately, the critical pedagogy we promote for teacher development grounds Freire's theory of critical pedagogy in the K–12 urban context of this country so that teachers understand that all of the standards that students will be tested on are taught when you employ a critical pedagogy.

Increasing the Impact of Teacher Education Research

Another challenge facing teacher education is the aesthetic of teaching in urban contexts. Existing metaphors of the teacher as a helpless victim or the teacher as a missionary and savior are extremely problematic. As educators, as writers, as advocates, we can use our voice, our influence, our positions as editors and contributors to create narratives of teachers as transformative agents. We can document the role of teachers as important participants in the transformation of urban schools, not as saviors per se but as collaborators with members of their communities. These narratives, which will emerge from critical research on teachers as critical pedagogues, can take the form of books, articles, chapters, and conference papers, but they can also take the form of Web sites and documentaries. Without developing studies and creating texts that transform this aesthetic, we simply acquiesce in the existing narratives for teachers. This narrative ends up dictating much of the information that is transmitted to teachers in pre-service teacher education and professional development.

As teacher educators and university-based researchers, we are also charged with creating better materials for pre-service and practicing teachers. At present, there exists a real gap between densely theoretical texts that are intended for doctoral students and university faculty and the very practical, pragmatic texts that are frequently peddled to teachers. Very few texts have been written explicitly for teachers that talk about the principles and practices of critical pedagogy. We have written this text to appeal to practicing teachers as well as teacher educators, but we recognize that it remains a text that will primarily be accessed by teacher educators and university-based scholars. We all need to do a better job of creating texts that are both theoretically sophisticated and immediately applicable for teachers, texts that can be incorporated into teacher education programs and influence practicing teachers.

Improving Coursework in Teacher Education

Another major challenge concerns the coursework of most teacher education programs. We recognize that this challenge falls partially on policymakers, as states often dictate course requirements to credential programs. However, we would argue that teacher credential programs have the responsibility to advocate to policymakers to rethink the current rigid and ineffective programming sequence. Credential programs often have limited space for coursework that is not predefined: a methods sequence, a foundations sequence, and fieldwork. There are few explicit spaces for the discussion of critical theory or the history or sociology of urban education. These subjects may be squeezed into a week's discussion during a foundations or methods course, but very little information can be processed in one week. Teachers will have a difficult time conceptualizing the applications of critical pedagogy if they have not had the opportunity to read and reflect upon the general principles of pedagogy in the immediate contexts where they will be working.

To create more meaningful discussions about critical pedagogy, teacher education courses have to change their structure and culture. At present, many teacher educators are reticent to assign anything that appears to be dense reading, and students are resistant to reading anything that appears to be too "theoretical" or removed from their teaching experience. Part of this can be addressed by creating more teacher-specific critical reading materials, but teacher education courses have to be re-imagined to include spaces where future teachers can read and discuss complex critical social theory.

In addition, it is important to consider the other learning spaces that exist for teachers outside of the university classroom. Traditionally, the two primary spaces of learning in teacher education are the university classroom and the K–12 classroom, where candidates transition from observing to leading instruction for a period of six to ten weeks. The transition from observer to supported participant fits in nicely with socio-cultural theories of learning through participation. However, socio-cultural theories of learning rely on novices being exposed to expert practice within the culture that they are destined to participate in. In the world of teacher education, however, pre-service teachers are not likely to witness effective critical pedagogy in the urban classrooms where they are student teaching. Given that this is the case, critical teacher educators must seek out other learning spaces for pre-service teachers. Simply "talking them through" critical pedagogy in our seminars is not going to work; they try to tell us this as delicately as they can, and sometimes their telling is not delicate at all.

There are many spaces within the community where adults do work effectively with youth and employ the principles of critical pedagogy. Whether they are after-school dance and theatre programs, sports leagues, community-based organizations, or neighborhood tutorials, numerous adults in the community are finding ways to engage and motivate youth that would prove very useful to those becoming teachers (see Akom, 2003 as one example). Teacher education programs should find ways for pre-service teachers to access these powerful learning spaces as they develop as critical educators.

Teacher education programs can also equip young teachers with the tools of critical research so that they can document and justify their innovative practices to a variety of constituencies including parents, colleagues, department heads, and administrators. Even though the pre-service teachers themselves are a primary audience for their own research, developing the ability to document student learning is an important skill for critical educators. As we stated earlier, our desire to adequately document our innovative approaches to teaching English led us into the world of research and has allowed our work to influence other educators.

In addition to developing teachers as researchers, teacher education programs need to develop their own research studies that document the myriad ways that beginning teachers are drawing upon critical pedagogy to make powerful connections with their students. We cannot rely on gut feelings or faith in our principles. We need to develop studies that show the possibilities, for the sake of our teacher education programs and for the benefit of our recent graduates, who need all of the support that they can get.

Improving Teacher Recruitment

The pool of future teachers will certainly be diversified when we diversify the college student body. However, universities in general, and teacher education departments specifically, should be working much harder to attract, support, and retain students of color. Each region and state has its own challenges in this area, but the following strategies can be generally applied:

- Diversify teacher education faculty.
- Create scholarships that target students of color.
- Recruit early and often—this includes going to high schools, community centers, churches, freshmen seminars, dormitories, sports teams, clubs, etc.
- Place strong teaching faculty in undergraduate courses that address issues of urban students of color.
- Create dual-degree programs that link bachelor's degree, master's degree, and teaching credential.
- Form pipeline relationships with urban districts to prepare and recruit urban high school graduates to join dual-degree programs and return to their communities to teach.

Limitations and Directions for Future Research

While we feel that the interwoven cases in this book have much to offer the fields of critical studies and urban education, we also recognize that our studies have their limitations. One advantage of working with a small number of examples is that the data are very rich. In our fifteen years working across a small number of sites, we managed to develop strong kinship networks with students, parents, teachers, and members of community-based organizations. These relationships allowed us to develop meaningful practices and collect meaningful data that we share in this book.

A drawback, however, is that we worked with a relatively small sample of students (about 300 students across the five studies mentioned here). It is extremely difficult to make any larger generalizations from such a small sample. It is also important to acknowledge that the sample is biased. We are unable to distinguish our personalities and the dispositions of our students fully from the principles of critical pedagogy under which we carried out the work. We have a mutual colleague who constantly asks, "How do you know it isn't just you?" Maybe we would have had success with these students had we never come across the readings of Paulo Freire. Maybe there are hundreds of other ways that educators could have been successful with these students that had nothing to do with critical pedagogy.

Furthermore, we are limited in the kinds of causal/correlational statements that we can make about the effects of critical pedagogy with urban youth. What we can say is this: youth who participated in these projects demonstrated complex academic skill development, their participation in the various activities exhibited motivation and engagement, they developed and demonstrated empowered identities, and they engaged in actions for advancing educational and social justice. We can also say that our students attended college in higher numbers than would have been predicted given their socioeconomic status and the graduation and college-going rates of their respective institutions. However, as we did not conduct controlled experiments, we cannot say definitively that critical pedagogy was the sole cause of these particular outcomes.

Finally, we were limited in our ability to impact the institutional cultures of academic underachievement at East Bay and South City high schools. To this day, both schools continue to fail large percentages of their low-income students of color. The same is true for the schools that fed our summer seminar. A look at the aggregate achievement of schools where we worked over the years would reveal a trend of consistent failure despite our documented successes with small segments. While social change is difficult to measure as an outcome, failure is not. If we had ultimately been successful in our charge, these schools and the communities that surround them would be different places by now. The students attending these schools would be receiving an education comparable to that of anyone in the United States. This, however, has not been the case.

Some of these limitations can be addressed with further research. Research can illuminate and document the practices of critical pedagogy across broader contexts with larger numbers of students. We would like to see more work that explores outcomes for students in classrooms where educators adhered to principles of critical pedagogy. What would an examination of student work reveal about their successes relative to their counterparts in similar classrooms that did not use critical pedagogy? What would comprehensive interviews with these students say about their sense of empowerment and their engagement with school? Would these studies permit us to draw definitive conclusions about the ability of critical pedagogical practices to raise grades, test scores, graduation rates, and college attendance?

Further research in critical pedagogy might reveal other practices that could inspire present and future educators. It would be ideal to create journals, Web sites, books, and documentaries that share inspired critical practices with other interested parties. For example, our work with youth popular culture was inspired by reading about critical language practices employed by Carol Lee in South Side Chicago. The assembling of such research studies would inspire practice and help us understand more about the similarities and differences of critical practices across multiple contexts. What, for instance, does critical pedagogy look like across elementary classrooms? What do these practices look like in work with the rural poor (a very significant population in our country)? What are some similarities and differences among work in urban and rural areas with similarly impoverished populations? Are there regional differences in the applications of critical pedagogy? If so, what informs these differences? And, at the end of the day, what, if anything, can be said about the core principles that tie all of these practices together?

Finally, we are in need of a great deal more research that explores the intersections between critical pedagogy and urban teacher development. We are less interested in what critical pedagogy looks like in a teacher education or professional development program than we are in how these programs ultimately generate critical educators (although the two are somewhat related). Future research should help us to identify essential skills and characteristics of critical educators and practices that help fashion those skills and characteristics. It does us no good to hold on to the belief that critical educators are born and not made. We need to develop projects and studies that help us understand the extent to which we are able to transform well-intended educators into critical educators who achieve results with students. Some studies have addressed these issues (see Duncan-Andrade, 2004, 2005b), but additional research is warranted.

Pedagogy, Love, and Revolution

Rarely, in conversations about reforming urban education, are the words pedagogy, love, and revolution juxtaposed. In fact, it is rare that the words love and revolution are associated with any facet of urban school reform. As we have spent the previous eight chapters discussing our philosophy and practice of pedagogy, we conclude with a conversation about love and revolution as these terms relate to critical pedagogy in urban education.

Teachers should love their students; this is the golden rule, a simple enough statement that does not require a book-length treatise. However, the questions of how revolutionary love differs from love traditionally defined and how it becomes manifest in urban classrooms are worthy of further discussion.

What is revolutionary love? How is it practiced in the context of education? And how can teachers be taught to love in this way? First of all we feel that revolutionary love is the love that is strong enough to bring about radical change in individual students, classrooms, school systems, and the larger society that controls them. Often love is defined by its inputs rather than its outcomes; instead of thinking about what teachers do to manifest revolutionary love, we are more interested in what happens as a barometer of this love. Even after all of these theories and practices are ingested, and even after tireless planning, something else will be required of teachers to achieve the kinds of outcomes that we describe in this book. That something else is not easy to predict, nor is it easy to quantify. It looks like endless dedication, an unyielding belief in the brilliance and potential of every student, and the commitment to stop at nothing to get kids to learn. It demands the energy and passion to present learning as an amazing opportunity for young people to prepare themselves to be engaged citizens and social actors. This something else is defined as never giving up. It is a continual search for more effective ways to help young people to learn and to demonstrate their learning in academically and socially powerful ways. This something else is revolutionary love. When teachers see revolutionary change in their students, classrooms, and schools, then they will know that they are practicing that sort of love.

Is it not possible to manifest revolutionary love without these outcomes. As educators, as researchers, as teacher educators, and as advocates for educational justice, we have to take responsibility for the failure of urban schools. If achievement results, student performance, and school climate do not look like we want them to, then it is because we have failed to manifest our revolutionary love. We know how to educate poor children. We have the knowledge and capacity. We lack the courage. We are cowards. Nothing angers us more than cowardice, because cowardice is the confluence of someone knowing what is morally right, having the capacity to act on that moral imperative, and not taking that action. Because the education system in this country has the knowledge and capacity to provide a quality education to all children and chooses to act as though it is tirelessly trying to figure out how to do that, we have systematic cowardice. Systematic cowardice, particularly in regard to services for young people, is the reflection of a morally bankrupt society. It is possible to educate any group of children if we love them enough to do what we need to do to educate them. As long as we continue to make excuses for our inability to do this, then we are not manifesting revolutionary love. And it is only that kind of love that is going to change our schools.

Love is never easy, because great love also means great pain. It means carrying a burden. It means suffering empathically. It means recognizing and reacting to inequitable conditions that we have the power to change. This revolutionary love is not easy to carry out, and it may exist more as an ideal than a reality. But it is important to the overall thread of this book. To be a part of the difference in urban education means more than ingesting a great amount of theory and creating innovative pedagogical practices. Of course, someone who aspires to this revolutionary love will study and they will develop innovative practices. But they will also stop at nothing short of success, and this commitment will drive them to do things they did not think possible.

An important component of revolutionary love is revolutionary courage. Our love of the students and our feelings of solidarity with them and their families provide us with the courage that we need to become the kinds of critical teachers we need to be. We do not claim to have mastered this love of which we speak. However, we can say that our feelings for students have inspired us to take great personal and professional risks that have resulted in some amazing outcomes for the learning and social development of our students. Love for our students has given us the courage to take on administration, to become public speakers and advocates, to engage in critical research, and to dedicate our time, energy, and personal resources to the struggle for educational justice. As in other drastic situations, love is what gives us the courage to do the unthinkable. It gives us the courage to sacrifice for causes greater than ourselves. This kind of love and courage can turn teachers into agents of change.

We believe revolutionary love is inherent in everyone and that what must be learned is the courage to unleash it. This can be learned through practice and through mentorship. For teachers, this means seeking out those who manifest revolutionary love and courage and working with and learning from them on a daily basis. These mentors, friends, and partners may be colleagues, students, or community members. They may also be pre-service classmates, or emerge from attendance at conferences, or even come from biographies and bibliographies—we may be apprenticed by the written words and lives of those who have come before us.

As teachers we instruct those around us about revolutionary love by leading public lives where our love for students and the world is open and evident. Students need access not only to the ideas and skills we seek to transfer. They also need to be able to access our love, and they need to be able to see how we draw upon that love to conquer our fears and to work with others for change. Really, what our students need access to is our revolutionary aesthetic. They need to see our theory of change in the world and how we act upon the world to carry out this model of change. If our revolutionary aesthetic is not compelling and reflected in the way we live, we cannot teach our students about revolutionary love. How can we share with them a life that we have not learned to live? It is not as though our students have to become "us," but in our actions they should see the potential for their own revolutionary life.

And what of this talk of revolution? This is a loaded and connotative word that we employ with a great amount of historical respect for what the term has meant, even as we seek to reclaim it for our own contemporary uses. A generation ago, the term revolution carried very specific connotations of a way of working against Western capitalist sexist white supremacist imperialism. It implied a set of social, economic, and racial conditions to be addressed and a strategy (collective action) for dealing with these conditions. At the dawn of the twenty-first century, we face many similar conditions, although the strategies for collective action have been reframed and political boundaries have been redrawn as a result of advances in technology and the continued globalization of accumulated capital.

Revolution remains an important ideal at the individual, psychological, social, and institutional levels. It remains a potent and motivating concept to believe that collective action can fundamentally transform what has stood as oppressive and total in our lives. Critical pedagogy can play a fundamental role in contributing to revolution on all of these levels. Raising individual academic performance among students attending urban schools is itself a revolutionary act. But a primary goal of critical pedagogy is to address the psychological impact of systematic oppression on young people today. While we frequently discuss the cultural outcomes associated with hegemony, we rarely address the psychological consequences of the domination of social thought and social space for those who are marginalized within these regimes of truth. In other words, while our young people are resilient and vibrant and full of love, we must recognize that dominant systems of thought can compel young people to engage in activities that cause great harm to themselves and to others. Past generations of critical scholars have referred to this condition as dysconsciousness, or the colonization of the mind (Fanon, 1967, 2004). These terms may be too simplistic in not accounting for conscious and subconscious resistance engaged in by our young, but they do accurately point to the relationship between hegemony and the mind-set and actions of the young people we teach. That being the case, some focus of the pedagogy of revolution has to be at the individual level; we must help these young people to feel better about themselves on the multiple levels of race, gender, class, sexual identity, and geography. A pedagogy that glosses over individual transformation in the cause of building larger collectives has missed the point. The only way that young people can become informed and empowered consumers of larger social collectives is if they are self-actualized and if they have begun the process of healing and loving themselves. Of course, these transformations can be concurrent, but it is unconscionable to deal with one without the other.

Tupac referred to young people fighting to break free of oppression as the "roses that grow from concrete." They are the ones who prove society's rule wrong by keeping the dream of a better society alive, growing despite the cold, uncaring, un-nurturing environment of the concrete. In a poem on this subject, Tupac wrote, "long live the rose that grew from concrete when no one else even cared" (Shakur, 1999, 3). He expanded this metaphor in his song "Mama's Just a Little Girl," writing:

You wouldn't ask why the rose that grew from concrete had damaged petals.
On the contrary, we would all celebrate its tenacity.
We would all love its will to reach the sun.
We are the roses.
This is the concrete.
And these are my damaged petals.
Don't ask me why…ask me how. (Shakur, 2002)

Despite the number of teachers who remain ineffectual at nurturing these roses in the concrete, we continue to be hopeful about the potential of critical pedagogy to improve urban classrooms. This optimism is spurred by the fact that most young people we encounter still come to school clinging to the hope that things will be different, despite overwhelming evidence that they won't be. Moreover, most teachers we encounter want to be great educators; they want to demonstrate the revolutionary love and courage that will meet their students' hopes and grow rose gardens in concrete. Contrary to prevailing public and government opinion, the majority of teachers we come across are more in need of guidance and critical support on how to be effective than they are of mandates and threats. We hope that the critical pedagogy we have described here will encourage, support, develop, and incite educators to grow roses in the concrete—educators who ask not why the roses' pedals are damaged but *how* we can grow more of them.

References

Acuña, R. (2003). *Occupied America: A history of Chicanos.* New York: Longman.

Adorno, T., & M. Horkheimer. (1999). "The culture industry: Enlightenment as mass deception." In S. During (Ed.), *The Cultural Studies Reader* (pp. 31–41). New York: Routledge.

aha! Process. (2007). "A platform for economic justice." Retrieved July 10, 2007, from *http://www.ahaprocess.com/files/PlatformForEconomicJustice.pdf.*

Akom, A. (2003). "Reexamining resistance as oppositional behavior: The Nation of Islam and the creation of a black achievement ideology." *Sociology of Education, 76* (October), 305–325.

Althusser, L. (2001). *Lenin and philosophy and other essays.* New York: Monthly Review Press.

American Institutes for Research. (2003). *High time for high school reform: Early findings from the evaluation of the National School District and Network Grants Program.* Menlo Park, CA: American Institutes for Research.

Anyon, J. (1981). "Social class and school knowledge." *Curriculum and Inquiry, 1,* 3–42.

Anyon, J. (1997). *Ghetto schooling: A political economy of urban educational reform.* New York: Teachers College Press.

Anzaldúa, G. (1984). "Speaking in tongues: A letter to third world women writers." In C. Moraga & G. Anzaldúa (Eds.), *This bridge called my back: Writings by radical women of color* (pp. 167–168). New York: Kitchen Table/Women of Color Press.

Anzaldúa, G. (1987). "Movimientos de rebeldía y las culturas que traicionan." In *Borderlands/la frontera: The new mestiza.* San Francisco: Aunt Lute.

Anzaldúa, G. (1996/2001). *Prietita and the ghost woman/Prietita y la llorona.* San Francisco: Children's Book Press.

Anzaldúa, G. (1997). *Friends from the other side/Amigos del otro lado.* San Francisco: Children's Book Press.

Apple, M.W. (1990). *Ideology and curriculum.* New York: Routledge.

Aronowitz, S., & H. Giroux. (1991). *Postmodern education.* Minneapolis: University of Minnesota Press.

Ashcroft, B., G. Griffiths, & H. Tiffin. (Eds.). (1995). *The post-colonial studies reader*. London: Routledge.

Banks, J. (1994). "Ethnicity, class, cognitive, and motivational styles: Research and teaching implications." In J. Kretovicks & E. Nussel (Eds.), *Transforming Urban Education* (pp. 277–290). Boston, MA: Allyn & Bacon.

Banks, J. (2001). *An introduction to multicultural education*. Boston, MA: Allyn & Bacon.

Barton, D., & M. Hamilton. (2000). "Literacy practices." In D. Barton, M. Hamilton, & R. Ivanic (Eds.), *Situated literacies: Reading and writing in context* (pp. 7–16). London: Routledge.

Blawis, P. (1971). *Tijerina and the land grants: Mexican Americans in struggle for their heritage*. New York: International Publishers.

Bourdieu, P. (1986). "The forms of capital." In J.G. Richardson (Ed.), *Handbook of theory and research for the sociology of education* (pp. 241–258). New York: Greenwood.

Bourdieu, P. (1990). *The logic of practice*. Cambridge, UK: Polity Press.

Bowles, S., & H. Gintis. (1976). *Schooling in capitalist America: Educational reform and the contradictions of economic life*. New York: Basic Books.

Burawoy, M. (1998). "The extended case method." *Sociological Theory, 16* (1), 4–33.

California Department of Education. (2006). Data collected on June 9, 2006, from *http://data1.cde.ca.gov/dataquest*.

Cammarota, J., & A. Romero. (2006). "A critically compassionate intellectualism for Latina/o students: Raising voices above the silencing in our schools." *Multicultural Education, 14* (2), 16–23.

Carnegie Corporation (2001). "Whole-district school reform." *Carnegie Reporter, 1* (2), 1–2.

Carnoy, M., & H. Levin. (1985). *Schooling and work in the democratic state*. Stanford, CA: Stanford University Press.

Carspecken, P.F. (1996). *Critical ethnography in educational research: A theoretical and practical guide*. New York: Routledge.

Collatos, A. (2004). "The post-high school trajectories of Futures students: Assessing access." Paper presented at the annual meeting of the American Educational Research Association, San Diego, California.

Council of the Great City Schools. (2007). *Beating the odds VII*. Washington, DC: Council of the Great City Schools.

Cushman, E. (1998). *The struggle and the tools: Oral and literate strategies in an inner city community.* Albany: SUNY Press.

D'Souza, D. (1995). *The end of racism.* New York: Free Press.

Darder, A. (1991). *Culture and power in the classroom: A critical foundation for bicultural education.* Westport, CT: Bergin & Garvey.

Darder, A. (1997). "Creating the conditions for cultural democracy in the classroom." In A. Darder, R. Torres, & H. Gutierrez (Eds.), *Latinos and education* (pp. 331–350). New York: Routledge.

Darder, A. (2002a). "Teaching as an act of love: Reflections on Paulo Freire and his contributions to our lives and work." In A. Darder, M. Baltodano, & R. Torres (Eds.), *The critical pedagogy reader* (pp. 497–510). London: Falmer.

Darder, A. (2002b). *Reinventing Paulo Freire: A pedagogy of love.* Boulder, CO: Westview.

Darling-Hammond, L. (1998). "New standards, old inequalities: The current challenge for African-American education." *The state of black America report.* Chicago: National Urban League.

Denzin, N. (1997). *Interpretive ethnography: Ethnographic practices for the 21st century.* Thousand Oaks, CA: Sage.

Delpit, L. (1987). "Skills and other dilemmas of a progressive black educator." *Equity and Choice, 3* (2), 9–14.

Delpit, L. (1988). "The silenced dialogue: Power and pedagogy in educating other people's children." *Harvard Educational Review, 58* (3), 280–298.

Delpit, L. (1995). *Other people's children: Cultural conflict in the classroom.* New York: The New Press.

Delpit, L., & J.K. Dowdy (Eds.). (2002). *The skin that we speak.* New York: The New Press.

Dewey, J. (1990). *The school and the society: The child and the curriculum.* Chicago, IL: Centennial Press.

Dewey, J. (1938). *Experience and education.* New York: Simon & Schuster.

Docker, J. (1994). *Postmodernism and popular culture: A cultural history.* New York: Cambridge University Press.

Du Bois, W.E.B. (1903/1996). *The souls of black folk.* New York: Penguin.

Duncan-Andrade, J. (2004). "Preparing for the urban in urban teaching: Toward teacher development for retention and activism." *Teaching Education Journal, 15* (4), 339–350.

Duncan-Andrade, J. (2005a). "An examination of the sociopolitical history of Chicanos and its relationship to school performance." *Urban Education, 40* (6), 576–605.

Duncan-Andrade, J. (2005b). "Understanding and supporting effective teaching in urban schools." *Educational Leadership, 62* (6), 70–73.

Duncan-Andrade, J. (2005c). "Your best friend or your worst enemy: Youth popular culture, pedagogy and curriculum at the dawn of the 21st century". *Review of Education, Pedagogy and Cultural Studies,* 26 (4), pp. 313–337.

Duncan-Andrade, J. (2007). "Urban youth and the counter-narration of inequality." *Transforming Anthropology, 15* (1), 26–37.

Duncan-Andrade, J. (forthcoming). *What urban schools can learn from a successful sports program: Ballin', best friends, and breakin' cycles.* New York: Peter Lang.

Emerson, R. (1841). "Self-reliance." Retrieved July 20, 2005, from *http://www.emersoncentral.com/selfreliance.htm.*

Fanon, F. (1967). *Black skin, white masks.* Translated by Charles Lam Markmann. New York: Grove Press.

Fanon, F. (1968). *Toward the African revolution.* Translated by Haakon Chevalier. New York: Grove Press.

Fanon, F. (1970). *A dying colonialism.* Translated by Haakon Chevalier. New York: Grove Press.

Fanon, F. (2004). *The wretched of the earth.* Translated by Richard Philcox. New York: Grove Press.

Ferguson, R., & H. Ladd. (1996). *How and why money matters. Holding schools accountable: Performance-based reform in education.* Washington, DC: Brookings Institution.

Finn, P. (1999). *Literacy with an attitude.* Albany: SUNY Press.

Fischer, C., M. Hout, M.S. Jankowski, S. Lucas, A. Swidler, & K. Voss. (1996). *Inequality by design.* Princeton, NJ: Princeton University Press.

Foucault, M. (1995). *Discipline and punish: The birth of the prison.* New York: Vintage Books.

Freire, P. (1970). *Pedagogy of the oppressed.* New York: Continuum.

Freire, P. (1997). *Teachers as cultural workers: Letters to those who dare teach.* Boulder, CO: Westview.

Freire, P. (1998). *Pedagogy of freedom.* Lanham, MD: Rowman & Littlefield.

Freire, P. (2004). *Pedagogy of indignation.* Boulder, CO: Paradigm.

Freire, P., & D. Macedo. (1987). *Literacy: Reading the word and the world.* New York: Continuum.

Gans, H. (1999). *Popular culture and high culture: An analysis and evaluation of taste.* New York: Basic Books.

Geertz, C. (2000) *Local knowledge: Further essays in interpretive anthropology.* New York: Basic Books.

Gilligan, C. (1982). *In a different voice.* Cambridge, MA: Harvard University Press.

Ginwright, S., P. Noguera, & J. Cammarota (Eds.). (2006). *Beyond resistance: Youth activism and community change: New democratic possibilities for policy and practice for America's youth.* New York: Routledge.

Giroux, H. (1983/2001). *Theory and resistance in education: Toward a pedagogy for the opposition.* South Hadley, MA: Bergin & Garvey.

Giroux, H. (1988). *Teachers as intellectuals: Toward a critical pedagogy of learning.* New York: Bergin & Garvey.

Giroux, H. (1996). *Fugitive cultures: Race, violence, and youth.* New York: Routledge.

Giroux, H. (2003). "Critical theory and educational practice." In A. Darder, M. Baltodano, & R. Torres (Eds.), *The critical pedagogy reader* (pp. 27–56). New York: Routledge.

Goodman, S. (2003). *Teaching youth media: A critical guide to literacy, video production, and social change.* New York: Teachers College Press.

Gorski, P. (2006). "The classist underpinnings of Ruby Payne's framework." *Teachers College Record,* February 9. Retrieved July 31, 2007, from http://www.tcrecord.org.

Gould, S. (1996). *The mismeasure of man.* New York: W. W. Norton.

Gramsci, A. (1971). *Selections from prison notebooks.* London: New Left Books.

Greenwald, R., L.V. Hedges, & R.D. Laine. (1996). "The effect of school resources on school achievement." *Review of Educational Research, 66* (3), 361–396.

Haberman, M. (2006). "Pedagogy of poverty: The pedagogy of poverty versus good teaching." Retrieved November 14, 2006, from *http://www.ednews.org/articles/610/1/Pedagogy-of-Poverty-The-Pedagogy-of-Poverty-Versus-Good-Teaching/Page1.html.*

Hanushek, E.A. (2001). "Efficiency and equity in education." *National Bureau of Economic Research Reporter,* Spring, 15–19.

Harvard Civil Rights Project. (2005). *Confronting the graduation rate crisis in California*. Boston, MA: The Civil Rights Project.

Herrnstein, R., & C. Murray. (1994). *The bell curve: Intelligence and class structure in American life*. New York: Free Press.

hooks, b. (1989). *Talking back: Thinking feminist, thinking black*. Boston, MA: South End Press.

hooks, b. (1994a). *Teaching to transgress: Education as the practice of freedom*. New York: Routledge.

hooks, b. (1994b). *Outlaw culture: Resisting representations*. New York: Routledge.

hooks, b. (2000). *Where we stand: Class matters*. New York: Routledge.

hooks, b. (2003). *Teaching community: A pedagogy of hope*. New York: Routledge.

Howell, M., & W. Prevenier. (2001). *From reliable sources: An introduction to historical research methods*. Ithaca, NY: Cornell University Press.

Hull, G., M. Rose, K. Fraser, & M. Castellano. (1991). "Remediation as social construct: Perspectives from an analysis of classroom discourse." *College Composition and Communication, 42* (3), 299–329.

James, C.L.R. (1938/2001). *The black Jacobins: Toussaint L'Ouverture and the San Domingo revolution*. New York: Vintage.

Joubert-Ceci, Berta. (2000). "Tribunal condemns U.S. crimes in Puerto Rico." *Workers World Newspaper*, December 7. Retrieved September 29, 2007, from *http://www.workers.org/ww/2000/vieques1207.php*.

Kincheloe, J. (2004). *Critical pedagogy primer*. New York: Peter Lang.

Kincheloe, J., & P. McLaren. (1998). "Rethinking critical qualitative research." In N. Denzin & Y. Lincoln (Eds.), *Handbook of research of qualitative research* (pp. 260–299). Thousand Oaks, CA: Sage.

Kohn, A. (2000). *The case against standardized testing*. Portsmouth, NH: Heinemann.

Kozol, J. (1978). *Children of the revolution: A Yankee teacher in the Cuban schools*. New York: Delta.

Kozol, J. (1991). *Savage inequalities: Children in America's schools*. New York: Harper-Collins.

Kozol, J. (2005). *The shame of the nation*. New York: Crown Publishers.

Ladson-Billings, G. (1994). *The dreamkeepers: Successful teachers of African American children*. San Francisco: Jossey-Bass.

Lave, J. (1996). "Teaching, as learning in practice." *Mind, Culture, and Activity, 3* (3), 149–164.

Lave, J., & E. Wenger. (1991). *Situated learning: Legitimate peripheral participation.* Cambridge, UK: Cambridge University Press.

Lazin, L. (Writer). (2003). *Tupac: Resurrection.* Atlanta, GA: Amaru Entertainment.

Lee, C. (2004). "Literacy in the academic disciplines and the needs of adolescent struggling readers." *Voices in Urban Education*, Spring, 14–25.

Levine, A. (2006). *Educating school teachers.* New York: Education Schools Project.

Loewen, J. (1995). *Lies my teacher told me: Everything your American history textbook got wrong.* New York: Touchstone Press.

Loomba, A. (1998). *Colonialism/postcolonialism: The new critical idiom.* New York: Routledge.

Lorde, A. (1984). *Sister outsider: Essays and speeches by Audre Lorde.* Berkeley, CA: The Crossing Press.

MacLeod, J. (1987). *Ain't no makin' it: In a low-income neighborhood.* Boulder, CO: Westview.

Marcos, Subcommandante. (1995). *Shadows of tender fury: The letters and communiqués of Subcommandante Marcos and the Zapatista Army for National Liberation.* Translated by Frank Bardacke, Leslie López, and the Watsonville, California, Human Rights Committee. New York: Monthly Review Press.

McIntosh, P. (1988). *White privilege and male privilege: A personal account of coming to see correspondences through work in women's studies. Working paper 189,* Wellesley College Center for Research on Women, Wellesley, MA.

McIntyre, A. (2000). *Inner-city kids: Adolescents confront life and violence in an urban community.* New York: New York University Press.

McLaren, P. (1994). *Life in schools: An introduction to critical pedagogy and the foundations of education.* New York: Longman.

McLaren, P. (1995). *Revolutionary multiculturalism: Pedagogies of dissent for the new millennium.* Boulder, CO: Westview.

McLaren, P. (2003a). "Critical pedagogy: A look at the major concepts." In A. Darder, M. Baltodano, & R. Torres (Eds.), *The critical pedagogy reader* (pp. 69–96). New York: Routledge.

McLaren, P. (2003b). *Life in schools: An introduction to critical pedagogy in the foundations of education* (2nd edition). Boston, MA: Allyn & Bacon.

McLaren, P., & J. Giarelli. (1995). "Introduction: Critical theory and educational research." In P. McLaren & J. Giarelli (Eds.), *Critical theory and educational research* (pp. 1–22). Albany: SUNY Press.

McNeil, L. (2000). *The contradictions of school reform: Educational costs of standardized testing.* New York: Routledge.

Meier, D. (1995). *The power of their ideas: Lessons for America from a small school in Harlem.* Boston, MA: Beacon.

Meier, D. (2000). *Will standards save public education?* Boston, MA: Beacon.

Moll, L. (2000). "Inspired by Vygotsky: Ethnographic experiments in education." In C. Lee & P. Smagorinsky (Eds.), *Vygotskian perspectives on literacy research: Constructing meaning through collaborative inquiry* (pp. 256–268). Cambridge, UK: Cambridge University Press.

Moll, L.C., C. Amanti, D. Neff, & N. Gonzalez. (1992). "Funds of knowledge for teaching: Using a qualitative approach to connect homes and classrooms." *Theory into Practice, 31,* 132–141.

Moraga, C., & G. Anzaldúa. (Eds.). (1984). *This bridge called my back: Writings by radical women of color.* New York: Kitchen Table/Women of Color Press.

Morrell, E. (2002). "Toward a critical pedagogy of popular culture: Literacy development among urban youth." *Journal of Adolescent and Adult Literacy, 46* (1), 72–77.

Morrell, E. (2004a). *Becoming critical researchers: Literacy and empowerment for urban youth.* New York: Peter Lang.

Morrell, E. (2004b). *Linking literacy and popular culture: Finding connections for lifelong learning.* Norwood, MA: Christopher-Gordon.

Morrell, E., & J. Duncan-Andrade. (2004). "What youth do learn in school: Using hip-hop as a bridge to canonical poetry." In J. Mahiri (Ed.), *What they don't learn in school: Literacy in the lives of urban youth* (pp. 247–268). New York: Peter Lang.

Morrell, E., & J. Rogers. (2007). "Students as critical public historians: Insider research on diversity and access in post Brown v. Board Los Angeles." *Social Education,* (70) 6, 365–368.

Morrow, R., & C. Torres. (1995). *Social theory and education: A critique of theories of social and cultural reproduction.* New York: SUNY Press.

National Center for Education Statistics. (2007). *National assessment of educational progress (NAEP).* Washington, DC: National Center for Education Statistics.

National Research Council. (2005). *Advancing scientific research in education. Committee on research in education.* Lisa Towne, Laures L. Wise, & Tina M. Winters, Editors. Center for Education, Division of Behavioral and Social Sciences and Education. Washington, DC: The National Academies Press.

Ng, J., & J. Rury. (2006). "Poverty and education: A critical analysis of the Ruby Payne phenomenon." *Teachers College Record,* July 18. Retrieved July 31, 2007, from http://www.tcrecord.org.

Nieto, S. (1992). *Affirming diversity: The sociopolitical context of multicultural education.* New York: Longman.

Noddings, N. (1992). *The challenge to care in schools: An alternative approach to education.* New York: Teachers College Press.

Noguera, P. (2003). *City schools and the American dream: Reclaiming the promise of public education.* New York: Teachers College Press.

Oakes, J. (1985). *Keeping track: How schools structure inequality.* New Haven, CT: Yale University Press.

Oakes, J., & M. Lipton. (2001). *Teaching to change the world.* Boston, MA: McGraw-Hill.

Oakes, J., J. Rogers, & M. Lipton. (2006). *Learning power: Organizing for education and justice.* New York: Teachers College Press.

Ogbu, J. (1990). "Minority education in comparative perspective." *Journal of Negro Education, 59* (1), 45–57.

Padilha, J., & F. Lacerda. (2002). *Bus 174.* New York: ThinkFilm.

Payne, C. (1995). *I've got the light of freedom: The organizing tradition and the Mississippi freedom struggle.* Berkeley: University of California Press.

Prillaman, R., & D. Eaker. (1994). *The tapestry of caring: Education as nurturance.* Norwood, NJ: Ablex.

Ravitch, D. (2000). *Left back: A century of failed school reforms.* New York: Simon & Schuster.

Rist, R. (1973). *The urban school: A factory for failure.* Cambridge, MA: MIT Press.

Rogers, J., E. Morrell, & N. Enyedy. (2007). "Studying the struggle: Co texts for learning and identity." *American Behaviorial Scientiest, 51* (3), 419-443.

Rothstein, R. (2004). *Class and schools: Using, social, economic, and educational reform to close the black-white achievement gap.* Washington, DC: Economic Policy Institute.

Said, E. (1978). *Orientalism.* New York: Vintage.

Schrag, P. (2003). *The final test: The battle for adequacy in America's schools.* New York: The New Press.

Schumacher, J. (Director). (1996). *A time to kill.* Los Angeles, CA: Warner Brothers.

Shakur, T. (1999). *The rose that grew from concrete.* New York: Pocket Books.

Shakur, T. (2002). *Better dayz* (Disc 1, Track 7, 4:09). Los Angeles: Interscope Records.

Shor, I. (1992). *Empowering education: Critical teaching for social change.* Chicago, IL: University of Chicago Press.

Smith, L. (1999). *Decolonizing methodologies: Research and indigenous peoples.* London: Zed Books.

Smitherman, G. (2001). *Talkin that talk: Language, culture, and education in African America.* New York: Routledge.

Solórzano, D., & D. Delgado-Bernal. (2001). "Examining transformational resistance through a critical race and LatCrit theory framework: Chicana and Chicano students in an urban context." *Urban Education, 36* (3), 308–342.

Storey, J. (1998). *An introduction to cultural theory and popular culture.* Athens: University of Georgia Press.

Strauss, A., & J. Corbin. (Eds.). (1997). *Grounded theory in practice.* Thousand Oaks, CA: Sage.

Strauss, A., & J. Corbin. (1999). *Basics of qualitative research: Techniques and procedures for developing grounded theory.* Thousand Oaks, CA: Sage.

Strinati, D. (2000). *An introduction to studying popular culture.* New York: Routledge.

Summitt, P., & S. Jenkins. (1998). *Reach for the summit.* New York: Broadway Books.

Tijerina, Reies López. (2000). *They called me "King Tiger": My struggle for the land and our rights.* Translated and edited by José Ángel Gutiérrez. Houston, TX: Arte Público Press.

Tyack, D. (1974). *The one best system: A history of American urban education.* Cambridge, MA: Harvard University Press.

U.S. Department of Education. (2005). "About the Institute of Education Sciences." Retrieved November 23, 2005, from http://www.ed.gov/about/ offices/list/ies/index.html.

Valencia, R. & D. Solórzano. (1997). "Contemporary deficit thinking." In R. Valencia (Ed.), *The evolution of deficit thinking: Educational thought and practice* (pp. 160–210). London, UK: The Falmer Press.

Valenzuela, A. (1999). *Subtractive schooling.* Albany: SUNY Press.

Vodovnik, Z. (2004). *Ya Basta: Ten Years of the Zapatista Uprising.* Oakland, CA: AK Press.

Vygotsky, L. (1978). *Mind in society.* Cambridge, MA: Harvard University Press.

Wachowski, A., & L. Wachowski. (1999). *The matrix.* Hollywood, CA: Warner Brothers.

Wenger, E. (1998). *Communities of practice: Learning, meaning and identity.* Cambridge, UK: Cambridge University Press.

Wild, N. (1998). *A place called Chiapas.* Victoria, BC: British Columbia Arts Council.

Willis, P. (1977). *Learning to labor: How working class kids get working class jobs.* New York: Columbia University Press.

Woodson, C.G. (2000). *The mis-education of the Negro.* Chicago, IL: Africa World Press.

Wright, R. (1940/1989). *Native son.* New York: Harper Perennial.

Wyrick, D. (1998). *Fanon for beginners.* New York: Writers and Readers Publishing.

Zinn, H. (1995). *A people's history of the United States.* New York: Harper Perennial.

Zirin, D. (2005). *What's my name fool?* Chicago, IL: Haymarket Books.

Zuberi, T. (2003). *Thicker than blood: How racial statistics lie.* Minneapolis: University of Minnesota Press.

Index

About the Authors

Jeffrey Michael Reies Duncan-Andrade is Assistant Professor of Raza Studies and Education Administration and Interdisciplinary Studies, and Co-Director of the Educational Equity Initiative at San Francisco State University's Cesar Chavez Institute (*http://cci.sfsu.edu/taxonomy/term/28*). In addition to these duties, he teaches a 12th grade English Literature class at Oasis Community High School in Oakland, CA, where he continues his research into the uses of critical pedagogy in urban schools. Before joining the faculty at SFSU, Duncan-Andrade taught English and coached in the Oakland public schools for ten years, and completed his doctoral studies at the University of California, Berkeley. Duncan-Andrade's research interests and publications span the areas of urban schooling and curriculum change, urban teacher development and retention, critical pedagogy, and cultural and ethnic studies. He has authored numerous journal articles and book chapters on the conditions of urban education, urban teacher support and development, and effective pedagogy in urban settings. He is currently completing a second book on the core competencies of highly effective urban educators.

Ernest Morrell is Associate Professor in Urban Schooling and Associate Director for Youth Research at the Institute for Democracy, Education, and Access (IDEA) at the University of California at Los Angeles. For more than a decade he has worked with adolescents, drawing on their involvement with popular culture to promote academic literacy development. Morrell is also interested in the applications of critical pedagogy in urban education and working with teens as critical researchers. The author of three other books, *Linking Literacy and Popular Culture: Finding Connections for Lifelong Learning* (2004), *Becoming Critical –Researchers: Literacy and Empowerment for Urban Youth* (Peter Lang, 2004), and *Critical Literacy and Urban Youth: Pedagogies of Access, Dissent, and Liberation* (2007), Morrell received his Ph.D. in language, literacy, and culture from the University of California at Berkeley.

Studies in the Postmodern Theory of Education

General Editors
Joe L. Kincheloe & Shirley R. Steinberg

Counterpoints publishes the most compelling and imaginative books being written in education today. Grounded on the theoretical advances in criticalism, feminism, and postmodernism in the last two decades of the twentieth century, Counterpoints engages the meaning of these innovations in various forms of educational expression. Committed to the proposition that theoretical literature should be accessible to a variety of audiences, the series insists that its authors avoid esoteric and jargonistic languages that transform educational scholarship into an elite discourse for the initiated. Scholarly work matters only to the degree it affects consciousness and practice at multiple sites. Counterpoints' editorial policy is based on these principles and the ability of scholars to break new ground, to open new conversations, to go where educators have never gone before.

For additional information about this series or for the submission of manuscripts, please contact:

Joe L. Kincheloe & Shirley R. Steinberg
c/o Peter Lang Publishing, Inc.
29 Broadway, 18th floor
New York, New York 10006

To order other books in this series, please contact our Customer Service Department:

(800) 770-LANG (within the U.S.)
(212) 647-7706 (outside the U.S.)
(212) 647-7707 FAX

Or browse online by series:
www.peterlang.com

FORCES THAT FORM YOUR FUTURE

Forces That Form Your Future by Kevin Gerald
Published by Insight Publishing Group
8801 S. Yale, Suite 410
Tulsa, OK 74137
918-493-1718

Unless otherwise noted, Scripture quotations are from the Holy Bible, New International Version, copyright © 1973, 1978, 1984 by International Bible Society. Passages marked KJV are from the King James Version. Scripture quotations marked AMP are taken from *The Amplified Bible, Old Testament*. Copyright © 1965, 1978 by Zondervan Corporation. *New Testament* copyright © 1958, 1987 by The Lockman Foundation. Used by permission.

ISBN: 1-930027-94-X
Library of Congress: 2003102782

Printed in the United States of America